D0871820

The Separate City

The Separate City

Black Communities in the Urban South, 1940–1968

Christopher Silver
and
John V. Moeser

THE UNIVERSITY PRESS OF KENTUCKY

Copyright © 1995 by The University Press of Kentucky

Scholarly publisher for the Commonwealth,
serving Bellarmine College, Berea College, Centre
College of Kentucky, Eastern Kentucky University,
The Filson Club, Georgetown College, Kentucky
Historical Society, Kentucky State University,
Morehead State University, Murray State University,
Northern Kentucky University, Transylvania University,
University of Kentucky, University of Louisville,
and Western Kentucky University.

Editorial and Sales Offices: Lexington, Kentucky 40508-4008

Library of Congress Cataloging-in-Publication Data

Silver, Christopher, 1951–
  The separate city : black communities in the Urban South,
1940–1968 / Christopher Silver and John V. Moeser.
    p.   cm.
  Includes bibliographical references and index.
  ISBN 0-8131-1911-1 (alk. paper) :
    1. Afro-Americans—Virginia—Richmond—Population. 2. Afro-
Americans—Virginia—Richmond—Politics and government. 3. Afro-
Americans—Georgia—Atlanta—Population. 4. Afro-Americans—
Georgia—Atlanta—Politics and government. 5. Afro-Americans—
Tennessee—Memphis—Population. 6. Afro-Americans—Tennessee—
Memphis—Politics and government. 7. Richmond (Va.)—Race
relations. 8. Atlanta (Ga.)—Race relations. 9. Memphis (Tenn.)
—Race relations. I. Moeser. John V., 1942– . II. Title.
F234.R59N48 1995
305.896′073075—dc20   94-23649

Contents

Tables, Maps, and Figures

Preface

The modern history and politics of Richmond, Virginia, have been the subjects of separate studies by each of the authors of this book. Both Christopher Silver's *Twentieth Century Richmond: Planning, Politics, and Race* and John V. Moeser and Rutledge M. Dennis's *The Politics of Annexation: Oligarchic Power in a Southern City* focused in one way or another on the city's white leadership structure. Silver's work examined the forces in the white community, the business community in particular, that shaped urban planning policy from 1900 through the 1970s. The Moeser/Dennis study concentrated on one major policy, boundary expansion, and how that policy was shaped by the politics of race.

Given our previous work in Virginia's capital city and, more generally, in the development of the contemporary urban South, and given also the important but inadequately understood role of the African-American community in that process, we decided to merge our interests in a comparative study. The three cities of Richmond, Atlanta, and Memphis were selected because they allowed us to examine the development of the black community in three unique contexts. When we embarked on this study in 1984, the number of African-Americans living in Memphis represented roughly half of the city's population, yet blacks were grossly underrepresented in city government. It would not be until 1991 that blacks elected a council majority and a mayor. Atlanta, by contrast, elected an African-American mayor and an African-American majority on city council more than ten years earlier, in 1973. Meanwhile, African-Americans assumed leadership of Richmond's city hall four years later than Atlanta but thirteen years earlier than Memphis. In short, relative to the timing of blacks emerging as dominant players in municipal government, each of the three cities represented a different point along a political continuum.

Another reason for selecting the three cities was that each represented a different political culture. Memphis had a long association with a political organization more characteristic of northern industrial cities—a machine. Boss Crump, whose support was based in part on the African-American vote, held sway during the first half of the twentieth century, his control ending only when a group of white, upper-class reformers successfully challenged his leadership in the 1950s. The postwar flirtation with reform was short-lived, however, as blacks, disenchanted by the reformers' failure to support black political aspirations, withdrew from the coalition with liberal whites. The dissolution of the reform movement created a vacuum that was quickly filled by segregationists, whose racist appeals struck a responsive chord among the white working class. For many years thereafter, Memphis remained deeply polarized racially.

The political culture of Atlanta was quite different. For years, white reactionaries were kept at bay by an alliance between the city's corporate elite and older, more conservative leaders of the African-American community. This alliance remained intact from the late 1940s through the mid-1960s and sustained a regime as different from mainstream southern politics as was the Crump machine. The alliance led to the election of Ivan Allen as mayor who, upon request of President Kennedy, traveled to Washington in 1963 to speak in support of civil rights legislation. Allen's Washington visit contrasted with the behavior of most southern politicians, who were bent on blocking such legislation.

The political culture of Richmond differed in still other respects. Power was held by the white upper class who were as suspicious of lower class whites as they were of African-Americans of any class. Richmond was not noted for its biracial coalitions, as was Atlanta; neither did it experience the level of racial enmity found in Memphis. Again, Richmond occupied a position on a political culture continuum midway between the other two cities.

The political cultures differed markedly among the three cases, and the variations affected dynamics both between the white and black communities and within the black community. Yet, in spite of the differences, a remarkable similarity in settlement patterns evolved in the African-American communities of all three cities. We argue that these developmental patterns are distinctive of the urban South and that the African-American community formed there in a manner unlike its counterpart of the urban North. The settlement pattern that appeared in southern cities constituted a relatively self-contained, racially-identifiable community separated from the larger white city. The South's separate city and the North's ghetto were similar in certain respects. Both, for example, were the products of racial segregation. But there were sufficient differences between the two that the term "ghetto" fails to capture the southern experience. We also argue that the formation of the separate city was not simply a matter of demographics. Rather, the physical contours of the black community were shaped by neighborhood/community development policy and urban renewal programs, often with black developers and civic leaders participating actively in the neighborhood spatial allocation process. Yet, it was the separate city that provided the staging ground for protests and political action, commonly initiated by younger blacks less tied to the white power structure and thus less patient with the accommodationist policy of the older, more conservative black leadership structure. We give considerable attention to the battle over public schools triggered by the 1954 Brown decision and the effect of that battle on political mobilization within the separate city.

Our exploration leads us also to a discussion of the class dynamics within the separate city. We are indebted to the important study of William Julius Wilson, *The Truly Disadvantaged*, which highlighted the relationship between national changes in the economy and the outmigration of the black middle classes from the older, inner-city African-American neighborhoods. The conclusions he draws from his study of Chicago are equally applicable to the southern separate city; namely, the increasing isolation of African-Americans living in inner-city poverty, and the collapse of once stable black neighborhoods as the more affluent segment of the population moves to new suburban subdivisions.

Like any scholarly work, this one is the result of contributions from many people. We are grateful for the role each person played, and while we alone are responsible for any shortcomings in our study, we wish to acknowledge the assistance we received along the way. Our field research in Memphis and Atlanta was generously supported by Dr. Laurin L. Henry, Professor Emeritus of Public Administration and former Dean of the School of Community and Public Affairs at Virginia Commonwealth University. While seeking primary sources in Atlanta and Memphis, we relied heavily on the excellent staff responsible for the Mississippi Valley Collection at the John Willard Brister Library, Memphis State University; the Special Collections Department at the Robert W. Woodruff Library, Emory University; the archivists at the Atlanta Historical Society; and the librarians of the Memphis-Shelby County Public Library. We are also appreciative of the assistance we received from the National Archives and the library staff at the Department of Planning and Community Development in the City of Richmond. Collecting voter registration data and election returns was made easier by the efforts of registrars in Fulton and DeKalb counties, Georgia; Shelby county, Tennessee; and the City of Richmond, Virginia.

The last chapter of this book, "Race, Class, and the New Urban Politics," was drawn from an article we wrote that appeared in the October 1994 issue of *Virginia Magazine of History and Biography*. We gratefully acknowledge the Virginia Historical Society, which authorized use of this material. Portions of chapters 2, 4, and 5 were drawn from "The Changing Face of Neighborhoods in Memphis and Richmond, 1940-1985," by Christopher Silver and included in *Shades of the Sunbelt: Essays on Ethnicity, Race and the Urban South*

(Greenwood Press, 1988), edited by Randall Miller and George Pozetta and republished here with their permission.

Karen Becker, Donna Kennon, Jane Peterson, and John Kirkley, all former graduate students in the urban and regional planning program at Virginia Commonwealth University, also helped a great deal with data collection and map preparation for the book. Ms. Becker is now a Ph.D. student at the University of North Carolina at Chapel Hill; Ms. Kennon is a transportation planner with the Virginia Department of Transportation; Ms. Peterson is a senior planner with the Planning Department, Chesterfield County, Virginia. We remember particularly Mr. Kirkley, whose outstanding academic performance in spite of severe disabilities was an inspiration to faculty and students alike and whose ready smile and love of life drew many friends. He died shortly after receiving his degree. We miss him and remember him with great fondness. We also gratefully acknowledge the fine work of Cindy Baumgartner in typing and retyping the entire manuscript.

We are also grateful to Professor Joel Schwartz, who invited us to the Columbia University Seminar on the City to present portions of our book and to the seminar participants for their helpful comments and suggestions. In addition, the comments made by professors Robert B. Fairbanks and John F. Bauman, both of whom read earlier versions of the book, were most helpful and guided us as we made revisions to the manuscript.

Dale Silver and Sharon Moeser are two very important people who deserve special recognition. We might still be collecting data had it not been for their persistent inquiries about our progress. We know well that each hour spent on this project during its ten-year gestation was an additional hour of household responsibility they had to assume. The forbearance and support of Dale, Wesley, and Jenny on the Silver side and Sharon, Jeremy, and David on the Moeser side proved to be a necessary ingredient for completing this study. Because we refused to relinquish all our responsibilities as husbands and fathers, however, the completion of this book took longer than anticipated, but in the long run, the study benefited, we believe, from its prolonged process of articulation. The dedication of this book to our families is but a small token of affection and appreciation.

1

The Rise of the Separate City

Our study of black community development in three southern cities from 1940 to the 1960s is conceptually wedded to two central issues. One is the heated contemporary debate regarding the race and class structure of the American city. The other, a bit less contentious but no less important, involves the historical discussion of black community structure in twentieth-century urban America. In the widely acclaimed study of urban poverty, *The Truly Disadvantaged* (1987), sociologist William Julius Wilson examined the problems of the urban black underclass within the context of the changing race and class structure of cities. He argued that African-American deprivation has increased markedly since the 1960s despite substantial social welfare expenditures to mitigate poverty. Wilson took on social welfare critics, such as Charles Murray, who argued in *Losing Ground* (1984) that the War on Poverty actually exacerbated the problems of city ghetto residents. According to Murray, social welfare expenditures undermined community and family institutions through disincentives to work, to be educated, and to be good citizens. Wilson's counter to this was simply that the War on Poverty actually missed the poor. Although the truly disadvantaged were bypassed in the social welfare programs of the 1960s, direct gains can be ascribed to the War on Poverty and the Civil Rights movement. These, however, tended to accrue only to the working- and middle-class members of the black community.[1]

Then, what explains the persistence and in some cities the enlargement of the "disadvantaged" segment in the decayed ghettos? In Wilson's view, it is the "sharp increase in inner city dislocations" that makes the 1970s and 1980s differ fundamentally from past periods. He stresses that the contemporary inner-city black community differed socially from the traditional ghetto. Until the late 1960s, as Wilson points out, the traditional ghetto "featured vertical integration of different segments of the urban black population." This meant that there was a middle class present in the community to serve as a "social buffer" to assist the disadvantaged. The outmigration of the African-American middle class in the 1970s and 1980s "made it more difficult to sustain the basic institutions [such as churches, stores, schools, and recreation facilities] in these neighborhoods." The increased "social isolation" of the disadvantaged eroded their affiliations with the community, undermined positive neighborhood identification, and weakened explicit norms and sanctions against aberrant behavior as the organization of inner-city neighborhood declined. Wilson maintains that the loss of the "historic" African-American community, not simply ineffectual public policy, explains growing inner-city poverty despite efforts to eradicate it.[2]

Wilson's explanation of the factors affecting the community transformation process rests on a narrow empirical base, however. He relies essentially on a comparison of the African-American community in Chicago in the 1940s (as portrayed in the classic study, *Black Metropolis* by Drake and Cayton) and data he collected for that city from the 1970s to substantiate a growing concentration of impoverishment in the city's predominantly African-American core since the 1940s. Wilson's Chicago data is supplemented by the work of historian Arnold Hirsch, whose *Making the Second Ghetto: Race and Housing in Chicago, 1940–1960* (1983) demonstrates that there was a rather dramatic restructuring of Chicago's black community prior to the 1960s, the result being the systematic removal of African-Americans from the inner core but maintenance of a ghetto through the machinations of public policy. What Hirsch suggests is not only that the ghetto shifted to accommodate downtown redevelopment in the post–World War II period and to preserve racial separation at the neighborhood level but also that the process of change during the 1940s and 1950s renewed the commitment to segregation. Without government sanctions, Hirsch suggests, demographic changes alone pointed to possibilities for greater racial integration in Chicago. Government actions reinforced the social agenda of whites to maintain strict racial segregation at the neighborhood level in the face of enormous growth in the city's African-American population between 1940 and 1960. In this fashion public policy and community pressures coalesced to enable Chicago to experience the creation of a "second ghetto."[3]

Hirsch's analysis sustains Wilson's contention that Chicago's "historic" black community remained cohesive through the 1960s, even though the second ghetto evidenced more obvious division along class lines than did the original ghetto. Growing black residential areas, coupled with the segregation of public housing projects from middle-income neighborhoods, reinforced this tendency. Hirsch readily admits that his study of the "second ghetto" essentially measures the white segregationist views and policies and does not try to explain the role of blacks in the community-formation process. Although Hirsch contends that blacks were not passive recipients of policy from a white-dominated power structure, neither *Making the Second Ghetto* nor Wilson's work specifically address how the black community contributed to the changing city structure and the essential character of urban black ghetto life. Sociologist Elijah Anderson's study of Philadelphia's black community supports Wilson's contention that "black social life in . . . the 1940s and 1950s appears to have been highly cohesive compared with the present situation."[4]

Whether there was one historic ghetto (as Wilson implies) or successive stages of ghetto development, as Hirsch (and other recent works) suggests, it is obvious that there is a discontinuity between the contemporary black community and its predecessor in twentieth-century Chicago. Does this pattern comport with the community change process experienced by blacks in other urban places? If so, to what extent is it possible to generalize from the Wilson and Hirsch studies to describe black community development in urban America in general? This book broadens the geographical focus of the debate to include the urban South and introduces the additional salient factor of black political culture in the community-development process, a perspective that has not received sufficient attention in the literature.

Indeed, the basic idea of "ghettoization" of blacks and its applicability to southern urban development throughout the twentieth century is a necessary starting point for reexamining the Wilson thesis. An abundant historical literature suggests that the black ghetto was commonplace in northern cities where the African-American population grew rapidly in a relatively short time. Gilbert Osofsky's *Harlem: The Making of a Ghetto* (1966), Allen Spear's *Black Chicago: The Making of a Negro Ghetto, 1890–1920* (1967), and more recently Kenneth Kusmer's *A Ghetto Takes Shape: Black Cleveland, 1870–1930* (1975), Joe W. Trotter, Jr., ed., *Black Milwaukee: The Making of an Industrial Proletariat* (1985), and Henry Louis Taylor, Jr., *Race and the City: Work, Community, and Protest in Cincinnati, 1820–1970* (1993), chronicle the "creation of a Negro community within one large and solid geographic area" in various northern cities, many of which absorbed large numbers of southern black migrants in the early twentieth century. As Osofsky points out in the case of Harlem, between 1910 and 1930 Harlem's black population increased from 91,709 to 327,706. In 1920, as James Weldon Johnson watched its phenomenal growth, he predicted that "it will be the greatest Negro city in the world." Chicago's black community was not as large as that of New York, but it rapidly absorbed a substantial contingent of southern black migrants, especially during World War I. Even as the population grew, as historian William Tuttle notes in his provocative study of the 1919 race riot in Chicago, "the expansion of the areas of black residence was negligible," with the new migrants contributing to the "drastically intensified density of the existing area" of the "Black Belt." Kusmer and Taylor go beyond the conventional explorations of ghetto formation in northern cities in the early twentieth century—which point not only to rapid black population and institutional growth but also to the machinations of the real estate industry—to emphasize the role of city-building processes, especially city planning, in black ghetto formation.[5]

In contrast to migration patterns to northern industrial cities, migration of rural blacks to southern cities during this period occurred on a much reduced scale and intensity. Gunnar Myrdal pointed out in his classic study of U.S. race relations, *An American Dilemma* (1944), that "Negroes did go to Southern cities but not nearly to the same extent as did the whites." In eleven of the twelve largest southern cities the African-American population decreased as a proportion of the total population between 1900 and 1940, not because of the absence of growth in the African-American population but because the rate of growth of the black population was slower than that of non-black residents. In the three southern cities highlighted in this book, from 1900 to 1940 there were differences in the rate of black population growth (as will be discussed in Chapter 2), but all three cities boasted substantial black communities that increased between 90 and 190 percent prior to World War II.[6]

Black population growth did not keep pace with increases in non-black residents, however. The black population of Memphis in 1940 was 121,498, which was a 143 percent increase over its 1900 population and slightly more than the black population of Chicago as determined by the 1920 census. Atlanta's black community numbered slightly more than 100,000 in 1940, and Richmond's African-American population exceeded 60,000. The growth rate of Atlanta's black community actually exceeded that of Memphis, even though the black population declined in proportion to the city's total population during this period. It was not so much population size or population growth rates but the dispersal of black population throughout the city that explains one essential difference between the northern and southern cities. In northern cities, "blacks crowded into dense central sections recently occupied by foreign born immigrants." In 1900, according to Brownell, black settlements in southern cities were "scattered," and the increased in-migration of rural blacks over the next four decades conformed to this dispersed pattern. At the same time, however, the "pattern in all southern cities during the twentieth century was one of advancing racial segregation, the increasing concentration of blacks in fewer, larger residential areas nearer the urban core."[7] Was this a belated approximation of the ghettoization of African-Americans that had already been fully institutionalized in northern cities, or did the black community in southern cities represent a different form?

The tendency toward increased concentration of the black population that gradually occurred in southern cities was a process dissimilar in several key respects to what happened in northern cities such as Chicago, New York, and Philadelphia. Two factors, significantly lower residential density and a wider spatial dispersion of black neighborhoods within the city, suggest a different settlement pattern in the urban South. Differences also hinge on the definition of "ghetto," which even the most cursory examination of the available literature shows to be plagued by vagueness. Geographer David

Ward offers a historical interpretation of the emergence of "the slum, the ghetto, and the inner city" that indicates not only how loosely the term ghetto has been applied to ethnic concentrations but also how its meaning has changed over time. In the nineteenth-century city, the term *ghetto* referred specifically to the "residential quarter of East European Jews," although it soon "acquired a more general meaning to describe the residential segregation of any minority in the slums of the inner city." In the American context, the ghetto and the slum became interchangeable, "where the newly arrived immigrants exacerbated social problems related to adverse living conditions and residential segregation." Ward also notes that "the term ghetto was not used with any consistency to describe segregated residential quarters until after World War II, when it was used to describe the extensive concentrations of blacks in northern cities." Ward defines the ghetto as an "exclusion from a more complex, segmented world defined by varied patterns of consumption," where "a limited access to resources is decisively compounded by environmental disabilities and ethnic or racial discrimination."[8]

Historians August Meier and Elliot Rudwick, in their classic history of African-Americans, *From Plantation to Ghetto*, equate ghettoization with "expansion of residential segregation," where a pattern of blacks "living in scattered enclaves about the town, with some individuals here or there living in white neighborhoods, was giving way to larger concentrations of blacks limited to one or two sections of a city." They contend that this was "accentuated" in cities of the border and northern states but less characteristic of southern cities in general. They also note that the rigidity and intensity of the process varied from city to city.[9]

In his description of urban black communities in *Dark Ghetto*, Kenneth Clark observed that "there are Negro residential areas in such Southern cities as Atlanta, Birmingham, and New Orleans, but the Negro ghetto in America is essentially a Northern urban invention." He goes on to point to the relatively greater prevalence of racially- mixed neighborhoods in the urban South, although he contends that increasingly in the 1960s it became more like the North in its discriminatory pattern. Yet another important difference, notes Clark, is that in southern cities, "where the pattern of segregation is so complete that the dark ghettos must be almost self-sufficient, there are a number of Negro-owned stores, restaurants, and banks." In contrast, blacks in northern cities are allowed to be involved at least "partially in the total city . . . whites are willing to open businesses within the ghetto, sensing a profit among the tenements." One major consequence, especially in northern black ghettos, is "insufficient economic resources within the ghetto to support its future development." By contrast, in southern urban black communities, economic and political resources were available to generate community improvements, and African-Americans relied on their own leaders to supply them.[10]

Another variation between northern and southern urban black communities involves the location and types of residences available under a system
of segregation. As Horace R. Cayton and St. Clair Drake observed in their
pathbreaking study of black community development, *Black Metropolis*
(1946), the Black Belt of Chicago embraced the "most rundown areas of the
city." The 8 square miles of Chicago's Black Belt in the mid-1940s was only
slightly larger than it had been in the 1920s, despite an increase of over
200,000 black residents. Considering Chicago as a whole, African-Americans
constituted less than 10 percent of the city's population in 1944, and except
for six small scattered residential clusters, African-Americans consumed
only a narrow strip of the city to the east and south of the stockyards.
According to Cayton and Drake, Chicago's Black Belt had a density of 90,000
blacks per square mile as contrasted with 20,000 whites per square mile in
the adjacent apartment districts. Overall, approximately one-half of the
"Black Metropolis" represented areas that had been designed as "blighted"
by the mid-1940s, and through the use of restrictive covenants, the boundaries of the black neighborhood remained fixed despite continued in-migration of blacks from the South in the 1930s. In marked contrast, the borders of
the black community in the urban South proved to be considerably more
fluid, and neighborhood densities were substantially lower, thus contributing to greater dispersal.[11]

The literature of urban black residential patterns, therefore, points to a
variety of differences between northern ghettos and the less concentrated but
equally segregated residential structure of southern cities. Yet, if the ghetto
was not the predominant community form in southern cities, is it possible
to offer a more accurate description than merely pointing to a more dispersed
residential settlement pattern? In place of the northern ghetto, as our examination of Atlanta, Memphis, and Richmond suggests, black community
development in southern cities involved a purer form of apartheid that
constituted nothing less than the formation of a "separate city" within the
context of the rapidly expanding southern metropolis. The idea of a "separate city" is premised on a number of demographic, social, economic, political, and institutional variables that will be examined in more detail in the
following chapters, but it is useful to set our notion within its proper
historical context.

Although it reached its most mature manifestation in the rapidly urban-
izing South after 1940, the "separate city" actually originated in the northern
black ghetto, especially Harlem in the 1920s. Spear notes that the New Negro
movement of the 1920s sought the "development of self-sufficient black
communities . . . a 'Black Metropolis' . . . that would provide within a self-
contained community all of the goods and services required by its people."
It was the goal of the New Negro movement leaders, as Spear puts it, to
"create their own cities—attractive communities, served by black business-

men, politicians and professional people and independent of white control."
James Weldon Johnson expresses this ideal in *Black Manhattan* when he refers
to Harlem as a "city within a city" that was "not a fringe . . . not a slum, nor
. . . a 'quarter' consisting of dilapidated tenements. It is a section of new-law
apartment houses and handsome dwellings, with streets as well paved and
as well lighted and as well kept as in any other part of the city." As he
concludes, "the Negro's situation in Harlem is without precedent . . . never
before has he been so securely anchored, never before has he owned the land,
never before has he had so well established a community life."[12]

The promise expressed by Johnson of the black city within a city dissipated in the case of Harlem. By the close of the 1920s, Harlem had become a
neighborhood "with manifold social and economic problems." According to
Spear, Harlem "confined blacks to a separate, self-contained section of New
York, limited them for the most part to menial jobs, and cut them off from
the mainstream of the city's political and social life. Rather than a black
metropolis, Harlem was a black ghetto . . . [that] was never self-sufficient,
but remained dependent upon the economic and political power of white
New York."[13] Not until 1989, in fact, would the descendants of Harlem's
golden era in the 1920s piece together the political wherewithal to elect a
black mayor in New York. In sharp contrast, that esteemed political prize
had been secured by African-Americans in major southern cities nearly a
generation earlier. By 1989, however, the promised black metropolis of
Harlem had become an empty, violent, decayed physical shell awaiting some
unknown fate on an island plagued with the miseries of excessive affluence
and abysmal deprivation. Harlem, the black city within a city, had become
the epitome of black Manhattan's abysmal deprivation. In contrast, although
it has its own enduring social and economic problems and characteristics,
including an increasingly visible "truly advantaged" element, the "separate
city" in the urban South nevertheless remained the foundation for black
economic and political ascendancy throughout the 1980s.

Depicting the "separate city" as it evolved in the southern metropolis in
the mid-twentieth century is the central purpose of this book. This necessi-
tates more than just charting demographic shifts within southern cities,
however. It is a related set of public policy initiatives that helped to fashion
the separate city from the historic black community in southern cities in
much the same way that the "second ghetto" emerged in Chicago after 1940.
The influence from key black community leaders in southern cities in these
public policy initiatives helped to sanction the idea of a separate black city.
It was the political consolidation, and the political isolation, of the southern
urban black community prior to the 1960s that not only sanctioned the notion
of a separate city for blacks within the emerging metropolis but also produced a backlash against traditional black leaders by a new generation raised
in relative comfort. These younger civil rights activists demanded freedom,

equality, and the dismantling of the separate city that had been so meticulously fashioned by their elders.

To appreciate common challenges facing urban blacks throughout the
United States from 1940 to the 1960s, one must recognize the similarities (not
just the differences) between southern urban black community development
and the deficiencies that plagued northern ghettos such as Harlem and
Chicago's Black Belt. First of all, the black community in the southern
metropolis was, like its northern ghetto counterpart, a product of discrimination by whites in the allocation of residential and commercial space for the
black community. Southern cities actually invented and made widespread
use of legal tools such as racial zoning to ensure residential separation on the
basis of race. Residential segregation in southern cities focused exclusively
on blacks as there were not sufficient numbers of other minority groups to
warrant that sort of districting process.[14]

Second, southern urban blacks were concentrated in the worst neighborhoods, in those areas either slated for demolition or at least determined to be
outside of the main lines of white residential development in the expanding
metropolis. As in the northern black ghetto, there were restrictions on the
ability of southern blacks to marshall economic resources sufficient to ensure
not only a full range of basic services in the black community but also a job
base adequate to provide decent incomes to its inhabitants. The black community was poor in general because it was denied access to the full range of
opportunities in the larger city dominated by whites.

Finally, African-Americans remained politically powerless within the
larger metropolitan areas throughout the formative years of the separate city
in the South. This stemmed in part from their confinement within an area
that was easily gerrymandered out of the political process. In the absence of
machine politics in most southern cities, black votes were not courted with
the same energy as in northern cities during the heyday of the "ghetto."
Atlanta, during the late 1940s, was an exception. As a result, however,
southern urban blacks opted for separate, independent political organizations. The political stakes for these groups were restricted to gaining a greater
share of public jobs or perhaps a seat on the school board. Eventually,
however, these independent black political organizations sustained black
political involvement in several southern cities during the era of urban
reform politics that began in the late 1940s. Political isolation enabled African-Americans to avoid the sort of alliances that crippled black political
aspirations in northern cities, where the climate seemed more conducive to
an active role in the power structure.

All of these similarities notwithstanding, the structure and the operation
of the black community in southern cities from the 1940s through the 1960s
diverged fundamentally from that of northern cities. To illuminate interre-
gional variations but also to show that the black community development

evidenced intraregional variations as well, this book examines three repre-
sentative yet distinctively different southern cities, Atlanta, Memphis and
Richmond. Each generated a different community pattern that varied from
the ghetto model, either in its traditional or "second ghetto" variety. For one
thing, the proportional size of the black population in these three southern
cities necessitated the allocation of a substantially greater share of the urban
space to accommodate their housing and nonhousing uses. In all three cities,
as early as the 1920s, the planning process took into account the future
expansion needs of blacks. Many African-Americans were consigned to the
old and rundown inner-city areas, but in all three a substantial proportion
were not. In all three cities, city leaders acknowledged that suburban areas
and new neighborhoods needed to be set aside for the black community to
ensure the maintenance of racially separated community development. In
addition, black developers and civic leaders participated actively in the
neighborhood spatial allocation process in these southern cities. To gain a
stake in the allocation process, Southern urban black leaders did not initially
challenge racial barriers to neighborhoods but emphasized instead the need
to broaden the array of choices and to secure improvements for blacks within
the context of an expanding separate black city.

The desire of the black economic elite in these three southern cities to
broaden the resource base of the community through black-owned enterprises also provided important sanctions for the separate city. All three cities
possessed a sizable and influential black economic elite whose prosperity
increased as the separate black city thrived. Even though the economic base
of the southern urban black community rested on a narrow range of service
industries, evidence from all three cities supports the contention that blacks
in the urban South from the 1940s through the 1960s served their own
community in matters such as financing, insurance, jobs, personal services,
and patronage, as well as offering a social life that rivaled that of the white
world in its depth and diversity.

Our examination of black community development in Atlanta, Memphis, and Richmond through the 1960s also reveals a degree of internal
diversity that has been obscured by a tradition in scholarship of emphasizing
the "culture of poverty" and qualities of the impoverished African-American
ghetto. Only as the southern separate black city reached a mature stage in
the 1960s and 1970s did the internal complexity of the black community
reveal itself, especially in the political arena. Only when blacks achieved
control of local politics in cities throughout the South and when, in fact, the
black separate city merged with and became coterminous with the city itself,
did the dormant conflicts within the black community come to the surface.
The flight of the black middle class to the outer city since the 1970s has
illuminated social and economic divisions that were present in the urban
black community throughout the twentieth century. Our study adds further

support to the argument advanced by historian Robin D.G. Kelly in a study of black opposition politics in Birmingham from the 1930s through the 1960s that the black poor did not share the same political agenda as the black middle class and that leading black organizations failed to address the needs of the black poor. The result, suggests Kelly, was a form of "infrapolitics," whereby the poor engaged in a dissident political culture that challenged traditional black leadership.[15]

As noted, the separate city in the urban South was in some respects like Hirsch's second ghetto in Chicago, that is, a creation of national and local public policy initiatives of the 1940s and 1950s. This is an important consideration in the South. Although the shifting spatial configuration of black neighborhoods in Atlanta, Memphis, and Richmond signified internal social, economic, and political realignments within the black community, these were not wholly spontaneous changes. They were prompted by public policies in the areas of education, housing, urban renewal, and transportation that blacks reacted to but could not control. The changing community characteristics in turn contributed to a redirection in racial politics during this crucial prelude to the full-fledged Civil Rights movement. It is one of our key assumption that the emergence of the "separate city" contributed directly to the increased political activism of African-Americans in the post-Depression urban South. In all three southern cities, new black leadership formed during and as a direct result of the community-development process of the 1940s and 1950s. This suggests that the Civil Rights movement of the 1960s must be viewed as not simply a reaction to centuries of discrimination and oppression but also an outgrowth of the cohesiveness and community identity fashioned in the separate city of the twentieth century.

The formation of the separate city also makes clear the obvious social costs associated with the restructuring of the southern center city. If we return to William Wilson's contention that the dismantling of the traditional black community explains why large, impoverished pockets of the black community in the inner city have slipped further into deprivation since the 1960s, the southern city demonstrates that there was a continuous process of community transformation from the 1940s through the 1960s, even before the Civil Rights movement emerged. The community diversity inherent in the separate city pattern, albeit within the context of continued segregation from the larger community, also explains why a new generation of blacks remain steadfastly opposed to revitalizing the residential core of southern and northern cities and instead continue to move toward their portion of the metropolitan fringe.

In sum, our comparative study examines both the influence of African-American populations on urban policy in the South and the effects of those policies and urban politics on southern blacks early in the Civil Rights era. It contributes to a growing literature on the history of black community development in the twentieth century and at the same time offers a counter-point to the northern-based "ghetto" literature that does not adequately explain the processes at work in southern cities. The selection of Atlanta, Memphis, and Richmond to represent the black community development in the South is based on two primary factors. First, each city stood at a different point on a continuum of black political leadership and policymaking during the formative period in the Civil Rights movement, and these differences persisted through the 1980s. In Memphis, for example, blacks comprised roughly about 48 percent of the city's population by 1980 and yet were able to secure only four of thirteen seats on the city council. Not until 1991 did the city elect a black mayor. In Richmond, blacks were denied a majority on the city council when city leaders annexed a large white suburban neighborhood in 1970 in order to reduce the black voting population well below a majority. With the help of white flight and a court-ordered single-member district government, blacks in Richmond secured a political majority and the may-oralty in 1977.

Since the 1940s black involvement in local government in Atlanta, Mem-phis, and Richmond has spanned a broad continuum. This reflects not only the number of registered black voters but also the structure of government and historic relationships between powerful constituencies. Variations in political participation by blacks also reflected the community develop-ment process that occurred differently in these three relatively different places.

A second factor in the selection of these three cities is their divergent political cultures, which mirror the wide political spectrum of the urban South. Memphis was unique among southern cities for its reliance on the political machine of Edward H. Crump for leadership during the better part of the half-century prior to his death in 1954. For a brief interlude during and after World War I, Memphis switched to a reform government but returned dutifully to the Crump fold in the late 1920s, after which the machine exercised unchallenged power, with noteworthy support from the black community. In the late 1940s and early 1950s, a new reform coalition com-prised of upper-class white businessmen, lawyers, educators and champi-oned publicly by the editor of the *Memphis Press-Scimitar*, challenged Crump for control of the city. Although seemingly more "progressive" than compa-rable white reform groups in Richmond and Atlanta, the Civic Research Committee (CRC) of Memphis began to unravel not long after it wrested political power following Crump's death. The conservative whites who replaced the CRC reformers in positions of leadership in Memphis in the 1960s rejected alliance with blacks and instead preyed on the racial prejudices of working-class whites (who had been the backbone of the Crump machine) to increase the political polarization between whites and blacks. The April

1968 assassination of Dr. Martin Luther King in a downtown Memphis motel was the culminating incident in a decade of stormy racial conflicts in the city.

The political culture of Atlanta during the 1940s and 1950s was appreciably different in tone and substance from that of Memphis. Atlanta had a rich tradition of biracial political coalition, prompted at least in part by a sense of noblesse oblige among Atlanta's upper-class whites whose business and political contacts reached to middle-class conservatives in the black community. This alliance was a unique fixture of Atlanta politics and anchored the electoral base of two Atlanta mayors, William Hartfield and Ivan Allen. These two white mayors were as atypical of white southern politicians as Crump's machine was unlike most southern urban political organizations. Atlanta cultivated the reputation during the Hartsfield era as a "city too busy to hate." Although the slogan was a clever bit of boosterism and characteristic of the bravado employed by the Atlanta business community, it proved to be a self-fulfilling prophesy. Whereas other cities exploded in interracial violence in the 1960s, even the most outrageous attempts to control blacks—such as the construction of "Peyton's Wall" to separate black and white neighborhoods—engendered an unequivocal but nonetheless restrained response from Atlanta's African-American civic leaders. Yet, the fact remains that irrespective of the biracial coalitions that paved the way for the election of a black mayor, Maynard Jackson, in 1973, the fundamental needs of the black community, particularly the majority of low-income blacks, received inadequate attention. During this important prelude to future black power in Atlanta, the black middle class engaged in a community-building process that was to have direct implications for future political participation but that also accounted for the growing problems of the "truly disadvantaged."

Richmond's political culture represents a hybrid of the Atlanta and Memphis experiences. Like Atlanta, Richmond's political power prior to 1977 rested with the city's white upper class. Characteristic of Richmond's power structure, indeed the power structure of Virginia, was the dominant role of a white aristocracy. Like the upper classes of both Atlanta and Memphis, Richmond's blue bloods had an instinctual aversion to the lower classes, believing that power should be exercised by those with sufficient levels of education and with the proper blood lines. Unlike the Atlanta model, however, Richmond's white leadership never cultivated a partnership with the black middle class except when it was necessary during elections to garner some black votes to win at-large seats on the city council. Even though Richmond's black leaders were active in the national Civil Rights movement, the movement had little direct impact on Richmond's local political agenda prior to the 1960s. Indeed, many of Richmond's white leaders were unsympathetic to the goals of the Civil Rights movement, although the virulent racism of other southern cities never held sway in its local politics. Richmond also lacked the sort of powerful and visionary mayor represented by a William Hartsfield or an Ivan Allen. It should be noted, however, that the appeals to black voters by Hartsfield and Allen and their endeavors to work closely with black professionals, should not be construed as a willingness on their part to share control of Atlanta with the black leadership. In this regard, Atlanta's mayors were cut from the same cloth as those of Memphis and Richmond.

The variations in overall political cultures of the three cities suggest a range of responses to the white leadership styles on the part of the black community. Although the development of black political leadership in southern cities occurred independently from that of white organizations, the changing approaches by African-Americans to influence in politics and policy were shaped in no small measure by the dominant political culture of the city. The separate city provided the community substructure for emerging black political power. The social divisions engendered by the separate city ensured, however, that even when blacks gained control of city government in the 1970s in Atlanta and Richmond and in Memphis in the 1990s, it was not the whole but rather a fraction of the whole that accounted for their success.

Given our desire to look at three southern cities simultaneously, we have chosen several policy areas related to black community development and political empowerment rather than trying to analyze every issue of importance to the black community. In Chapter 2, we attempt to set the stage for our policy analysis by examining the process of black community development in all three cities both prior to 1940 and in the following two decades when the "separate city" took shape. This predominantly demographic analysis also includes attention to emerging patterns of leadership within the black community of all three cities. In Chapter 3, we look at the issue of school desegregation, both as a cornerstone of the growing Civil Rights movement and as a political mobilizing issue in the emerging black separate city. We then turn in Chapter 4 to a discussion of public policy initiatives related to community development, including attention to public housing, urban renewal, highway construction, restructuring of the downtown through various civic improvement projects, and experimentation with neighborhood planning to guide the neighborhood change process. All of these policy initiatives were in process as the school desegregation battles were being waged and helped to ensure that segregated residential patterns would endure even when the legal system of segregation crumbled.

Finally, we link the idea of the separate city to the early foundations of black empowerment and black political mobilization around such issues as education, community development, and the failure of public policy to address effectively long-standing needs of the expanding and increasingly consolidated black community. As the separate city emerged, it became evident that there were internal divisions within the black community that reflected a structural divide between an empowered black middle class and the larger working class and disadvantaged who were not able to transform black power into public policy successes. The "separate city" from which the South's new African-American leadership emerged was, on the one hand, a political triumph, but also an admission of the profound social ineffectiveness of decades of struggle to eliminate racial barriers in the southern metropolis. The consequences of these successes and failures are what southern urban leaders must grapple with in the 1990s. The urban South, indeed urban America, now reaps what it sowed in the critical decades of the 1940s through the 1960s.

2

Community Change and Community Leadership

In the fall of 1940 black academician Benjamin E. Mays returned to the South and to his former home of Atlanta. In 1921 he had begun his professional career there as a mathematics instructor at Morehouse College. Raised in the impoverished rural backwaters of South Carolina, Mays escaped temporarily to the racially-tolerant world of New England for his education. When he returned to the South in the 1920s, he saw more vividly in Atlanta than he had in his native South Carolina how "the cruel tentacles of race prejudice reached out to invade and distort every aspect of southern life." Mays' second return to Atlanta in 1940 as the newly appointed president of Morehouse was also, in his view, a call to battle for black rights in a city that had improved imperceptibly during a generation-long absence. "In the 1920s, and even when I came back in 1940," he later reminisced, "Atlanta was so depressing in its black-white relations that I saw no difference between it and Birmingham or Memphis. As I appraised bad human relations in the South, I ranked Birmingham No. 1, Memphis No. 2, and Atlanta No. 3." Political powerlessness, rigid segregation in all public facilities, and the threat of humiliation or intimidation when venturing out of "black Atlanta," these were his memories of Atlanta in the early 1920s. Yet, as Mays looked around Atlanta in 1940, it seemed no less hostile toward blacks and even more rigidly divided than it was in the 1920s into two separate and unbridgeable worlds, one white and one black.[1]

Within the context of a separate black urban world, however, Mays soon discovered that Atlanta in 1940 stood on the threshold of a new era of change in race relations. All of the efforts by whites to constrict the black world produced a degree of black cohesion that posed a new challenge to white dominance. The spirit of rebellion, or at the very least of change, in black Atlanta, was symptomatic of broader regional forces at work in the early 1940s. In October 1942 Mays traveled to Durham, North Carolina, for an historic assemblage of southern black leaders that gave rise to the Southern Regional Council (SRC). Out of that gathering came the "Durham Resolution" that challenged the white South to improve race relations by allowing voting rights, civil rights, employment opportunities, and unrestricted access to public services.[2] The organizer of this unique gathering of black educators, ministers, businessmen, editors, physicians, social workers, labor leaders, and civil rights workers was Gordon B. Hancock, a sociologist teaching at Virginia Union College in Richmond, Virginia. Like Mays, Hancock used both the college classroom and the church pulpit to decry the conditions endured by blacks in southern society. Hancock's eagerness to formulate and disseminate the Durham Resolution owed to his perception of rising black militancy, especially in the urban South, and to a desire to remain in step with the changing and restless black community.[3]

Hancock's personal development and professional career mirrored that of Mays. He, too, grew up in rural South Carolina and left the South to secure a college education in the North. Like Mays, he returned to the South in 1921 to teach at an all-black college, Virginia Union, located on the northern edge of Richmond. In his sociology classes at Virginia Union, Hancock examined critically the conditions of blacks in the South and trained his students to garner the factual data to support their observations. Hancock's career as a racial spokesman encompassed the difficult decades of the 1920s and 1930s. He was, as biographer Raymond Gavins put it, a member of "the South's black vanguard . . . during the interregnum between Washington and King." In the classroom he influenced a new generation of black leaders through his pioneering explorations of southern race relations. As a leader in the Interracial Commission, founded as a biracial study group in 1919, Hancock advocated integration through biracial cooperation. In January 1944, as a follow-up to the Durham gathering that he so masterfully orchestrated, Hancock joined with fellow academics Luther P. Jackson and Charles S. Johnson, Plummer B. Young, publisher-editor of the Norfolk *Journal and Guide,* Howard Odum, a white sociologist from the University of North Carolina, and Rufus E. Clement and Mays from Atlanta's black academic establishment to launch the SRC as a replacement for the Interracial Commission. Its goal was "to improve 'economic, civic and racial conditions in the South [and] to attain through research and action programs the ideals and practices of equal opportunity'."[4]

More than Hancock's influence as the SRC organizer, it was his role as minister to the large and devoted black congregation at the Moore Street Baptist Church in Richmond's Jackson Ward that connected him to the black community. Moore Street Baptist was not a silk-stocking institution but a relief agency and spiritual nourisher in the heart of Richmond's most prominent black neighborhood. The congregation grew from 500 members when Hancock began his ministry in 1925 to nearly 2,000 parishioners by the early 1940s. This growth corresponded to the increasing concentration of black Richmonders in the Jackson Ward neighborhood. As a founder of the Richmond branch of the Urban League in 1923 and through involvement with the biracial Richmond Council of Social Agencies (RCSA), Hancock worked for racial improvement through community organizations as well as through education and his ministry. In 1929, for example, the RCSA produced a detailed assessment of the social and economic needs of the city's black residents. Although the report documented authoritatively the problems confronting the city's increasingly concentrated black community, it engendered little direct public effort to deal with the city's pervasive black poverty.

Instead of challenging injurious public policies, black leaders such as Hancock addressed the needs of the masses directly through church-sponsored initiatives. As Hancock saw it, institutional change came too slowly. Ironically, Hancock's writing, teaching, and community activism motivated a new generation of black leaders to demand institutional responses to the problems of the black community. Whereas Hancock sought to build bridges between the races on behalf of blacks, by the 1940s new leaders in Richmond's black community seemed to be looking for something other than an "interracial bridge"; black Richmond was moving decidedly in the direction of self-sufficiency and self-determination and was not precisely in step with Hancock's brand of cooperation.[5]

Lieutenant George Washington Lee faced a situation in Memphis in 1940 that was distinctly different from that of Mays and Hancock. At the time, Lee was struggling to maintain his stature as the self-proclaimed black militant who stood up for black rights while retaining influence within the city's powerful white Democratic political machine. Memphis in 1940 was on the frontier of southern race relations, separated spatially and ideologically from the liberal currents that flowed through the southeastern cities and that supported a discernible interracial dialogue in places such as Atlanta and Richmond. A lifelong Republican, Lee chose in 1940 to abandon overt race militancy to accommodate the autocratic city leader Edward Crump and to become, in the eyes of his detractors "a brown screw in the Crump machine." When Crump used police intimidation to expel from Memphis a prominent and outspoken black businessman, the usually outspoken Lee raised no protest. Yet, neither did other leading black Memphians, who, like Lee, had nurtured black pride and black economic independence along the city's famed Beale Street over the previous decades. Lee, the insurance executive, Bert Roddy, a barber and chain store operator, and Merah Steven Stuart, an insurance company executive and future president of the local NAACP chapter, had been the leading voices of black militancy since the 1920s. By the early 1940s, however, Crump's Memphis no longer tolerated even verbal defiance from its black citizens, and all three fell obediently into step.[6]

The multitalented Lee was a unique combination of businessman, politico, and intellectual, who, during the 1920s and 1930s, succeeded relatively well in all three areas. Lee consistently spoke of the futility of accommodation and his repeated denunciations of the Interracial League (which was the local offshoot of the Interracial Commission) suggests how he differed philosophically from Hancock and Mays. Lee criticized the black ministers in Memphis who supported interracial organizations and denounced especially Memphian E. Sutton Griggs for his interracial pronouncements. As Lee asserted, "we've got too many apostles of peace at any price, too many preaching about the glories of the other world, and too few pointing out the hell of the world in which we now live."[7]

By 1940, however, the weight of the Crump machine, which previously practiced tolerance toward blacks in exchange for votes, now sought to crush completely any vestiges of black political independence. As for Lee, who had always evidenced a streak of opportunism, Crump's new tactics did not engender greater militancy but a willingness to fall in obediently behind the city's white political leadership. Some black Memphians, such as Stuart, counseled blacks not only to appear loyal but also to adopt a conservative posture to secure improvements for the race. As Stuart remarked, "Radicals get in the limelight of popularity. Conservatives get things done. . . . They want the same thing . . . [except that] a conservative Negro is a radical who has grown ripe—and practical. Both are at heart for the full, legal rights of the race."[8]

The streak of conservatism that in 1940 became the hallmark of black political survival in Memphis also touched the black communities of Atlanta and Richmond. Whereas Lee appeared to be more obsequious toward the Crump machine in the early 1940s than Hancock and Mays were toward their respective white counterparts, there was an underlying conservatism that guided race relations in all three southern cities. In one sense, the accommodationist spirit of the early 1940s marked the culmination of one-half century of development in the black community under the guiding hand of Jim Crowism. In all three cities the black community had grown into an increasingly politically cohesive and spatially separate world by the 1940s. The black leadership in Atlanta, Memphis, and Richmond pressed for change and community improvement and were also motivated in the early 1940s toward a goal that can be best described as "community preservation." The social and economic processes of urban development since the late nineteenth century had produced a tangible racial asset, "a black community," that could serve as the foundation for increased black prosperity. The separate black community was something to build on, to improve and to conserve, within the racially charged atmosphere of the early 1940s.

In the period from the early 1940s through the mid-1960s, the community-building and -improvement process followed lines already demarked in the early 1900s, although in spatial terms the changes were greater in the latter period. The enlarged and separate black urban world no longer blended into that of whites, as the accommodationists had hoped and advocated, but became even more separate. Blacks sought a more substantial share of the fruits of urban development but within the context of a separate black city within the city. Blacks in the Atlanta of Mays, the Richmond of Hancock, and the Memphis of Lee after 1940 also transformed community conservation and development into a form of political protest that enlivened the Civil Rights movement. To appreciate the growing political force of blacks in all three cities in the post–World War II era, it is essential to link politics to the evolution of the black community. It was the pre-1940s community that nurtured and sustained black leaders such as Mays, Hancock, and Lee and, paradoxically, the sort of community preservation and revitalization that fueled the racial battles engaged in by a subsequent generation of black leaders. Even though the black communities in Atlanta, Memphis, and Richmond confronted common problems related to survival in a hostile white world, they also forged unique versions of the separate black community. The distinctive socioeconomic pattern of development of the black community in each city in turn contributed to variations not only in the quest for civil rights but also in the future political culture of cities throughout the South.

The Black Community in Formation: Pre-1940s

The black community in southern cities in the early 1940s was a product of more than one century of development under the powerful influence of slavery, Reconstruction, Redemption, and the peculiar institution of the New South, Jim Crowism. Historians Richard Wade and Ira Berlin demonstrate that cities provided a place for black culture and community to flourish in the South under slavery. The post–Civil War decades witnessed a broadening of the functions and institutional base of the southern urban black community to accommodate the influx of displaced rural blacks. The result was an increasingly complex urban black community vying for a place, both in a spatial and an organizational sense, within the dominant white society. Robert Purdue's study of African-Americans in Savannah from 1865 to 1900 points to relatively fluid race relations that provided sufficient latitude for black community development. Howard Rabinowitz's comparative study of race relations in Atlanta, Montgomery, Nashville, Raleigh, and Richmond, spanning essentially the same period, shows that "blacks successfully built communities around their own churches, schools, welfare institutions, societies, and businesses." In the case of Nashville, Raleigh, and Richmond, these communities sustained local black political power long after federal Reconstruction ceased to protect their civil rights. Yet, by the turn of the century, there was an unmistakable trend toward a physical, social, and economic separation of those black communities that had grown up since 1865. White hostility, Rabinowitz notes, "forced blacks to think of themselves as a group apart and encouraged the development of a definite ethnocentrism."[9]

The imposition of a rigid and all-encompassing system of racial separation in southern cities by 1900 did not necessarily mean a full-scale retreat from the promising civil rights advances of the Reconstruction era. Rabinowitz argues that the acceptance by blacks and their white Republican allies of a segregated society represented a pragmatic compromise in the face of increasing racial tensions. For most whites the transition from exclusion to integration was too profound to be acceptable. "Segregation replaced exclusion as the norm in Southern race relations," claims Rabinowitz. "In the process, the stage of integration had been largely skipped." De facto segregation gave way to de jure segregation, according to C. Vann Woodward, because those who had sought to guarantee fair treatment of blacks caved in under pressure from reactionaries. Rabinowitz suggests, however, that "black attitudes were perhaps as important as anything else in explaining the timing of the decision to legalize what previously had been left to custom." Black resistance to de facto segregation, especially from the new generation of black youths who had been born to freedom, who had followed the white-prescribed path of self-improvement, and who challenged continued indignities from whites, gave white society an excuse to legalize the system of separation. As Rabinowitz concludes, "given white fears generated by black resistance in word and deed at the end of the 1880s, it is not surprising that white southerners were quick to seize the opportunity presented by the North's defection from the fight for equal rights. It was the opening they had been looking for since the Civil War and such limited flexibility in race relations as there had been would now be eliminated."[10]

Atlanta

The growth and change in the black communities of Atlanta, Memphis, and Richmond after 1900 bore the unmistakable imprint of Jim Crow. Yet, in none of these three cities did Jim Crowism produce instantly the segregated city. Atlanta is a good case in point. There the dispersed pattern of black residential settlement that characterized the late nineteenth century was modified after 1900 by a process of controlled physical expansion. According to historian Richard J. Hopkins, African-Americans in late nineteenth-century Atlanta had been "just as mobile residentially as most whites." In the aftermath of the Atlanta race riot in 1906, however, the lines of demarcation between white and black neighborhoods ceased to be as fluid, and guiding black residential expansion became a matter of public concern and eventually public policy. Whereas it was possible in pre-1906 Atlanta to find "at least one black household on every street" in the city and numerous white neighborhoods "honeycombed with all-black alleyways and side streets," in the decade after the riot "the citywide dispersion of blacks was much less apparent."[11]

As a direct consequence of the 1906 riot, black businesses were forced out of the central business core. They shifted, in tandem, to form what soon became a thriving black business district along Auburn Avenue, the place black residents and managers affectionately called "Sweet Auburn." At the same time, white real estate brokers blocked black residential expansion along the periphery of the central business district. The dispersed pockets of poor black housing in Central and South Atlanta—in particular the communities of Pittsburgh, Summerhill, and People's Town—merged into a continuous mass of black residences extending westward from the fringe of downtown toward Atlanta University. Although the "Old Fourth Ward" on Atlanta's East Side, with its preponderance of black businesses along Auburn Avenue, remained a cohesive black enclave, physical expansion of the city's black community between 1906 and 1940 occurred almost exclusively to the west of the central business district. By 1940, well over one-third of Atlanta's African-American population lived on the West Side. Still, only the broad outlines of the separate black city could be seen in the pre–World War II era. Jim Crowism had made a deep imprint on the social structure of Atlanta, but the process of racial segregation was far from complete.[12]

The growing concentration of black residences on the city's West Side was a carefully orchestrated effort. On June 16, 1913, Atlanta enacted a zoning ordinance to legalize residential segregation according to race. Like racial zoning ordinances enacted in numerous other southern (including Richmond) and northern cities, Atlanta's followed the basic formula set forth in the Baltimore plan of 1910. The city assigned a racial designation to every city block based on the race of the majority of residents. From that point onward, blacks would not be allowed to move into white blocks (and vice versa), although it left to private determination those blocks that were presently inhabited equally by whites and blacks. In 1915, however, the Georgia State Supreme Court declared the Atlanta racial zoning ordinance unconstitutional because it infringed on "the right of the individual to acquire, enjoy, and dispose of his property." When the city revised its ordinance to exempt residences acquired before passage of the ordinance, the Georgia High Court upheld the legality of racial zoning in 1917.[13]

The euphoria of Georgia's segregationists faded quickly when the U.S. Supreme Court unanimously struck down a similar racial zoning ordinance from Louisville, Kentucky, later that year. In the landmark decision *Buchanan v. Warley* the court ruled that the denial of the full use of property "from a feeling of race hostility" constituted inadequate grounds to sustain racial zoning. Like most southern cities intent on legalizing residential segregation, Atlanta was not dissuaded by *Buchanan v. Warley*. Besides Atlanta, southern cities such as Norfolk, Richmond, New Orleans, Winston-Salem, Dallas,

Charleston, South Carolina, and Birmingham all passed new racial zoning legislation after the *Buchanan* decision. Other cities discussed the topic seriously and looked to consultants to find a workable approach to planned apartheid.[14]

Cleveland planning consultant Robert Whitten prepared Atlanta's Zoning Plan in 1922, the most celebrated post-*Buchanan* attempt to link legalized residential segregation to comprehensive planning. Actually, what Whitten proposed differed little from the city's original racial zoning scheme except that it employed the nomenclature of conventional land use districts along with a set of racial designations. Whitten defended racial zoning on the grounds that the Atlanta Plan allowed "adequate areas for the growth of the colored population," that residential separation would instill in blacks "a more intelligent and responsible citizenship," and that racially homogenous neighborhoods promote social stability. Even in its new guise, Atlanta's racial zoning plan never made it past an initial court review.[15]

What is significant to note is that this renewed attempt to implement racial zoning was part of a major metropolitan planning initiative by planning consultant Warren Manning to make Atlanta not only "a beautiful, orderly place," but also "the wonder city of the Southeast." It was a widely held tenet of planning in the 1920s that controlled growth of black neighborhoods was necessary to produce a socially better city. Even though the explicit racial designations in the city's zoning plan had to be removed, the "controlled segregation" objective of race-based planning guided public policy and private real estate decisions in Atlanta over the ensuing decades. According to recommendations in the 1922 plan, Atlanta's black residential expansion was to be confined to the west and southeast sections of the city. That was, in fact, exactly the direction of black residential expansion from the 1920s onward. Even without the powerful legal tool of zoning, white and black Atlantans proved adept at guiding the process of black residential growth in conformity with the prescription in the 1922 plan through the use of deed restrictions and an assortment of racially sensitive real estate practices.[16]

The controlled physical expansion of the black community in Atlanta in the 1920s and 1930s did not relegate blacks just to neighborhoods of older housing abandoned by whites, however. It was not solely the product of white segregationists either. African-American entrepreneur Heman E. Perry constructed hundreds of houses for black clients on a 200-acre tract he acquired in the West Side in the early 1920s. Although Perry's real estate empire collapsed in that decade, his community building fueled the inexorable westward push of black Atlanta and opened up areas of new housing to the city's growing black middle class. At the time of his initial development in the West Side, the city's fashionable black neighborhoods remained on the East Side. As middle-class blacks migrated westward, Hunter Street, which bisected the West Side from the edge of downtown past Atlanta University to Mozeley Park, began to rival "Sweet Auburn" as the hub of black business and social life in Atlanta. In the West Side itself, black residential expansion remained circumscribed well into the 1930s. When, for example, an African-American physician purchased three lots in the 1930s in the still all-white Mozeley Park subdivision just beyond the existing black community, he encountered threats of violence from the neighborhood and temporarily abandoned plans to breach the color line.[17]

It was not long thereafter, however, that the pressures generated by African-American population growth (coupled with black displacement from neighborhoods around the central business district) opened the West Side to new black housing developments and undermined efforts to prevent racial change in existing white neighborhoods. Whereas neighborhoods responded individually to the threat of racial change in the 1920s and 1930s, by the 1940s accommodating black residential expansion while maintaining segregated residential patterns became a centerpiece of city policy. White city leaders accepted the expansion of black Atlanta toward the west and south-west, but they also supported West End white neighborhoods in controlling changes in the boundaries that separated blacks from whites. Competition for residential space in the West Side was only one of the many struggles for power between blacks and whites in Atlanta from the 1940s onward, but it was uniquely important in one sense. In the West Side, white recalcitrance to social change was tempered by a process of negotiation with blacks over the future racial composition of the area. In the process of creating a completely segregated city, whites in Atlanta accepted negotiation with blacks over the issue of neighborhood change in order to counteract pressures toward residential integration. Through a neighborhood planning process based on negotiations between whites and blacks, the separate city took a significant step toward realization.[18]

The origin of the interracial dialogue in planning for neighborhood development can be traced to the 1930s in conjunction with the Public Works Administration (PWA) low-income housing program in Atlanta. Federal officials, recognizing the "considerable difficulty in endeavoring to develop a white project, and a colored project in the same community," welcomed the aid of a local biracial coalition headed by white businessman Charles F. Palmer and Atlanta University's African-American president, Dr. John Hope. Although whites and blacks worked through separate committees to plan for the nation's first public housing projects—Techwood Homes for whites and University Homes for blacks—Palmer and Hope supported a single slum-clearance and housing-development package for Atlanta. Furthering the objective to give equal attention to black and white housing needs, the Atlanta Housing Authority (AHA) was created in 1938. By 1940, the AHA had completed or begun work on nearly 5,000 public housing units, approximately 40 percent of which were for white occupancy. At the time, it represented one of the largest public housing programs in the nation. Over the next two decades, however, public housing, slum clearance, urban renewal, and neighborhood planning, which had been pursued in the 1930s through a unique sort of biracial cooperation, generated conflict between whites and blacks in the struggle to control Atlanta. These struggles were further complicated by efforts on the part of black leaders to gain a voice in the city's public schools.[19]

The black community development pattern of Richmond prior to 1940 differed from Atlanta's not only in the degree of interracial cooperation but also in its physical and social manifestations, especially since the turn of the century. Actually, in 1900 there was little difference in the size of the black population of the two cities. Atlanta's black population of 35,727 in 1900 was only slightly larger than Richmond's black population of 32,230. Between 1900 and 1940, however, the growth rates of the black communities of Atlanta and Richmond diverged sharply, with the 1920s proving to be the pivotal decade. Whereas Atlanta's black population grew by 44 percent during the decade, Richmond's black community actually *declined* slightly. Even though the 1930s brought a similar growth rate in the black community of both cities, by 1940 Atlanta's black community of more than 100,000 residents was nearly twice that of Richmond.[20] Population growth pressures, as noted, pushed Atlanta's black community well beyond the urban core by the 1940s. In contrast, Richmond's black community remained largely within the boundaries prescribed by whites during the heydey of Jim Crow in the early 1900s. And Richmond seemed determined to use public policy to bring about the desired pattern of racial residential segregation.

Richmond

Richmond was the first city south of the Potomac River to embrace racial zoning following enactment of the Baltimore plan in 1910. In 1911, immediately after a decision of the Virginia Supreme Court upholding the legality of a local zoning ordinance, Richmond's city council passed a racial zoning ordinance. The law designated neighborhoods as either white or black (based on the existing racial composition) and prohibited occupancy by new residents of the opposite race. The intent was to freeze the existing configuration as well as to control future expansion of black neighborhoods. The Richmond residential segregation law received the blessing of the state's highest court in 1915 and until the U.S. Supreme Court decision in *Buchanan v. Warley* in 1917, the city administered it with vigor. Even after 1917, as one contemporary noted, Richmond remained "a hotbed of strong opinion favoring preservation of the strict integrity of both races." Two more attempts to fashion a legally defensible racial zoning scheme failed to overcome the precedent set in the *Buchanan* decision. The editor of the *Virginia Municipal Review*

Atlanta Black Population, 1900–1980

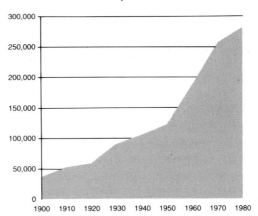

Figure 1A

Black Percent of Atlanta Population
1900–1980

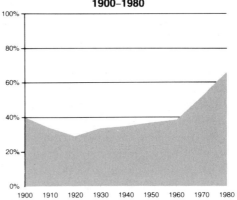

Figure 1B

Atlanta Black Population
Percent Growth Over Decade

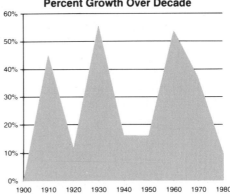

Figure 1C

voiced the prevailing local sentiment following a final negative verdict (the *Deans* case) by the Virginia courts on another racial zoning law in 1930: "a gradual and natural encroachment of the colored population into white neighborhoods" now will confront Richmond with "a problem of increasing significance . . . whose solution deserves the thought and discussion of leaders of both races."[21]

There was some movement of African-Americans into predominantly white neighborhoods both *before* and *after* the 1930 decision, but not to the extent predicted by proponents of legalized residential segregation. Growth in Richmond's black neighborhood occurred principally in those areas close to the core that were in transition from residential to commercial uses. The most notable change in racial occupancy took place in the Jackson Ward neighborhood located to the north of the central business. Since the early nineteenth century a large concentration of Richmond blacks had resided adjacent to this white middle-class neighborhood both to the north in an area known as Apostle Town and to the west in New Town. After 1900 these pockets of black population actually spread inward toward the urban core as the expanding central business district induced white middle-class residents to abandon Jackson Ward for developing suburbs to the north and west. In effect, white middle-class neighborhoods leapfrogged over Apostle Town and New Town as the growing black community pushed into the heart of Jackson Ward. Although the edges of Jackson Ward had long served as the social and economic hub of Richmond's black community, after 1920 the entire ward became synonymous with black Richmond. According to sociologist Charles Knight, writing in the 1920s, the consolidation as Jackson Ward as a black neighborhood owed largely to the fact that "Marshall Street had been rapidly changing from a residence street into a business street, and it is apparent that those parts of Clay and Leigh Streets in this vicinity are destined for the same usage in the near future." Even though most whites had moved out by the end of the decade, many retained ownership of housing. The relatively low rate of home ownership among black residents in Jackson Ward, coupled with the rapid exodus of whites, produced "a central-city ghetto, or something very much like it."[22]

The existence of a highly concentrated black community in Richmond's Jackson Ward offers a contrast with the community pattern of Atlanta in the pre-1940 period. For one thing, Atlanta's black West Side was an amalgam of suburban neighborhoods built in early twentieth century and thus constituted relatively good housing stock in those areas where blacks replaced whites as residents. Jackson Ward housing was built largely in the early to mid-nineteenth century, and much of it was in deteriorated condition by the time blacks replaced whites in the early 1900s. The Jackson Ward structures were far too large and too expensive for a single low-income black family, so most were subdivided into two or more units, and others became boarding houses. Most important, whites retained ownership, and white absentee owners sought to maximize their returns by encouraging over-crowding. In addition, Jackson Ward was geographically self-contained, being cut off from the expanding suburbs to the east and north by Shockoe Valley (through which ran the tracks of the Seaboard Air Line) and to the south and west by commercial and industrial areas. The fixed boundaries of Jackson Ward, along with the absence of space for new housing construction within the community, required a substantially higher population density than in Atlanta's West Side to accommodate the growing black population. White Richmonders, through racial zoning but especially through real estate practices, kept black Richmond confined largely to what was emerging as a Jackson Ward "ghetto." The black separate city would not be formed until after the 1940s and embrace an area greater than one-half of the entire city of 1940.[23]

In marked contrast to Atlanta, Richmond offered virtually no new housing for African-American during the 1920s and 1930s. The formation of the Renters' and Consumers' Protective Association in Richmond in 1919 led to a proposal, endorsed by the Richmond Chamber of Commerce, to create a stock company for the development of moderately priced homes for blacks on a suburban site. The proposal aimed directly at reducing the population density of Jackson Ward and included a range of improvements such as street paving, alley cleanup, and demolition of substandard housing. As the spon-sors put it, "Jackson Ward will have such a cleaning up as it has never known. . . . Additional housing will be provided in another quarter for the overflow of Jackson Ward, with paved streets, sewers, lights, gas, water and car service; so that the entire colored working population can easily reach places of employment and be able to live under attractive conditions, and, when they desire, to acquire homes of their own."[24]

Not only did this scheme fail to materialize, but overall private housing developments produced only a handful of new houses for African-Ameri-cans, most of which were rental units in cheaply constructed four-family apartment buildings. The absence of new housing construction available to blacks left even relatively prosperous black families with no alternative except to crowd into Jackson Ward's old and increasingly dilapidated houses.[25]

Moderate growth rates in Richmond's black population between 1900 and 1940 made it possible for Jackson Ward to accommodate an increasing proportion of blacks. Yet, it should be emphasized that barriers to black migration into neighborhoods beyond Jackson Ward, not just slow popula-tion growth, hastened the consolidation of the city's black ghetto. There were several other pockets of black residences southwest of the downtown in the Randolph area, and to the east in Church Hill and in Fulton. These other older neighborhoods continued to attract new black residents as the demarcations

Richmond Black Population, 1900–1980

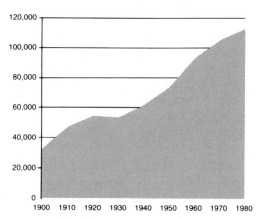

Figure 2A

Black Percent of Richmond Population 1900–1980

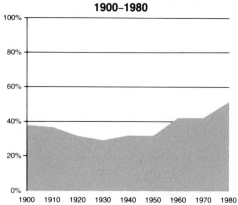

Figure 2B

Richmond Black Population
Percent Growth Over Decade

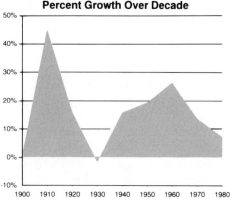

Figure 2C

between white and black neighborhoods became more rigid after 1900. Yet, it was the growing importance of Jackson Ward to black community life in Richmond that explains black opposition to a Public Works Administration (PWA) housing project for the neighborhood in the mid-1930s.

African-American leaders initially favored the proposed low-rent apartment project that would have been located near Virginia Union College north of the Jackson Ward community. White residents of the adjacent Sherwood Park neighborhood had a different view. They strenuously opposed what they regarded as a breach of the residential color line and convinced the project organizers to seek a new site. The nearly two years of conflict over selection of a new site led to the demise of the original limited-dividend housing proposal. In 1935, however, the PWA again expressed interest in constructing public housing in Richmond. This time the Mayor's Advisory Committee on Housing, a biracial steering group, proposed a site that they thought neither whites nor blacks would oppose in the northern section of Jackson Ward. The project called for slum clearance as well as for the construction of several hundreds of low-income housing units. Although some white absentee land owners in the proposed area objected to the plan, it was black homeowners, led by the ad hoc Home Owners Committee, that determined to stop the project. George W. Howell, chairman of the Home Owners Committee, appealed to federal officials to reject Richmond's request to clear and rebuild a portion of Jackson Ward on the grounds that it would force black property owners to become renters. As Howell noted:

> Property in this area consists mostly of (sic) Negro Owned Homes, which are obtained by hard labor, economic living and extreme thrift on the part of the purchasers. In many instances these homes represent the entire savings of Negro families. To deprive us of our homes, reduce us to the status of renters and not provide any decent locality where we shall go, is most inconceivable on the part of our Government. . . . We are satisfied where we are and do not wish to depart from the homes we own, since after this area is rebuilt, we have no possible chance to buy in the rebuilt area.[26]

Prominent black community organizations, especially the black Ministerial Union and the biracial Urban League, supported the project but suggested that residents should be involved in the planning process and that a more selective version of clearance should be undertaken so as to affect only the "undesirable houses." Federal land appraiser Richard D. Stimson urged that condemnation proceedings be initiated against land owners to break down resistance, and key members of the local housing coalition agreed. In response, the chairman of the Mayor's Advisory Committee, William H. Schwarzschild, said that he would "never vote for the Government to condemn this property against the wishes of the colored people." By September 1935, after having secured options on only one-half of the 150 parcels of land in the project area, Richmond learned that its public housing project had been a victim of cuts in federal appropriations for slum clearance. Actually, by September, black and white members of the Advisory Committee had come up with a new site that would require the demolition of only four structures. When news came that Richmond had been removed from consideration as a site for public housing, seventeen leading black organizations penned an unequivocal appeal in support of the project on the new site: "We unhesitatingly state that failure of this project would be a great blow to our people, hundreds of whom were looking forward to the opportunity of moving from the dilapidated, unsanitary shacks which they now occupy, into modern houses, at a rental they can afford to pay."[27]

The failure of the Richmond PWA project contrasts sharply with the success of Atlanta's initial housing program and reflected sharp differences between the two cities in their approach to community-development matters. Indeed, it was somewhat surprising that Richmond got as far as it did with the PWA project given that its mayor, J. Fulmer Bright, was a vehement anti-New Dealer. Atlanta's mayor, William Hartsfield, used his Washington connections skillfully to secure urban improvement and relief funds for his city. All that Richmond got from federal government was a study by planner Harland Bartholomew that documented the deteriorated state of its housing, especially in the old and congested Jackson Ward neighborhood. When the Virginia legislature responded in 1938 to a national trend to empower cities to create housing authorities to be eligible for public housing funds under the Federal Housing Act of 1937, Mayor Bright fought the local initiative. He insisted that housing problems should be resolved by local businessmen and that federal involvement only exacerbated the problem: "I believe that these very Federal housing projects, now being constructed to relieve the ills of which we complain, will in themselves constitute the slums of the next generation, 20 years hence." In 1939 he vetoed a City Council resolution sponsored by the biracial Richmond Advisory Committee on Housing that called for the creation of a local public housing authority. Whereas Atlanta entered the 1940s with a vigorous program to clear slum areas and to rebuild them with low-income housing, Richmond's political leadership allowed the community-development process to follow a natural and seemingly unplanned course, so long as it remained within the prescribed boundaries of existing black residential concentrations. After 1940, as a direct consequence of another set of public initiatives aimed at restructuring the core of Richmond, the physical integrity of Jackson Ward was destroyed, and with it went the social and economic core of Richmond black community.[28]

Memphis

The pre-1940 pattern of black community development in Memphis offers another variation to those of Atlanta and Richmond. More so than in the other two cities, the residences of African-Americans in Memphis were widely dispersed throughout the city in the twentieth century. Sociologist Thomas Woofter found in his 1928 study that the Memphis black population, which was only slightly greater than Richmond's, occupied nearly three times more urban space. Blacks occupied 28 percent of the residential land in Memphis, which amounted to a density of 21 persons per acre. In contrast, Richmond's black community squeezed into only 10 percent of the residential land and boasted a substantially higher residential density of 46 persons per acre. Between 1910 and 1920 the number of black homeowners in Memphis increased by 70 percent, whereas Richmond's proportion of black homeowners rose by a more modest 22 percent. According to Woofter, the increase in black home ownership in Memphis occurred as blacks from the center city migrated to outlying neighborhoods where single-family housing and home ownership possibilities were more prevalent. Memphis had no single black concentration such as Jackson Ward or the more spacious West Side of Atlanta to accommodate population growth or to absorb displacees. As a result, the city's rapidly growing black population in the 1920s and 1930s fanned out to the north and south of the central business district in search of new housing. Between 1900 and 1940 the city's black population grew from 49,910 to 121,498, with the greatest concentrations located in the midtown area. The spectacular growth of the Memphis-Shelby County black population in the 1930s by nearly 28,000 persons occurred principally as a result of migrants from impoverished rural areas coming to the metropolis. Accommodating this sudden population growth reinforced the tendency of the city's blacks to disperse to many neighborhoods. Over the next three decades, however, the Memphis black community consolidated from two sprawling clusters into a single expansive and highly segregated entity that encompassed the entire core area.[29](See Fig. 3.)

There is no evidence that Memphis joined with Richmond and Atlanta in the movement to legally control racial change in neighborhoods through racial zoning. At a time when most southern planning consultants advocated racial zoning, a comprehensive plan for Memphis prepared by planner Harland Bartholomew in 1924 studiously avoided any reference to the racial implications of zoning. Yet, it should be noted that the designation of new multifamily housing, commercial, and industrial zones by Bartholomew coincided precisely with existing black residential clusters. Local attorney and Chairman of the Chamber of Commerce City Planning Committee Wassell Randolph acknowledged that racial considerations played a role in determining future land uses. In Memphis, he noted, African-Americans lived principally in "the less desirable sections of the city," particularly in the industrial corridor stretching south of the central business district along the Mississippi River. "We have a sort of natural zoning of the races," he observed. The city's 1923 zoning ordinance merely reinforced the natural

Memphis Black Population, 1900–1980

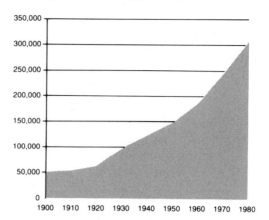

Figure 3A

Black Percent of Memphis Population 1900–1980

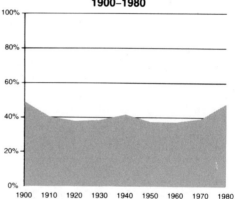

Figure 3B

Memphis Black Population Percent Growth Over Decade

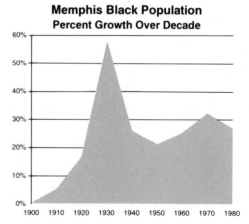

Figure 3C

separation prescribed by existing land use and topography. What allowed Memphis the luxury of eschewing racial zoning to achieve racial separation was the plentiful supply of undeveloped space for new white neighborhoods along the fringes of the city. The aggressiveness of Memphis's annexation efforts from 1899 to 1919 gave the city ample space for residential expansion beyond the core. Between 1922 and 1930, Memphis experienced a housing boom (Richmond, in contrast, experienced a slump) that resulted in the construction of more than 10,000 single-family homes in new East Memphis subdivisions beyond the outer parkway. This parkway served as the demarcation not only between the old city and the new but also between white and black Memphis. As long as black population growth could be accommodated through infiltration into older neighborhoods to the north and south of Beale Street and inside the parkway perimeter, white Memphians saw no need to depart from their traditional reliance on "natural zoning" to ensure racial separation.[30]

Blair T. Hunt, principal of Booker T. Washington High School and a prominent member of the Memphis black community after World War I, acknowledged the influence of "natural zoning" as well as the dispersed character of the city's black community: "Whenever you had seemingly a residential area of blacks, it was close to a bayou or a railroad track. I suppose because the land was cheap or cheaper, and no doubt, that's why we settled. But we lived in patches. There was no big black belt, no solid black belt anywhere in this city of Memphis. Then in the course of time, the Negros began to expand their residential areas." Pockets of black affluence emerged along Linden Street in the "silk-stocking" seventh ward, but most Memphis blacks lived in modest frame houses in the most undesirable locations.[31]

The condition of housing in the pre-1940 period offers a more precise demarcation between white and black neighborhoods. According to a survey of Memphis housing financed by the Works Progress Administration (WPA), approximately 50,000 housing units were in substandard condition, which accounted for approximately 77 percent of the residences of black Memphians. In contrast, only 35 percent of the white population lived in substandard units. The statistics pertaining to black occupancy of substandard housing would have been even more dismal except for the city's aggressive slum-clearance and public housing campaigns during the 1930s. Memphis rivaled Atlanta in procuring federal assistance for slum clearance and demolished nearly 1,000 "shacks" by the end of the decade. By 1938 the Memphis Housing Authority (MHA) operated 1,124 public housing units in two separate complexes, one for whites and the other for blacks. Even as Richmond's city council remained deeply divided over the issue of creating a local public housing authority, Memphis embarked on three more slum-clearance and public housing projects that increased the city's assisted housing inventory to 3,337 units by 1941.[32]

The initial strong support in Memphis for a public housing program, a program that became anathama to both whites and blacks by the 1950s, owed to several factors. Certainly, the eagerness of Boss Edward Crump to secure federal largess to bolster the local economy during the Great Depression was an essential factor. The aggressive development program of Crump's hand-picked housing czar, MHA Executive Director Joseph A. Fowler, never endured either a public debate or a process of negotiation between blacks and whites. One reason was that the MHA slum-clearance activities of the 1930s involved principally sparsely populated areas adjacent to the central business district and posed no direct threat to established black or white neighborhoods. Moreover, Memphians had complained about the severe housing blight in its central business area and accepted the involvement of the local housing agency to root out the problem by clearing slums. What Memphians did not realize was how public housing and slum clearance would significantly alter the social morphology of the city as the program expanded after 1940. Public housing construction fostered the concentration of blacks south of the central business district and served as a determining factor in black residential expansion that marked the decades after 1940.[33]

Black Community Patterns: 1940–1970

In Atlanta, Memphis, and Richmond, segregation of neighborhoods by race was a process under way, but still quite incomplete, in 1940. Although the spatial configuration of the black residential areas differed among the three cities in 1940, over the next three decades all moved toward total physical separation from the white world. Atlanta in 1940 was the most mature case among the three in the trend toward a separate black city within a growing metropolis, and yet it was still racially integrated. According to 1940 census data, 55 percent of Atlanta's census tracts were predominantly white, with black residents making up less than 10 percent of the total tract population. In contrast, only 45 percent of Richmond's tracts were predominantly white in their population composition in 1940. Memphis offers an even more striking contrast to the Atlanta pattern, with less than one-third of its tracts possessing a black population of less than 10 percent in 1940. In the case of Memphis, the wide geographical dispersion of black residents also represented an emerging spatial split within the black community itself between relatively affluent and poorer neighborhoods (see Maps 1, 2, and 3).[34]

Atlanta

Atlanta in 1940 possessed relatively few mixed-race tracts, that is, tracts whose black population ranged between 10 percent and 70 percent. Only 19

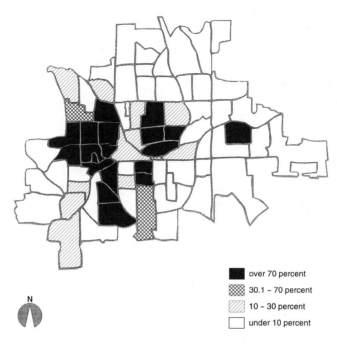

over 70 percent

30.1 – 70 percent

10 – 30 percent

under 10 percent

N

Map 1. Percentage of Black Population in Atlanta Census Tracts, 1940

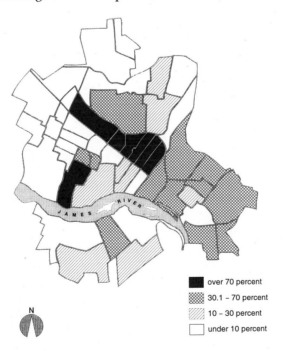

over 70 percent

30.1 – 70 percent

10 – 30 percent

under 10 percent

N

Map 2. Percentage of Black Population in Richmond Census Tracts, 1940

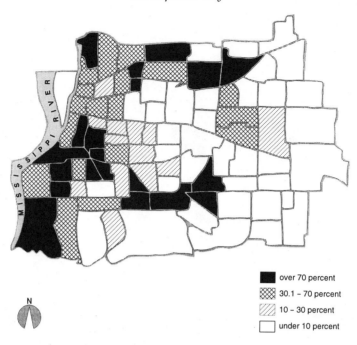

over 70 percent
30.1 – 70 percent
10 – 30 percent
under 10 percent

Map 3. Percentage of Black Population in Memphis Census Tracts, 1940

percent of the city's tracts could be categorized as mixed-race, although most of these had a black proportion ranging from 10 to 30 percent. Mixed-race tracts offered areas for black residential expansion without necessarily prompting wholesale displacement of whites. The availability or lack of unavailability of mixed-race tracts in 1940 offer an indication of how much room was left in the existing neighborhoods for black expansion without expanding into exclusively white areas. In the case of Atlanta in 1940, there were few mixed-race tracts and thus relatively little room for black residential expansion without directly going into predominantly white neighborhoods. In contrast, both Memphis and Richmond had approximately 40 percent of their census tracts in the mixed-race category. In Richmond, for example, only 15 percent of its residential tracts in 1940 were predominantly black. With enough room to absorb additional black population growth in its mixed-race tracts through white outmigration, Richmond and Memphis seemed less likely than Atlanta to experience competition between blacks and whites over neighborhoods that in 1940 were still predominantly white. Although in all three cities after 1940 the black community became increasingly spatially concentrated, Atlanta was clearly further along in the process on the eve of World War II. This helps to explain why Atlanta gave the issue of controlled racial change in its West Side neighborhoods such a prominent place in its public planning agenda as early as the 1940s. City leaders in Memphis and Richmond paid less attention in its planning process to racial change in neighborhoods until the late 1950s.[35]

The comparatively small proportion of mixed-race neighborhoods in Atlanta in 1940 owed to the tremendous growth in its African-American population from 62,769 in 1920 to 104,532 in 1940 coupled with local efforts to control where that growth was located. In other words, the mixed-race tracts of 1920 became predominantly black tracts by 1940. It should not be assumed, however, that white Atlantans were victims of a large-scale black invasion of their neighborhoods. Quite to the contrary, the wholesale abandonment of neighborhoods by whites in Atlanta often occurred at the first sign of a crack in their racial hegemony or where new black housing development occurred first and led to "all black enclaves adjacent to white districts."[36]

The location of African-American households in Atlanta in 1940 and 1960 confirms the relatively high degree of residential segregation (Map 4). Census tract data for 1940 reveal that nearly 90 percent of the city's 28,315 black households crowded into one-third of Atlanta's seventy-four census tracts. In addition, the incidence of homeownership among black households in Atlanta was low. Only 13 percent of the city's black households were homeowners compared to a 32 percent rate for white Atlantans. The spatial distribution of black homeowners in the 1940s suggests that black affluence related to residence in the city's West Side. Map 5 shows that census tracts closest to the central business district had the lowest rates of homeownership. What stands out from the census data is the small number of tracts overall in Atlanta where black homeownership exceeded 10 percent. Only eight city tracts showed black homeownership rates above 10 percent. There appears to be no connection between the degree of racial mixing and the incidence of black homeownership in Atlanta's census tracts in 1940. Those tracts with the lowest proportion of black residents also had the lowest incidence of homeownership. It seems that location was the more salient factor. In general, West Side tracts adjacent to Hunter Street (west of Walnut and Vine Streets) had the highest homeownership rates among black households. Yet, the predominant pattern was that rental and homeownership areas intermingled to form a single residential concentration with a remarkably low overall rate of homeownership.[37]

Memphis

Whereas the black community in Atlanta clustered largely in the western one-third of the city in 1940, black households in Memphis could be found all over the city, with representation in approximately three-quarters of its residential census tracts. Black neighborhoods tended to cluster around the central business, and white residential areas stretched eastward into the fringes of Memphis, although there were ample mixed-race neighborhoods to the north and south of the central business district in 1940 to accommodate

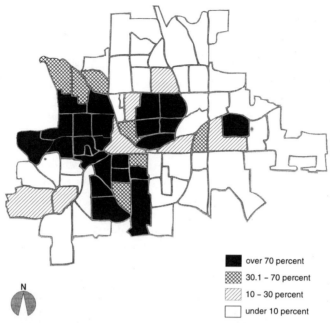

N

Legend:
- over 70 percent
- 30.1 – 70 percent
- 10 – 30 percent
- under 10 percent

Map 4. Percentage of Blacks in Atlanta Census Tracts, 1960

black residential expansion without encroaching on predominantly white areas. Some black families lived in most areas of Memphis by 1940. In only seven of its seventy-five tracts did black households make up less than 2 percent of the total. Even with this wide geographical dispersion, most blacks in Memphis in 1940 lived either north of Jackson Avenue or south of Poplar Avenue, with the neighborhoods in between ranging from 10 to 55 percent in black occupancy. One reason for the bifurcated pattern in the black community was the persistence of a white residential wedge that extended from the edge of Memphis's central business district eastward to the growing suburbs. Over the next forty years, blacks filled in the already segregated neighborhoods to the north and south of this white residential corridor, but the white wedge persisted. As illustrated in Map 6, there was little change in the locus of predominantly black neighborhoods from 1940 to 1950, although the 1950s brought increasing black presence in both North and South Memphis. After 1960 the area of greatest expansion of the city's black community was South Memphis (see Map 7).

The changing spatial configuration of the Memphis black community from 1940 to 1960 evidenced an emerging socioeconomic as well as geographic split. In terms of the rate of homeownership and income levels, North Memphis was becoming the more affluent black area. Actually, in 1940

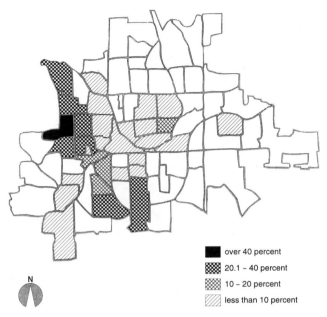

over 40 percent

20.1 – 40 percent

10 – 20 percent

less than 10 percent

*Includes data from those census tracts where blacks constituted 10 percent or more of the households.

Map 5. Percentage of Black Owner-Occupied Households in
Atlanta Census Tracts, 1940

the majority of the tracts with the highest proportion of black homeowners
was in South Memphis. By 1950, however, the incidence of black homeownership in South Memphis declined, and the six predominantly black census
tracts in North Memphis boasted homeownership rates of 53 percent or
greater. In several North Memphis neighborhoods, the black homeownership rate exceeded 60 percent. In contrast, the average homeownership
rate in the thirteen predominantly black census tracts in South Memphis
was 29 percent in 1950. It should be noted that the overall homeownership
rate among blacks in Memphis vastly exceeded that of blacks in Atlanta
(see Table 1, Map 5).

The notably greater incidence of tracts in South Memphis with declining black homeownership after 1940 was not simply a result of unplanned
population shifts, however. The location of public housing projects in Memphis contributed significantly to the transformation of South Memphis to an
area of renters. Of the 3,337 public housing units constructed in Memphis
prior to 1950, 2,220 were built south of Poplar Avenue, and all were designated for black occupancy. Only 280 units of public housing for families were
built in North Memphis over the entire life of the program. The rest of the
public housing went into Central Memphis.[38]

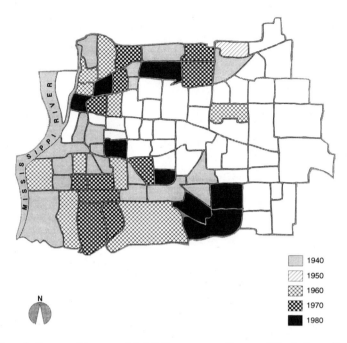

Map 6. Census Tracts with 70 Percent or Greater Black Population, Memphis, 1940-1980

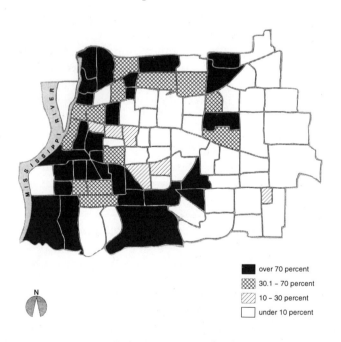

Map 7. Percentage of Blacks in Memphis Census Tracts, 1960

Table 1. Black Families at 80 Percent or Less of Median Income,
Memphis, 1950

Census tract	Total black families	Black families 80% or less Number	Black families 80% or less Percent	Census tract	Total black families	Black families 80% or less Number	Black families 80% or less Percent
North				South			
1	960	690	72	40	3,070	2,095	68
2	770	390	51	41	2,965	2,295	77
3	980	345	35	42	750	655	87
4	890	535	60	43	465	380	82
5	175	90	51	44	1,090	880	81
6	1,155	720	62	45	1,595	1,105	69
7	620	270	44	46	820	610	74
9	860	420	49	47	470	320	68
10	335	205	61	48	2,030	1,395	69
14	235	145	62	49	1,650	1,100	67
18	1115	685	61	50	910	645	71
90	900	630	70	51	1,585	1,140	72
Total	8,995	5,125	57	52	675	490	73
				53	1,810	1,100	61
Central				54	2,165	1,445	67
19	720	505	70	55	835	515	62
20	420	335	80	57	815	545	67
21	830	625	75	58	475	290	61
22	595	480	81	59	155	115	74
23	1,535	1,105	72	60	640	295	46
24	1,625	1,210	74	61	555	305	55
28	1,055	610	58	62	265	145	55
30	285	155	54	63	340	235	69
32	155	125	81	65	855	550	64
34	185	135	73	66	300	180	60
35	325	260	80	67	1,775	1,235	70
36	285	240	84	68	910	570	63
37	155	130	84	76	665	475	71
39	315	245	78				
Total	8,485	6,160	73	Total	30,635	21,110	69

* Eighty percent of median income in Memphis in 1950 was $1,881.

The location of public housing also influenced the income differential between the northern and southern sections of black Memphis. North Memphis boasted a greater proportion of the city's more affluent blacks in 1950, with five of its ten predominantly black tracts possessing an average family income greater than 80 percent of the median family income for all Memphis families. African-American living in neighborhoods just to the east of the downtown were largely low-income, and this band of black poverty extended into South Memphis, following a line corresponding closely to the location of public housing projects. Of the twenty-eight predominantly black census tracts in South Memphis in 1950, all but three were very low-income. Only in one tract did the majority of black residents have an annual income above 80 percent of the city median. Although poverty was a pervasive problem of the black community as a whole in Memphis after 1940, there is evidence of an expanding poor black section extending from the city's core into South Memphis that remained separated spatially from more affluent black neighborhoods to the north of the downtown. The emerging black belt in South Memphis after 1940 was in many respects as varied from the black northside as it was from the white world from which it was separating (see Map 6 and Table 1).

The changing spatial distribution of African-Americans in Memphis must be viewed in the context of the city's territorial expansion through annexation after 1940. Map 8 shows annexations in Memphis from 1940 to 1970. In 1940, for example, black neighborhoods extended north from the central business district to the city line. The addition of 35 square miles of territory in the 1950s, much of it north of Wolf River, provided space for white residential expansion within the city limits but beyond established black neighborhoods. Annexation to the east and southeast was intended to bring the newly built white suburbs into the city as well as to provide space for further development. At the same time, city leaders pressed for annexation of land in South Memphis (toward the Mississippi state line) to supply additional areas for development of black neighborhoods in order to reduce pressures on Southeast and East Memphis neighborhoods. The politics of annexation, along with the politics of public housing, slum clearance and neighborhood planning, all influenced the evolving form of the black community in Memphis between 1940 and the 1960s.[39]

Richmond

Richmond offers a variation on both the Atlanta and Memphis models. As in Atlanta, black community change in Richmond after 1940 represented a sort of inexorable flow in one direction. Richmond's East End was comparable to Atlanta's West Side in absorbing the greatest influx of blacks between 1940 and 1960 (see Map 9). At the same time, the development of new white neighborhoods occurred in a predominantly westerly direction. Even though Jackson Ward in central Richmond remained the social, economic, and institutional heart of the city's black community and boasted the highest residential densities of any black census tracts in 1940, blacks already represented between 30 and 70 percent of the residents in three-quarters of the city's East End tracts by this time. Chamberlayne Avenue, which bisected

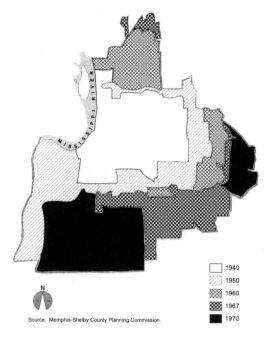

Source: Memphis-Shelby County Planning Commission.

	1940
	1950
	1960
	1967
	1970

Map 8. Memphis Annexations, 1940-1970

Richmond from its northern to southern boundaries, served as a rough dividing line between predominantly white neighborhoods to the west and predominantly black and mixed-race neighborhoods to the east. Gradually, after 1940 the black middle class moved out of Jackson Ward and into the older white suburbs to the north (but primarily on the east side of Chamberlayne Avenue) and directly eastward into Church Hill. In 1940 black and white neighborhoods coexisted in various sections to the east of Chamberlayne Avenue. By 1970 blacks predominated in all but one census tract in the eastern half of Richmond (see Map 10).

Public policy, especially in public housing, highway construction, urban renewal, and comprehensive planning, encouraged this segregated residential pattern. In the Church Hill area alone, the city built 1,848 (64%) of its 2,885 public housing units prior to 1970. Nearly all the rest were put in central Richmond in Jackson Ward (east of Chamberlayne Avenue). The concentration of public housing in the East End not only furthered segregation of the black community but also fostered class division within the black community itself, as evidenced by the concentration of middle-class neighborhoods in northeast Richmond and poorer black areas in the East End.[40]

In 1940 this split was hardly noticeable, however. Those black neighborhoods with the lowest homeownership rates were adjacent to the older

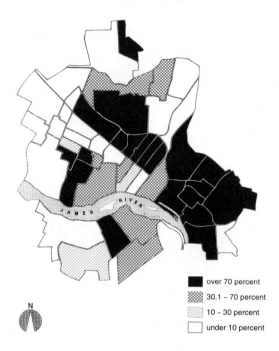

over 70 percent

30.1 – 70 percent

10 – 30 percent

under 10 percent

N

Map 9. Percentage of Blacks in Richmond Census Tracts, 1960

commercial and industrial areas strung along the James River. In fact, the East End showed a relatively high rate of homeownership (between 20.1 and 40%) in black neighborhoods in 1940. The highest black homeownership rates in Richmond in 1940 were in the tracts just to the north of Jackson Ward and on the south side of the James River adjacent to the white middle-class neighborhoods of Woodland Heights and Forest Hill (see Map 11). Unlike Memphis, where black homeownership was highest in predominantly black tracts, in Richmond black homeownership was more prevalent in the mixed-race tracts than in the segregated ones. By 1950, as in the case of Memphis, there was a growing division within the black community on a class basis. Richmond possessed (like Memphis) a white residential wedge extending from the central business district westward to the exclusive West End, but this did not constitute a barrier between major social segments of the black community as it did in Memphis. Rather, the social divide in black Richmond followed a line north of Church Hill at the eastern edge of the city to where it intersected the Richmond-Petersburg Turnpike (eventually Interstate 95) just north of the central business district. To the north of this line were the formerly white neighborhoods to which the black middle class migrated during the 1950s and 1960s (see Table 2). To the south and east, in Jackson Ward, and in the expansive East End area dominated by the Church Hill

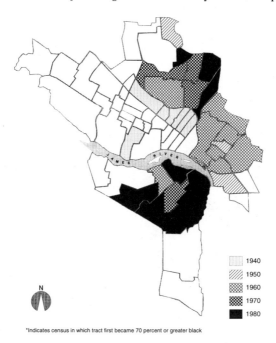

*Indicates census in which tract first became 70 percent or greater black

Map 10. Census Tracts with 70 Percent or Greater Black Population,
Richmond, 1940-1980.

neighborhood, resided the city's largest concentration of low income blacks.
Since Richmond did not launch a major urban renewal program until the late
1960s, considerable racial change in neighborhoods occurred only after 1970.
Displacees from urban renewal and other public improvement projects filled
the few remaining pockets of white residences to the east of Chamberlayne
Avenue, especially in Highland Park. The only other major change after 1970
was a substantial increase in low-income blacks in South Richmond in the
Brainbridge-Blackwell-Hull Street area, hastened by public housing construction and urban renewal displacees.[41]

Census data for 1960 indicate that the highest proportion of African-
American owner–occupied housing in Richmond was in North Richmond
and in some East End tracts (see Map 9 and Table 2). Renters continued to
predominate in the black community's traditional center, the Jackson Ward
neighborhood, as well as those tracts located immediately to the north of the
city's central business district. Pockets of black residences in the city's West
End, in Church Hill, and in North Richmond had owner-occupancy rates
well over 50 percent during the 1950s and 1960s. After 1960, however, as the
black middle class sought better housing outside of the traditional boundaries of black Richmond, the status of Church Hill as a mixed-income black

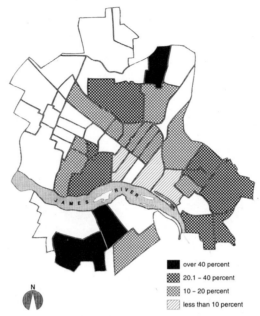

<table>
<tr><td>■</td><td>over 40 percent</td></tr>
<tr><td>▦</td><td>20.1 – 40 percent</td></tr>
<tr><td>▨</td><td>10 – 20 percent</td></tr>
<tr><td>▨</td><td>less than 10 percent</td></tr>
</table>

*Includes data from those census tracts where blacks constituted 10 percent or more of the households.

Map 11. Percentage of Black Owner-Occupied Households in
Richmond Census Tracts, 1940

neighborhood changed significantly. The outmigration of middle-class blacks not only depopulated the East End but also made it a rival to Jackson Ward as a locus of black poverty. Although lacking the institutional substructure that had made Jackson Ward the hub of black life through the 1940s, Church Hill became during the 1960s and into the 1970s the symbol of manifold social and economic problems confronting impoverished blacks in Richmond.[42]

The socioeconomic split reflected in the changing black neighborhood pattern in all three cities foreshadowed a future division among black community leaders along political lines. In the 1940s the black community may have appeared to most observers as a cohesive entity cordoned off from white areas. As suggested in the preceding analysis, however, there were demographic indications that the black communities in Atlanta, Memphis, and Richmond were internally diverse, an amalgam of subcommunities linked together by race for survival in a hostile white world, but certainly not a homogenous community. Matters of community leadership and political power were secondary concerns given the limited role for blacks in public decision making in 1940. Yet, it was during the 1940s and 1950s that the issue of who spoke for the interests of African-Americans became a

Table 2. Homeownership/Renter Rates among Blacks
in Richmond, 1960

Census tract	Total black families	Black 80% or less		Black renter-occupied	
		Units	Percent	Units	Percent
East					
E-2	1,258	519	51	503	49
E-3	1,202	610	56	489	44
E-4	1,172	402	36	708	64
E-5	1,147	342	33	707	67
E-6	1,067	160	18	722	82
E-7	1,352	702	55	583	45
E-8	1,161	292	28	760	72
E-9	1,208	279	35	527	65
Total	9,567	3,306	40	4,999	60
Central					
N-1	653	129	21	494	79
N-2	774	171	25	523	75
N-3	1,215	227	20	926	80
N-6	1234	129	11	1,047	89
N-7	695	196	29	473	71
N-8	458	161	36	286	64
Total	5,029	1,013	21	3,749	79
North					
N-4	1,029	426	52	393	48
N-9	1,279	534	53	471	47
N-10	1,036	226	44	287	56
N-11	1,097	195	59	137	41
N-12	1,759	10	67	5	33
Total	6,200	1,391	52	1,293	48
West					
W-7	1,691	897	55	723	45

* Expressed as a percentage of the total number of black-occupied housing units.

matter of considerable importance in the black communities in all three cities. The internal struggle for leadership in the evolving black separate city foreshadowed the emergence of black political power in the 1970s, especially in Atlanta and Richmond, and later in Memphis. To understand the transformation in local black leadership in the Civil Rights era and the emergence of black political power in Atlanta, Memphis, and Richmond, it is important to examine the nascent black community power structure of the 1930s and 1940s.

Black Community Leadership

Memphis

Leadership in the black community of Memphis throughout the first half of the twentieth century, particularly during the reign of Edward H. Crump, revolved around political influence. The political role of black Memphis was an anomaly in a region otherwise characterized by complete disenfranchisement, but then Boss Crump was a rather atypical southern urban politico. This is not to underestimate the role of black entrepeneurs, professionals, and religious leaders as community notables. Beale Avenue in Memphis was a center of black business and professional life whose influence reached well beyond the confines of the city. Yet, in a southern city where a growing African-American population retained voting rights during the heyday of disenfranchisement, it is little wonder that politics found its way into most community institutions. Given the importance of black voters in the revival of the Crump machine in the 1920s, blacks who delivered blocks of votes gained an entrée to the white power structure that could bring individual rewards as well as possible improvements for the black community.[43]

In the 1940s, however, black leadership in Memphis was in an obvious state of transition. In the late 1930s Robert R. Church, Jr., the black Republican who had worked closely with the Democrat Crump since the 1920s, broke with the machine. This act of defiance by Church not only brought on him the full wrath of Crump's legendary vindictiveness but also marked the beginning of what the Church family described as "the most tyrannical decade in the history of Memphis for Colored citizens." The split between Crump and Church was not, in fact, a complete break between the white power structure and the black community but rather a power struggle between the aging Church and his ally, J.D. Martin, and Crump. Even with the removal of Church and Martin from Memphis politics, black Memphians continued to vote for Crump. Throughout the 1940s until the mid-1950s blacks "accepted accommodation," even though in other southern cities the politics of protest signaled a new relationship between the black community and the prevailing power structure.[44]

If there was a meaning to the rupture between Church and Crump in the 1930s, it was that "blacks had lost their last significant exercise of political independence" until they coalesced to challenge, rather than to accommodate, white power in Memphis.[45] Church may have recognized the futility of further accommodation, or, as his critics suggest, he overestimated his importance to the Crump machine. Whatever the explanation for Church's ill-fated challenge to Crump, over the next two decades black political involvement operated on the basis of what might be described as "strategic accommodation." On the one hand, African-Americans supported white leaders who proclaimed sensitivity to the needs of the black community. During the 1940s this included Crump candidates as well as opponents of the machine. On the other hand, for the first time the black community fielded its own candidates for select offices (see Chapter 3), although every attempt was made to secure candidates acceptable to both whites and blacks. More important, however, was the simultaneous development of the organizational basis for separate black activism that by the early 1960s nurtured a new brand of leadership in black Memphis.

Ralph J. Bunche's portrait of black community leadership suggests that in Memphis blacks created their own machinelike structure to adapt to political life under Crump. This arrangement had its origins in the mayoral election of 1919 when Church promised the reform candidate, Rowlett Paine, solid black backing in return for "certain civic services," including paved streets, additional schools, and black police officers in black neighborhoods. Paine retained black support in his 1923 reelection bid because of his largess during the first administration, and Church's political cronies took charge of the political mobilization effort throughout black sections of Memphis. As reported in the Memphis *Commerical Appeal* on November 3, 1923, Bert M. Roddy, Waymon Wilkerson, Lieutenant George Washington Lee, T.H. Hayes, and Reverent B.J. Perkins led rallies in North and South Memphis and "brought out a total of more than 1,500 colored voters . . . to hear enthusiastic appeals for the straight Paine Administration ticket."[46]

Paine's comfortable margin of victory may have minimized the perceived contribution of African-American voters, or it may have been, as one commentator noted, that "there was practically no organized demand made by them [black leaders] to force the issue after the mayor assumed office." Whatever the circumstances, Paine failed to retain black allegiance for a third term, and despite a campaign platform that called for "just treatment of Negroes," blacks sought to unseat him in the 1927 election. Church's crony, George Lee, organized the West Tennessee Civic and Political League, which claimed to control nearly one-half of the registered black voters, and immediately endorsed Watkins Overton, who was Crump's ticket to regaining political control of the city. Overton noted that black disaffection with the incumbent stemmed from "broken promises" as well as "the building of an obnoxious city crematory in the choicest Negro residential district of the city." For his part, Overton promised more parks, swimming pools, and hospital facilities for blacks, because, as he claimed, "the general improvement of the Negroes as citizens is part of the general plan for improvement of the South." In contrast to Paine's initial pledge to employ blacks in key city positions, Overton openly opposed the appointment of black policemen and firefighters or integration of public parks.[47]

Overton's landslide victory consummated the political marriage between the black Republican machine led by the Church-Lee-Martin triumverate and Crump's Democratic organization. Bunche contends that there were few tangible benefits to the black community from this alliance beyond the ability "to quash traffic tickets and secure a few appointments of Negro teachers." J.D. Martin, whose drugstore was "a kind of mecca for powerful Negroes to gather and discuss things," offered support to Bunche's view. He admitted that after his break with Crump there was little he could do for the black community "because Crump's machine need do him no favors whatever; it owes him no political debt." According to Reverend Blair T. Hunt, whose ties to the Crump machine survived the Church schism, a great many black voters continued to support Crump candidates during the 1940s, even after he had forced both Church and Martin to leave Memphis. Crump confiscated Church's property for $80,000 in back taxes that the city previously overlooked as a favor. Robert Church, Jr., whose father was probably the wealthiest black in the United States in the early 1900s, left Memphis impoverished. Crump later had the elegant Church family home burned down on the pretext of testing some new fire-fighting equipment. The Memphis boss also had the name Church expunged from the public by instructing the City Commission to change the name of Church Park and Auditorium to "Beale Avenue Park and Auditorium." Martin's drugstore received regular visits from the police, and, under the threat of arrest, he also left the city.[48]

The systematic dismantling of Church's business and political empire showed not only the power of the Crump machine but also the fragility of black political influence. Crump, moreover, could still rely on Lee and Hunt to secure black votes for the organization. Lee, Hunt, and the majority of black voters remained loyal, historian David Tucker noted, because Crump continued "to offer paternalism—welfare, health care, public housing, schools, playgrounds, and personal favors," which seemed more than blacks could count on in other southern cities. In comparison, the Crump "machine provided security for blacks and delivered a better share of city services and less brutal police treatment than did white rule in southern cities where blacks did not vote."[49]

It was not simply an overbearing political environment that accounts for the reticence of black leaders in Memphis. Long before Crump evidenced his intolerance for independent political action, the black community showed a decided inability to maintain its own organizations. Twice during the 1920s, the local chapter of the NAACP lost its charter for lack of membership. Under a new charter and a new president, Aaron Brown, Jr., the local revived in 1930. Yet, Brown, a former instructor at LeMoyne College in Memphis, noted the difficulty of keeping it going because "the Negro has been deceived by his leaders so many times that the confidence is low." Even more telling was his view that the black community suffered from factionalism that transcended political party affiliation and centered on matters of class. Attempts to organize independent political action was stymied by established black as well as by white leaders.[50]

Little apparently changed when Merah S. Stuart, an African-American insurance executive, took over as president of the local NAACP branch later in 1930. During his five-year term, according to critics, the Memphis branch failed to push the agenda of the national organization because Stuart "was more concerned with the exploitation of the Negroes in favor of his insurance company than with the welfare of the group." This view was not universal as some regarded Stuart as an outspoken defender of black rights. He was, in any case, a protégé of Dr. Joseph Edison Walker, the founder of the Universal Life Insurance Company which by the early 1930s was among the top ten black insurance firms in the country. Walker's original refusal to pay obeisance to Church led to his social and political ostracism in the 1920s. When Church refused support for Walker's appointment to the Republican National Convention in 1932, Walker switched parties and established the Independent Business and Civic Association (later renamed the Shelby County Democratic Club) in consort with the Crump machine. To broaden his base of power beyond black Democrats, Walker sought to control other key organizations in the black community. Through Stuart, his longtime associate and the vice-president of Universal Life, he resuscitated and controlled the NAACP and in 1937 organized the defunct Urban League. He exanded his influence in black business circles by organizing the Negro Business League to promote black enterprise in the city.[51]

In the aftermath of the Crump-Church split, Walker emerged as the dominant figure in black Memphis. He did so by controlling not only the major political institutions but also by expanding his business interests to include banking—his Tri-State Bank founded in 1946 was the only black-owned bank in Memphis—and by supplying the financial backing for three new churches, one of which was named after him. Walker used the pastorship of one of his churches, the Mississippi Boulevard Christian Church, to lure Hunt into his political fold after Crump died in 1954.[52]

It was in 1948, however, that Walker first tested his political strength by openly breaking with Crump to join a coalition of liberals and organized labor to back the anti-Crump candidate for the U.S. Senate, Estes Kefauver. It was significant that three of the city's predominantly black precincts went for Kefauver. Walker convinced black businessman Taylor C.D. Hays and Reverend James A. McDaniel, president of the Urban League, to join the defection. Reverend Dwight V. Kyle, pastor of the Avery Chapel A.M.E. and a member of the local NAACP, became the first black to run for Congress (this time on the Progressive ticket) since the early 1900s. Walker used the successes of 1948 as a stepping stone to his own political aspirations. By joining forces with white liberals such as Edmund Orgill and by luring George Lee, who controlled the local Republican party, away from Crump, Walker forged a coalition capable of eliciting wide support for black candidates. He recognized, moreover, the need to expand the black electorate and, prior to his 1951 run for the Memphis Board of Education, organized a massive voter-registration drive. In concert with Lee and two other black insurance executives, L.B. Matlock and A.A. Gilliam, Walker organized the Non-Partisan Voters Committee in 1951 and within a few months increased the number of registered black votes by nearly 12,000. By the early 1950s the two black insurance executives, Walker and Lee, "monopolized black political leadership" in Memphis. Although Walker's bid for a seat on the Memphis Board of Education fell considerably short and showed that Crump still controlled a sizeable chunk of the black electorate, it was obvious by the early 1950s that black candidates could make a solid showing in political contests without white backing.[53]

Most important, the Walker candidacy broadened the base of African-American leadership in Memphis. McDaniel served as the first black member of the newly formed Civic Research Committee, a group that eventually spearheaded the overthrow of the Crump machine, and joined Lee and Walker in the Non-Partisan Voters Committee. Walker also recruited LeMoyne College's President Hollis F. Price, Reverend Roy Love, who later ran for a seat on the Board of Education, attorney A.A. Latting, Dr. A.N. Kitrelle, and *Memphis World* editor Lewis O. Swingler. Civic clubs and church leaders, many of whom previously avoided political involvement, supported efforts to expand the black electorate. In particular, the politicization of black ministers such as McDaniel and Love marked a profound shift among the city's traditionally reticent religious leaders. In the past, the ministers who got involved in politics were loyal to Crump. Although most avoided politics and did not support the Boss, they were, as Reverend A.E. Campbell reminisced, "careful in avoiding conflict with him." As the events of the 1940s and early 1950s showed, there was a long road yet to travel for full participation in local politics. Still, the new black boss of Memphis, Joseph Walker, and his coalition of black elites, were in the process of changing the face of black politics in Memphis and, in effect, the black community itself by the early 1950s.[54]

Atlanta

Politics was not the measure of leadership in Atlanta's black community that it was in Memphis in the early 1940s. Political scientist Clarence A. Bacote noted in his widely cited assessment of Atlanta politics from 1869 to 1955 that the 1920s and 1930s were the "nadir" in political influence emanating from the black community. The Atlanta Civic and Political League formed in 1934 to encourage blacks to register despite the existence of a white primary and a poll tax. The League stressed that the white primary did not apply to special elections. In the early 1920s, for example, black voters twice helped to defeat a bond issue that neglected their interests. On the third go around, city officials promised that one-third of the funds would go into black schools. With support from the black community, the bond issue passed. Black voters also played a key role in preventing the recall of Mayor James L. Key in 1932. Yet, the white primary severely limited black influence in most elections and blunted black interest in political involvement. The League claimed a membership of approximately 2,500. Given that there were only 2,106 registered black voters in Atlanta in 1939, however, the ACFL's membership claims were probably inflated.[55]

Aggressive black voter registration efforts in the mid-1940s, prompted by the elimination of the white primary and the poll tax, created the base for a more significant political role for blacks in Atlanta. Yet, even before the voter-registration campaigns, blacks exerted remarkable influence in Atlanta affairs on the strength of professional and business leadership. The social structure of Atlanta's black community in 1940 contained a sizable "upper class" drawn from business and professional circles and linked by affiliation and tradition to the black educational institutions that made up the Atlanta University Center. It was this African-American elite that white Atlantans consulted on matters of race relations, involved in biracial coalitions to support various improvement projects such as public housing and urban renewal, and negotiated with on highly sensitive matters such as regulating the real estate market and residential shifts to preserve residential segregation. Indeed, the emergence of black political militancy in the early 1960s constituted a reaction by newly enfranchised blacks not only to white Atlantan policies but also to the domination of black community affairs by a black elite long enmeshed within the politics of the white establishment.[56]

Atlanta's black professional and business class in 1940 ranked second only to New Orleans' in its size and influence in the South. Leading black businesses in Atlanta centered in the fields of real estate, banking, and insurance and were offshoots of the business empire of Heman E. Perry during the 1920s. The son of a Texas grocer, Perry drew on his experience with the Equitable and Manhattan Life Insurance companies and founded the Standard Life Insurance Company in Atlanta in 1911. The instant success of the insurance venture enabled him to branch out into a number of other areas, including banking, real estate, and several service industries. Although Perry's speculation in real estate led to his demise in the mid-1920s, his personal collapse did not impede the expansion of black-owned businesses in Atlanta. Three of Perry's former employees founded the Citizens Trust Company in the early 1920s. It survived the Great Depression and by the 1940s had become the largest black-owned bank in the country and a controlling force in many other business concerns in black Atlanta.[57]

As the number and scope of black businesses grew from the 1920s through the 1940s so, too, did they separate physically and in their marketing efforts from white Atlanta. After the Atlanta race riot of 1906, black-owned businesses left the central business district and located initially on Auburn Avenue in the city's East Side. "Segregation forced the development of Auburn Avenue as a black business center," and in turn the separation of black business gave rise to new black entrepeneurs. Between 1910 and 1930, the number of black professional and business concerns in Atlanta's central business district declined from forty-eight to fourteen. White property owners refused to lease to new black businesses. At the same time, the number of black-owned businesses overall increased markedly. Most of the new businesses were small, family-run affairs that were in retail and service sectors, with well over one-half being either restaurants, grocery stores, or hairdressing and barbering shops. Still, there were forty-four general physicians, fifteen dentists, four real estate firms, four law offices, and one bank to serve Atlanta's black community in 1930. The number of black businesses increased during the 1930s, and by the early 1940s new large-scale enterprises, especially in real estate, made their mark on black Atlanta.[58]

Perhaps the most important change in African-American business life in the 1930s and 1940s was its migration from Auburn Avenue to the West Side in conformance with the prevailing demographic shift under way in the city. The shift of black business from Auburn Avenue to Hunter Avenue adjacent to Atlanta University further separated it from the white side of Atlanta and underscored the emergence of a "dual system" of business in the city. Some black leaders quietly acknowledged that segregated business actually helped black entrepeneurs because it encouraged black economic self-reliance. In the view of one prominent black Atlantan, the coexistence of separate business sectors supported by "educational institutions of higher learning for both races" bred "progress" for the Atlanta black community.[59]

The proximity of Atanta's new center of black commerce to the black academic world was more than physical, however. The city's black intellectuals employed by the Atlanta University Center produced not only a new generation of professionals but also, through activist faculty and administrators, exerted substantial control over the business and organizational life of black Atlanta. L.D. Martin, who founded the Citizens Trust Company in the 1920s and remained its president until the 1940s, chaired the Economics Department at Atlanta University. His business partner, J.B. Blayton, also served on the economics faculty. The President of the Atlanta Mutual Building Loan and Savings Association, John P. Whittaker, served as Registrar of Atlanta University. The University's president, John Hope, had served on the Board of the Citizens Trust Company since the 1920s. Charles E. Maxey, who founded the Southeast Fidelity Fire Insurance Company in 1949, also served simultaneously on the Atlanta University faculty. T.M. Alexander, a leading real estate broker in Atlanta, remained active in the affairs of Morehouse College long after graduation. Alexander's connections reached not only into the academic community but also, through it, to the upper echelons of the Atlanta black community.[60] The overlapping memberships between Atlanta's leading businesses and the Atlanta University Center (of which Morehouse was a part) accentuated the "eliteness" of those wielding economic power in the black community. Through the Atlanta University connection, moreover, key black elites interacted with their white counterparts in Atlanta. Education and social class defined the participants in the Atlanta interracial dialogue that was a trendsetter in race relations throughout the South.

Atlanta's business-professional-academic elite could not wholly detach itself from issues that affected the African-American masses, however. A tradition of self-help in the black community nurtured a spirit of noblesse oblige on the part of the black elite. The wife of John Hope, for example, formed a Neighborhood Union in 1908 to address the health and educational needs of poor blacks living close to Morehouse College. By 1915 her efforts led to the city's first and only settlement house. Throughout the 1920s the academic community in Atlanta functioned as a voluntary social welfare agency. Hope himself worked hard to improve housing in Atlanta's black community and was the only official black member of the prestigious local group that secured the nation's first public housing projects in the mid-1930s. Hope had been useful to the white housing reformers because as president of Atlanta University he was able to procure without a fight the land used for the black project. Like his white counterparts, Hope operated through private negotiations and unofficial committees. While the exercise of his influence in the white community redounded to the benefit of the black community, Hope's style of leadership left the Atlanta black elite vulnerable to charges of accommodation or, at worst, collusion with whites out of individual self-interest.[61]

One wealthy and influential real estate broker, W.H. "Chief" Aiken, made no effort to obscure his links to the white business world. His association with one of the city's leading white banks provided the mortgage funds necessary to sustain development of nearly 1,000 new houses for blacks in Atlanta's West Side in the late 1940s. He served as one of the three black members of an "unofficial" committee established by Mayor William Hartsfield in 1952 to oversee real estate practices in the West Side communities to ensure peaceful maintenance of residential segregation. Hartsfield's intent was to bring together influential black and white community leaders from the West Side to negotiate the process of racial change in order to prevent blockbusting and possible violence. Also representing black real estate interests was T.M. Alexander, a fellow member of the Empire Board of Real Estate. The third African-American member, A.T. Walden, had practiced law in Atlanta since 1919 and was a prominent member of several black political organizations. Although the mission of the West Side Mutual Development Committee (WSMDC), as Hartsfield called it, was to safeguard black interests, it also served directly the cause of residential segregation. It conformed to the local style of using private negotiations rather than public debate when dealing with civil rights issues. Hartsfield made this position clear in his response to a call from a grand jury in early 1960 to establish an "offical" biracial committee to deal with racial tensions. He rejected the suggestion, noting that the races in Atlanta already enjoy "perfect communication over here [at City Hall] and that the proposed aims of a citywide biracial committee were already being accomplished by a number of smaller committees on which blacks serve," such as the WSMDC. In the absence of political pressure from black leaders, Hartsfield decided for himself who best represented black interests.[62]

Political power through the vote may not have been a tool available to Atlanta's black community in the 1940s, but efforts to increase political influence began in earnest. Complementing the voter-registration efforts launched by the Walden-led Atlanta Civic and Political League (ACPL) in the 1930s was the Women's Civic League formed in 1940 by a black social worker to register "underprivileged" black women. Even with repeal of the poll tax by Governor Ellis Arnall in February 1943 and a stepped-up voter registration campaign conducted jointly by the ACPL, the NAACP, and the Atlanta *Daily World*, there were only about 3,000 black registered voters in 1945. A special election in Feburary 1946 for a vacant congressional seat (in which the white primary did not apply) sparked renewed voter-registration efforts. The number of eligible black voters in the city rose to 6,876. African-American votes were instrumental in the outcome of the special election because Helen Douglas Mankin defeated the favored Tom Camp on the strength of solid support from black precincts.[63]

The elimination of the white primary in April 1946, coupled with the gubernatorial race in the fall and the success of the special election in February, spontaneously politicized Atlanta's black community. In 1940 Bunche describe the black ministers of Atlanta as an impediment to the civil rights movement. "That more progress has not been made in bettering the social, economic, and political life of the Negro," he wrote, "is in large measure the fault of the ministers, who direct the social thinking of so large a part of the population." By 1946, however, many black ministers were active in a coalition of black organizations, the All-Citizens Registration Committee, that increased the number of registered black voters in Atlanta to 21,244 by May. They continued throughout the summer to support an educational campaign to inform new voters of the issues at stake in the upcoming election. As Bacote noted, "consequently, the local branch of the NAACP reactivated its citizenship schools in the twenty-one precincts where Negroes were concentrated, with college teachers volunteering as instructors. Negro ministers opened their churches for forums on public affairs." A permanent nonpartisan umbrella organization, the Atlanta Negro Voters League, formed in 1949, and made its initial presence felt by backing the successful reelection bid of Hartsfield.[64]

Further proof that the political mobilization of the 1940s represented a permanent change in Atlanta's black community came about shortly after the 1949 election. Bacote notes that the influence of the black vote resulted in the hiring of black police officers, suppression of race baiting, and "in city planning the city fathers began looking at the needs of all citizens regardless of color," with the result being "better streets, lights, sewers, water, and sidewalks [that] have made Negro neighborhoods attractive." The election of Dr. Rufus E. Clement, President of Altanta University, to the Board of Education in 1953 by a margin of 10,000 votes indicated that blacks could elect their own leaders. Clement not only secured solid support from black voters but also garnered considerable backing from the white community. The election of a black to the Atlanta school board could not have come at a more critical juncture. With the *Brown* decision just over the horizon, Atlanta proved that black political leaders could garner biracial backing. Given the explosive issues that would jolt most southern cities in the 1950s and 1960s, the willingness of a segment of Atlanta's white community to accept such radical social and political change was an auspicious event.[65]

Richmond

Black church leaders in Richmond represented key community influentials, not only in religious affairs but also in politics and social reform. One student of black politics in Richmond contended that from 1940 to the mid-1960s, the ministers "held a disproportionate amount of power and influence." Gordon Hancock, as a professor at Virginia Union and as a practicing minister, contributed a nationally recognized figure to Richmond's ministerial ranks. But in local political organizations and social reform groups, there was a wide array of local black leaders besides ministers. Two black professionals, attorney Oliver W. Hill and physician Dr. J.M. Tinsley, took center stage in the politicization of the black community in 1940s. It was during this period that politics usurped business as the centerpiece of black community organizational life in Richmond. The demise of Jackson Ward as an economic hub of black Richmond also shifted attention from black business to a new age of political life.[66]

This was a notable change from the 1920s and 1930s, however, when black businesses in Jackson Ward supplied the leading community figures. Maggie Lena Walker, the first female bank president "anywhere," and John

Mitchell, the publisher-financier-politico, dominated black community affairs throughout the 1920s. Giles P. Jackson, an attorney and organizer of the Negro Exhibit at the Jamestown Exposition in 1907, completed Richmond's black triumvirate. When Jackson died in 1924, the white Chamber of Commerce, "for the first time in its entire history took cognizance of the death of a citizen who was not a member of its body and adopted resolutions expressing sorrow." Mitchell's death two years later did not evoke a similar note of sympathy from white Richmonders because of his open criticism of white repression. The black community overlooked the failure of Mitchell's Mechanics Savings Bank (known popularly as "John Mitchell's Bank") and acknowledged his valiant stand against lynching in the early 1900s. Mitchell was joined in a futile quest for the governorship of Virginia in the 1920s on an all-black ticket that included Maggie Walker as a candidate for the superintendent of Public Instruction in Richmond. When Mitchell died in 1926, the mantle of black leadership in Richmond passed to Walker. Not only had Walker launched a local Council of Negro Women, but she also served as director of the NAACP, as a board member of the Urban League, and, with Hancock, as a member of the Virginia Interracial Commission. She was, as one writer put it, "the focal point of the Richmond black community where all knew and revered her." Her death in 1934 left a noticeable void in the black community leadership structure.[67]

Political activity declined as well, and after Walker's death black Richmond marshaled only 1,527 registered voters in 1936. Only through its political clubs, the most important of which was the Richmond Democratic League, did blacks exercise even a modicum of political influence in the interwar period. The hostility of Mayor J. Fulmer Bright, who served in that office continuously from 1924 to 1940, neutralized all efforts by blacks to influence local politics. Bright consistently secured "the poor white vote on the basis of his record of 'No Negroes on the city payrolls—city jobs for hard working white men'." Bright's refusal to hire blacks for city jobs became an issue in the 1936 mayor campaign. During the campaign, a memorandum circulated stating that Roy Dudley, his challenger, intended to discharge whites to make jobs available for blacks. Dudley publicly denied the allegation and claimed that Bright simply sought to inject the race issue into the campaign. Although Dudley sidestepped the black hiring issue—there were in 1936 sixty-one black employees (out of 2,000 city workers) in positions such as orderlies, cooks, and maintenance workers—he received solid support from black voters, albeit in a losing effort. The problem was that only about 1,500 blacks voted in the 1936 election.[68]

Four years later, however, African-Americans claimed a decisive role in ousting Bright. This seems a bit of an exaggeration since Gordon B. Ambler defeated Bright by over 5,000 votes and the total black vote amounted to only 2,400. Yet, what was significant in the 1940 election was the demonstrated success of voter-registration efforts. Through the combined work of Tinsley, the NAACP local, and Roscoe C. Jackson of the Democratic Voters' League, the number of black voters increased by more than 50 percent over the 1936 figure. Those blacks who voted in 1940 supported a winner and found in Ambler a progressive white political leader willing to give attention to problems that had long plagued the black community, especially substandard housing. Ambler's victory signaled the beginning of a political reform movement in which black Richmonders eventually played a prominent part. By the end of the decade the black community, with white support, actually elected a prominent black attorney to Richmond's city council.[69]

The difficulty in increasing the number of eligible black voters was a poll tax that remained in force until the U.S. Supreme Court declared it unconstitutional in 1946. After its removal, Dr. W.L. Ransome organized the Richmond Civic Council (RCC) as an umbrella voter-registration organization representing nearly eighty black church, civic, fraternal, business, and education groups in the city. Within one year the number of registered voters grew to more than 8,000 not just because of the registration campaign but also because attorney Oliver Hill announced his candidacy for one of seven positions in Richmond's General Assembly delegation. Hill finished eighth in the 1947 election, a mere 187 votes behind W.H.C. Murray, the labor candidate who also picked up a share of the black vote. Despite allegations that white labor had not reciprocated in supporting Hill, both Hill and Tinsley maintained that the Murray forces backed Hill, and he urged retention of a labor-black coalition.[70]

The coalition bore fruit for Hill and the Richmond black community one year later. Having failed in an attempt to gain the backing of the interracial Richmond Citizens' Association, Hill ran as an independent candidate for one of nine seats on Richmond's newly reconstituted City Council. Ransome's Richmond Civic Council supplied the organizational backing for Hill. The same array of leading black ministers who backed Hill in the previous election—including Dr. Joseph T. Hill, Reverend K.D. Turner, Dr. C.C. Scott, Dr. J.A. Brown, Reverend R.R. Fitzgerald, Reverend A.M. Walker, and Hancock—supported his second try at political office. Support from white laborites, in concert with an enlarged black electorate, produced 9,097 votes for Hill and made him the first black to sit on Richmond's city council since the late nineteenth century. Ironically, Hill won his seat by 263 votes over the labor candidate, a reversal of the outcome of his previous candidacy.[71]

It seemed fitting that the black RCC should have representation on the new city council because it actively supported the charter reform campaign of the biracial Richmond Civic Association (RCA) that resulted in the new city manager-council form of government. Blacks recognized clearly the advantage of a government structure premised on a merit system of hiring (as contrasted to the political basis for city government jobs under the old system), that promised a wide range of urban improvements, and that did away with the Democratic primary. Even before the new city council took the oath of office, Richmond opened the public library to black patrons and hired several black police officers. Changes seemed to be happening even before Hill had a chance to act.[72]

The marriage between the black RCC and the biracial RCA proved short-lived, however. The release of a plan for a downtown expressway that would slice through several central city neighborhoods, both black and white, led to a referendum in conjunction with the June 1950 councilmanic election. Ironically, Ransome's RCC joined with former mayor Bright to oppose the expressway, whereas councilman Hill offered "cautious" support for the highway plan prepared by planning consultant Ladislas Segoe of Cincinnati. Hill contended that "the Segoe Plan was much less destructive than other plans under consideration." That position might have cost him a few precious votes among black and white opponents of the expressway. The expressway went down to defeat by the wide margin of nearly 4,000 votes, but Hill lost his bid for reelection in 1950 by only forty-six votes.[73]

Despite Hill's narrow defeat, the Richmond *Afro-American* proclaimed another victory for the black community. Given that Hill received 12,488 votes (over 3,000 more than in 1948), his candidacy obviously drew strong support from white as well as black voters. Overall, the black vote clearly aided other RCA candidates, and their endorsement of Hill in the 1950 election would likely be followed by future endorsements of black candidates. "Black leaders were confident that their cooperation would be rewarded," noted Dwight Holton, "but more importantly, blacks appear to have held the balance of power in the selection of several of the new councilmen." Perhaps less noticed was the apparent split within the black leadership over the expressway issue. Hill's support of the Segoe plan stood in contrast to Ransome's unequivocal opposition. Even more curious was the collaboration between Ransome and his longtime foe, Bright. The expressway issue was divisive in more than a physical sense.[74]

The Hill-Ransome split that began in the privacy of the RCC gatherings exploded across the pages of the Richmond *Afro-American* in the 1952 councilmanic election. Hill opposed Ransome as a council candidate (Hill himself chose not to run again because of his involvement in the *Brown* case) and worked secretly with the RCC and RCA to come up with a suitable alternate. Hill regarded Ransome as too old and too conciliatory to white business interests. Hill endorsed David C. Deans, a black life insurance executive, and got the RCA to back his nomination. Before the Deans nomination became public, Ransome announced his own candidacy. Although the RCC originally endorsed Ransome, it decided by a close vote to establish a Joint Campaign Committee for Deans and Ransome. The fighting between the Hill and Ransome camps continued throughout the weeks leading up to the June election. The result was a decisive defeat for both candidates. In turn, the RCA lost two seats on the city council. "It was all too obvious," notes Holton, "that the Civic Council's in-fighting had wreaked havoc upon black political strength in Richmond." It took nearly a decade to regain the political momentum engendered by Hill in 1948 and carried through to the 1950 election. In the meantime, Richmond's black community searched for new leadership during a period of tremendously disruptive community change.[75]

Change in the black communities of all three cities in the 1940s was not a consequence of any single set of factors. A complex interface between three principal community variables—population growth, social reorganization, and the formation of new leadership—transformed the black community in Atlanta, Memphis, and Richmond. As this chapter suggests, there were variations in the community change process in all three places, although they displayed a common trend toward increasing consolidation and separation through segregation. In all three cities, public policy initiatives beginning in the 1930s with the public housing and slum-clearance programs also influenced the black community-development process. Even though all three southern cities had access to the same federal pool of urban development resources, the local political culture affected directly the allocation of these resources in black community development. Community change fueled political involvement as the black community sought to have a greater say in public policy issues. No issue received more attention than challenging segregation in public education and public places, even though black neighborhoods became increasingly segregated. This fight is the centerpiece of the next chapter.

3

School Desegregation and the Rise of Black Political Independence

As noted in Chapter 2, prior to World War II Atlanta, Memphis, and Richmond became increasingly differentiated along race lines as the black community in each city became geographically more separated from the white community. The development process leading to the formation of the separate city differed among the three localities as did the development pattern itself. In Atlanta, through private agreements negotiated by leaders of the two communities, black population growth was accommodated by directing expansion westward from the downtown. Atlanta's development process relied heavily on racial zoning and on federally sponsored slum-clearance and public housing programs. Richmond's separate city, like Atlanta's, also tended to expand in one direction, though, in Richmond's case, the direction was eastward rather than westward. Moreover, in the pre-1940 period, community development in Richmond was less planned than in Atlanta, a difference that stemmed largely from Richmond's aversion to federal New Deal programs and the preference to allow the private market to determine the fate of black neighborhoods. Meanwhile, the separate city in Memphis evolved out of two socially and geographically distinct areas of black population, with the more affluent residents cut off from the poorer areas by a wedge of white neighborhoods. Community development in Memphis combined the use of "natural zoning," rather than the explicit race-based zoning codes prevalent in Atlanta and Memphis, with federally funded slum-clearance programs.

Irrespective of these differences, the fact remains that the black community in all three cases was never able to control its own destiny. Even in Atlanta, where private arrangements affecting African-American neighborhoods were agreed to by a few representatives of the black elite, black neighborhoods were always subject to forces rather than controlling and directing them. In varying configurations, black Atlantans, Memphians, and Richmonders lived separately and unequally from whites, with this separation having the full force of custom and law. Most lived in inferior housing that was concentrated in segregated neighborhoods and suffered marginal employment, inadequate health care, and underfunded Jim Crow schools.

Laws forced them to seats at the back of the bus, restricted them to separate seating in theaters and auditoriums, and gave license to deny them seating altogether in restaurants and other public accommodations. Seldom allowed to visit museums, libraries, and zoos on the same basis as whites or even drink from the same fountain, blacks lived as second-class citizens with few resources to change their condition.

During the 1950s and 1960s, however, a dramatic upheaval shook the South. Legal barriers began to fall under pressure from the federal courts and new legislation enacted by Congress that contributed to greater political empowerment of blacks. Atlanta, Memphis, and Richmond all experienced the changes, and although the impact of the Civil Rights movement varied from city to city, the fact remains that never again would social relations be the same. The era of accommodation and paternalism gave way to political resistance and protest. The day of black independence was dawning.

Perhaps the single most explosive issue that signaled the beginning of a new era and around which blacks mobilized for political action was public education. Certainly other issues were also important in galvanizing blacks, but the events surrounding the U.S. Supreme Court's *Brown v. Board of Education of Topeka* emboldened a new black leadership. In Richmond, particularly, the battle over school desegregation led directly to the formation of a new and powerful black organization, an organization that later engineered the election of the city's first black majority on the city council and the city's first black mayor. In Atlanta and Memphis as well, the education issue set into motion new forces and personalities that together would alter significantly the political relationships between blacks and whites.

In this chapter we examine the school issue and the role it played in changing the social and political agenda of Atlanta, Memphis, and Richmond. It begins prior to 1954 when the storm clouds of change were gathering. The South did not lack for warnings, but the warnings fell on deaf ears. As a consequence, when the U.S. Supreme Court's decision suddenly undermined a century of legal segregation in schools, it struck heavily not only the ill-prepared cities but also the region as a whole. For urban blacks, the victory was tarnished by the tremendous costs associated with it.

Prelude to Brown

Witnessing the events leading up to *Brown* were three journalists: Ralph E. McGill, editor and publisher of the *Atlanta Constitution*; Edward J. Meeman, editor of the *Memphis Press-Scimitar*; and Virginius Dabney, editor of the *Richmond Times-Dispatch* and, like McGill, a recipient of the Pulitzer Prize for editorial writing. Compared to the vast majority of whites in the South, these three journalists were decidedly progressive in their views and rallied through their writings a small but growing cadre of white southern liberals during the 1940s and 1950s.

All three had urged racial reform, although each in a distinctive way. McGill and Meeman, neither born to wealth and privilege, couched their arguments in moral terms and appealed to their readers' conscience. Dabney, a Virginia patrician, argued reform largely in terms of Jeffersonian democracy and simple prudence. His argument was that unless change was forthcoming and directed by the enlightened elite of the South, the voices of reason would be overcome by the cries of northern militants and demagogues of both races. Of the three, Meeman was more restrained on the race relations question. Given the Memphis political climate, Meeman believed that he could ill afford to take on two liberal causes (race relations and political reform) and decided to concentrate on denouncing the Crump machine and championing the cause of governmental reform. In the process, he decried Crump's exploitation of blacks. Although they could vote under Crump, blacks, according to Meeman, were "mere pawns," who, if they fell afoul of the machine, were "arrested without right, beaten up by police, and denied legal rights." Later, Meeman also served as a key organizer and member of the Memphis Committee on Community Relations created to foster communication between black and white leaders and to avert racial unrest during the post-1954 protest campaigns over segregation.[1]

In contrast, McGill and Dabney were much more direct about racial matters. They advocated reform in race relations and the need for whites to work cooperatively with blacks in achieving greater equality. Both played leading roles in promoting and participating in the South's interracial dialogue prior to 1954. Eleven years before the *Brown* decision, McGill presided at a meeting in Atlanta that was attended by over 100 prominent southern whites, one of whom was Virginius Dabney. They had gathered to respond to the Durham Resolution issued earlier in 1942 by a group of southern African-Americans who had convened in Durham, North Carolina (see Chapter 2). In a 1943 *Times-Dispatch* editorial, Dabney characterized the "Durham Statement," as a "landmark in Southern race relations, and probably the most important document of the kind since the War Between the States." The Durham conferees, who had excluded black leaders living outside the South, were intent on resolving problems in the South by involving only the indigenous black leadership, believing that white leaders in the region would respond better to the more moderate positions of their black counterparts than to the more stridently phrased and encompassing manifestos crafted by northern black leaders. The African-Americans meeting in Durham were apprehensive about the growing racial unrest in the South and about their own credibility in the black community should they fail to make any headway in improving the status of blacks.[2]

They urged the white South to demonstrate greater fairness to blacks and to provide evidence of greater opportunities for southern blacks, although they stopped short of calling for an end to segregation. They made it clear that without some tangible evidence that white leaders were willing to make some concessions, the black masses would begin to turn increasingly to black "extremists" outside the South who would demand nothing less than complete abolition of all segregation and discrimination.[3]

The group of whites who convened in Atlanta the year following the Durham gathering endorsed the challenge from the black leaders. They unanimously declared that the document written at Durham was "so frank and courageous, so free from any suggestion of threat and ultimatum, and at the same time shows such good will, that we gladly agree to cooperate." Following the Atlanta conference, the response that the white participants had written was printed and circulated with more signatories added. Those at the Atlanta meeting also proposed that still another meeting be arranged, only this time the gathering would be biracial and consist of representatives from the Atlanta and Durham gatherings. This proposal was favorably received by the blacks.[4]

Convening in Richmond on June 14, 1943, black and white leaders from throughout the South came together, with Gordon Hancock providing the keynote address. Writing in his influential study, *In Search of the Silent South*, historian Morton Sosna notes that Dabney would have chaired the meeting in Richmond had it not been for a controversy that stemmed from a January 1943 article he had authored in the *Atlantic Monthly*. In the article, entitled "Nearer and Nearer the Precipice," Dabney had commented that "a small group of Negro agitators and another small group of white rabble-rousers are pushing this country closer and closer to an interracial explosion which may make the race riots of the First World War and its aftermath seem mild by comparison." Dabney went on to criticize both A. Philip Randolph for planning a Washington, D.C., protest march and Roy Wilkins of the NAACP for saying that American blacks desired social equality with whites. Dabney believed that such militancy was counterproductive and would only lead to more troublemaking from white demagogues in the South. The article generated such intensive criticism, notably from whites who supported integration and from African-Americans such as Langston Hughes and P.B. Young, the relatively moderate editor of the *Norfolk Journal and Guide*, that Dabney thought it politically wise not to serve as conference moderator.[5]

Given the importance of the meeting, it is interesting that neither of the Richmond daily papers, the *Richmond Times-Dispatch* and the *Richmond News-Leader*, nor the weekly black paper the *Richmond Afro-American* covered the proceedings. Because both Dabney and Hancock were columnists, one can only conclude that the participants wanted to meet privately. Either they failed to contact the news desks or else convinced the news managers not to report the events. Dabney later referred to the meetings in an editorial and made specific reference to Hancock's speech. Hancock reiterated many of the same issues raised at the Durham meeting. A particularly salient point in Hancock's address shows that he had read Dabney's *Atlantic Monthly* piece: "Negro leadership in the South can be strangled or strengthened. . . . If the South resents interference from outside elements, then there must be a greater liberalism in the South in dealing with Negro leadership; and inter-racialism must not be synonymous with a 'motion to lay on the table' every proposal for social and economic advance. . . . It makes a world of difference to the cause of race relations whether the capital of the Negro race is in New York City or Atlanta."[6]

In editorializing on the dialogue that had begun between black and white leaders in the South, Dabney stressed Hancock's phrase about making "a world of difference to the cause of race relations whether the capital of the Negro race is in New York City or Atlanta." Dabney made it clear that unless some concessions were made to blacks, then the black leaders responsible for the Durham Resolution might be repudiated by the larger southern black community, resulting in a power vacuum that might be filled by more "radical" forces from the North. To prevent interracial strife, which Dabney believed would occur should the more moderate voices of the black South fail to elicit any substantive response from southern whites, concrete action was necessary. In particular, Dabney called for the abolition of segregation on streetcars and buses in Virginia, the appointment of African-American police officers to patrol the black neighborhoods of Virginia's cities, and the hiring of an all-black staff at the Piedmont Sanitorium at Burkeville, a hospital for black tuberculous patients. Dabney reminded his statewide readership that about fifteen southern cities already had black police officers; that in Georgia, Kentucky, Maryland, and West Virginia, all-black staffs had been appointed for black hospitals; and that segregation on public transit systems was less stringently enforced. In Dabney's view, repeal of segregation law for streetcars and buses would not be a revolutionary act. In addition to his cry of alarm to stave off intervention by northern black "radicals" and to reinforce the position of southern black moderates, Dabney concluded with the prophetic warning that "the best way to provoke bitter race clashes in this region over an indefinite period is for the whites to turn their backs on the legitimate appeals of the Negroes for justice. The crisis is upon us, and we shall ignore it at our peril."[7]

The letters written in response to Dabney's editorial were "in almost unprecedented numbers." African-American writers were unanimously in support of the proposals, and about three-fourths of the whites were supportive. Dabney also circulated copies of the editorial to the leading southern newspapers. With the exception of a small weekly journal in Kinston, North Carolina, however, no other white newspaper in the South supported Dabney. Even McGill's *Atlanta Constitution* remained silent. Virginia's political leadership also offered no response, and none of the proposals was implemented during the 1944 Virginia General Assembly. Finally, in 1950 the state legislature considered bills to eliminate segregation on intrastate and interstate public transit and to create a state commission on race relations, but they failed to pass.[8]

What Dabney had feared came to pass; even liberal whites were turning their backs on black appeals for justice. By maintaining the status quo, Virginia legislators not only undermined moderate and conservative black leadership and provided no alternatives for blacks except mass protest, but they also contributed to the hysteria that later developed in the Old Dominion and other southern states when the Supreme Court ordered the abolition of segregated schools. It was precisely this kind of inaction and failure to embrace moderate reform that prompted McGill to write a column, "One of These Days It Will Be Monday," the title referring to the fact that decision day for the U.S. Supreme Court usually fell on Mondays and that a school desegregation order was inevitable.

The southern liberal cause floundered, but not all was lost, however. Black and white leaders who had gathered in Richmond in 1943 decided to hold another joint meeting. In 1944 they congregated in Atlanta where steps were taken to form the Southern Regional Council (SRC) whose purpose was to fulfill the objectives established a year earlier at the Durham conference. Among the southerners identified with the Council were McGill, Dabney, and Morehouse College President Dr. Benjamin Mays. Although the Council proved unsuccessful in persuading politicians to support its program, it kept communication channels open between blacks and whites and addressed some important racial issues. Its role was to work quietly behind the scene to advocate greater racial equality. Yet, even its moderate positions (for instance, the SRC initially did not endorse school integration) drew fire from intransigent whites. It was viewed by Georgia's former governor Eugene Talmadge as a communist-inspired organization. More than once Ralph McGill found it necessary to counter these charges. Even with all of the editorializing from Meehan, McGill, and Dabney, the pronouncements of black and white leaders meeting in Richmond and Atlanta, the efforts of the new regional biracial organization, and the growing impatience and restiveness of the black masses—in spite of all of this—no significant legislative initiative occurred between the 1940s and 1954. The consequence, of course, was that the 1954 *Brown* decision came "like a thunderclap," to use McGill's expression, bringing a storm that had been building for years in the South but that most southern lawmakers ignored until it struck.[9]

Ironically, the Court's desegregation order and the death of boss Crump occurred the same year. Historian Hugh Graham noted that with Meeman's bête noire dying in May of 1954, "Meeman's lifelong devotion to freedom and democracy was to be sternly challenged as the Supreme Court thrust an issue of great divisive potential into Memphis' civic arena." In an editorial following the *Brown* decision, Meeman pleaded for time and patience from the courts. He wrote that the ruling was not unexpected and urged his readers to accept it, observing that compliance would improve the image of the United States before the rest of the world. "Our preachments on democracy and dignity and equal opportunity of man," he penned, "will ring truer to Asia's fermenting millions when they learn that here in America equality was not graded by complexion." As Graham pointed out, Meeman's editorial may not have been the most direct expression of approval, but within the context of his readership in the Mississippi Delta and the Yazoo Basin, even these evasive words were boldly affirmative.[10]

McGill also had anticipated the Court's desegregation order. As late as the early 1950s, McGill, like Dabney and many other southern white liberals, supported the principle of separate but equal treatment of blacks provided that in actuality their treatment was equal to that of whites. (Later, during the 1960s, McGill abandoned this position and argued that segregation was wrong and had imposed tremendous burdens on the South.) In a 1953 column, McGill wrote that "segregation is on its way out and he who tries to tell the people otherwise does them great disservice. The problem of the future is how to live with the change." When a year later the Court declared school segregation unconstitutional, the Atlanta editor never reminded his readers of the earlier warnings and failed to comment significantly on the *Brown* decision until five months later, concluding his observations with the simple admonition to obey the law.[11]

Dabney sat in his *Richmond Times-Dispatch* office when word of the *Brown* decision came across the wire. Unlike McGill, Dabney had not anticipated the Court's total repudiation of the "separate but equal" doctrine. Also, unlike his counterpart in Atlanta, Dabney issued an immediate editorial response. On Tuesday May 18, 1954, the day after the momentous decision, Dabney's column appeared in the *Times-Dispatch*. Entitled "What the Segregation Decision Means to the South," the editorial urged "calm and unhysterical appraisal of the situation by the officials and people of Virginia." Dabney proceeded to suggest that more time was necessary for the South to make the necessary adjustments, that full integration would take a long time to achieve.[12]

Had more opinion leaders across the South possessed the foresight of Ralph McGill and followed his advice to plan ahead for the day when school desegregation would be the law of the land, the *Brown* decision might not have been so traumatic. Second, editors such as Dabney and Meeman might not have found it necessary to plead for more time from the Court to allow the South to adjust to its decree.

Richmond

Once the high court announced the *Brown* decision on May 17, 1954, most leading officials in Atlanta, Memphis, and Richmond urged calm and refrained from demagoguery. That neither Atlanta nor Memphis had local elections may have contributed to the relative calm in both cities. For sure, the absence of electoral contests denied anyone the opportunity of capitalizing on the decision as an excuse to prey on the fears of desegregation opponents. Only in Richmond were there councilmanic elections, but the turnout was low, and race was not an issue. In fact, the *Times-Dispatch* reported that "this year's candidates failed to settle upon a single dominating issue."[13]

Two days after this election, Richmond hosted the first Southwide official discussion of the *Brown* decision. In a meeting closed to the press at the Hotel John Marshall, nine governors and forty-one other leaders from fifteen southern states shared views about the court ruling. Whatever hope may have existed for constructing a united front in the South was dashed shortly after the meeting got under way. It was clear that no consensus prevailed, and the fifteen states represented fell into one of three different camps. West Virginia, Maryland, and Kentucky indicated that they would comply with the Supreme Court decision and begin efforts to desegregate their schools. Georgia, South Carolina, and Mississippi remained defiant and expressed no intention to integrate. Between the two extremes were the other states, including Tennessee and Virginia. The best the conferees could achieve was a noncommittal statement issued at the conclusion of the meeting that each state would pursue its own course of action.[14]

In less than two years, however, opinion throughout the South began to crystallize. Increasingly, the mood across the South shifted from tacit acceptance to resistance. Virginia and Tennessee, like other border areas, began to close ranks with the Deep South states. This remarkably fast turn of events was precipitated by the Supreme Court's *Brown* II decision on May 31, 1955, and by African-American insurgency, which was both aggressive and highly publicized. Of the two precipitating events, the Court's implementation decision was the less threatening because it lacked a deadline for compliance. It left the specifics of implementation to district judges who were more sensitive to local political climates. Black insurgency, on the other hand, produced serious worries for white segregationists.[15]

Insurgent action took many forms. In 1955–1956, there was the dramatic bus boycott in Montgomery, Alabama, that launched the civil rights career of Dr. Martin Luther King, Jr. At the same time, a more encompassing boycott of white businesses occurred in Orangeburg, South Carolina. Parallel to the boycotts and other types of nonviolent mass action were legalistic and institutionalized forms of protest. Legal and institutional actions tended to be directed at school desegregation. Indeed, among all the points of conflict, school segregation became the focus of white belligerency. Urged by the national leadership, National Association for the Advancement of Colored People (NAACP) branch organizations during the summer of 1956 filed some sixty petitions before local school boards seeking compliance with the Court's implementation decree. Similar action had been taken a year earlier following a 1954 strategy conference in Atlanta called by the NAACP five days after *Brown* I. This first round of petitions, although engendering bitterness and some reprisals, included fewer appeals than the second round and was eventually forgotten. The second round, however, evoked deep hostility and contributed significantly to the spread of white belligerency. Increasingly, sentiment favored Massive Resistance.[16]

The Massive Resistance campaign was fueled largely by politicians and journalists. Chief among the latter was the editor of the *Richmond News Leader*, James Jackson Kilpatrick. Unlike McGill, Meeman, and Dabney, all of whom had at one time or another challenged the forces of racial bigotry (albeit with differing amounts of gusto), Richmond's other newspaper editor became the ardent champion of white resistance. Kilpatrick, perhaps more than any other proponent of segregation, broadened the appeal of the resistance campaign and made it "respectable." In one of his books, *The Southern Case for School Segregation*, published in 1962 after Virginia's Massive Resistance struggle was over, he claimed that while the fight was on, "I was on a horse and the pen was a lance." Kilpatrick borrowed heavily from such pre–Civil War southern patriarchs as John C. Calhoun and popularized the old doctrine of interposition, a theory long ago laid to rest but disinterred in the 1950s by Georgia Governor Herman Talmadge and a Virginia county attorney, William Old. The interposition argument provided the constitutional justification for southern defiance, and Kilpatrick exploited it for all its worth.[17]

According to the theory, the federal union constituted a compact of sovereign states, each with the power to assert its sovereignty and defy what it considered unconstitutional federal rulings. In the case of school desegregation, the doctrine meant that the state could interpose its sovereignty between local school officials and federal courts, at least until the issue was settled by constitutional amendment. Inasmuch as the *Brown* decision was viewed by interpositionists as an illegal amendment to the Constitution rather than simply an interpretation of the document, a state had the right to resist the court order until the Constitution was properly amended.[18]

Kilpatrick editorials that embraced interposition appeared in pamphlet form and circulated throughout the South. In just eighteen months from the beginning of the *News Leader* campaign in late November 1955, legislatures in eight southern states, including Georgia and Virginia, had passed interposition measures. Tennessee took a somewhat less extreme position, as it was prone to do throughout the Massive Resistance era, and simply registered its opposition to the *Brown* decision.[19]

Immediately after *Brown* I, Virginia attempted to follow a fairly moderate course of action. At the 1954 southern summit convened in Richmond, for example, it steered a middle course between the extremes of compliance and defiance. By *Brown* II, however, the Old Dominion abandoned this course and offered leadership to the upper South in a program of Massive Resistance and supported the Deep South with a potent justification for defying the Court. Virginia's relatively dramatic shift from moderation to defiance owed to the potent fusion of Senator Harry Byrd's political machine with James Kilpatrick's pen. Byrd found a strong ally in Kilpatrick. Writing to Governor Lindsay Almond in 1958, Byrd said, "I have great respect for Jack, who has, in a very brilliant fashion, aroused the country to the evils of the Supreme Court's decision."[20]

The interposition resolutions, which owed their existence in part to Kilpatrick's editorializing, were but the warmup to the main event. Interposition merely provided the rationale to maintain segregated schools. The resistance legislation itself followed in short order. The Virginia Massive Resistance laws called for a state Pupil Placement Board that would review all African-American applications to white schools. Although the purpose of the law was never directly set forth, the obvious intent was to block any efforts by blacks seeking to attend white schools. Should the federal courts order a school to integrate, then the state empowered the governor to close the school and attempt to reopen it on a segregated basis. Should a local school district admit blacks, whether voluntarily or under court order, the governor could also withhold funds from all schools in that district. In such an eventuality, the locality could operate its schools by using strictly local funds or else close its schools and use a tuition grant program to assist students in attending private schools.[21]

The Virginia legislature also mounted an offense against organizations that fought for integration. The NAACP felt the brunt of the assault because of its highly visible stand against interposition. In addition to a large membership (the Virginia Conference was larger at that time than any other in the South), the NAACP filed more school suits in Virginia than in any other southern state. In addition, as Andrew Buni notes, the General Assembly passed legislation that required individuals and groups that sought to influence public opinion or state policy and solicited funds for litigation to register with the State Corporation Commission and to furnish information on the group's finances and activities. Furthermore, any groups found to be engaged in barratry (the persistent incitement of law suits) would be guilty of criminal offense.[22]

Determining the effects of these "anti-NAACP" laws on the civil rights organization is difficult, although one observer with the Southern Regional Council asserted that the laws contributed to a 14 percent decline in Virginia black voter registration from 107,152 in 1957 to 91,757 in 1958. An additional factor, however, was probably the short-term loss of interest in electoral politics that followed the 1957 gubernatorial race. Benjamin Muse notes that the laws and the subsequent legislative investigations were largely responsible for the NAACP's losing about one-third of its membership from 1956 to 1958. In contrast to the statewide 14 percent reduction of black registrants from 1957 to 1958, however, black voter registration in Richmond during that same period increased by 14 percent from 12,345 to 14,089. This upsurge in the city's figures resulted largely from efforts of another group closely allied with the NAACP, namely, the Crusade for Voters.[23]

This new organization emerged as a consequence of the alarmingly low level of black political preparedness for a statewide tuition grant referendum held in January 1956. By the lopsided vote of 304,154 to 146,164, Virginians supported the convening of a limited constitutional convention called for the purpose of amending Section 141 of the Virginia Constitution. The purpose of amending the document was to permit a publicly funded tuition grant program for students to attend private and presumably segregated schools rather than integrated public schools. Two months later, forty delegates met in Richmond for the convention and voted unanimously to amend the constitution. The governor then called a special session of the General Assembly that proceeded to establish a tuition grant program. Obviously, nothing less than the future of public education was at stake. Yet, although blacks represented roughly one-third of the city's voting age population, African-Americans comprised only 18 percent of all registered voters. More troublesome was the fact that only 22 percent of voting age blacks were registered. The black voter turnout on the day of the referendum also could have been higher. About 8,000 blacks, or 69 percent of eligible black voters, cast ballots with the vast majority of blacks voting against the proposal to call a constitutional convention.[24]

An ad hoc group known as the Richmond Committee to Save Public Schools had been organized to defeat the proposal. To have failed in this endeavor was bad enough (64 percent of Richmond voters supported this convention), but to have witnessed such an abysmal response in the black community was doubly tragic. Some of the younger African-Americans involved with the ad hoc group believed that the root of the problem was a weak and ineffective Richmond Civic Council (RCC), a loosely organized confederation of over eighty black civic, labor, business, educational, fraternal, and religious organizations that endorsed candidates and sponsored voter-registration campaigns. The governing structure of the RCC tended to protect the local autonomy of individual ministers, lodge presidents, and leaders of civic organizations. Ministers exercised most of what leadership there was. They were the one group within the Council that had regular contact with a large proportion of the black population. Yet, many of the ministers were older, much too cautious, and, consequently, unwilling to engage in any significant protest action lest it disrupt their limited access to the white community. Some of the ministers supplemented the income they derived from congregational giving. Although this was often an economic necessity, the willingness to accept any kind of additional assistance often led to rumors that white politicians could purchase support in some quarters of the black community.[25]

The younger blacks in the ad hoc group were professionally trained, primarily as doctors, lawyers, and educators. Like the ministers, they were occupationally tied to the African-American community inasmuch as the vast majority of their patients, clients, and students, respectively, were black. Unlike some of the ministers, however, they were sufficiently secure financially that they were beyond suspicion of "supplementing" their income through collaboration with white politicians. Because of their professional status as well as their choice of neighborhoods (many black professionals lived in Barton Heights or near Virginia Union University), these leaders of the nascent Crusade for Voters were somewhat removed from the black masses in Jackson Ward and Church Hill. They were Richmond's version of what W.E.B. DuBois labeled the "talented tenth," highly educated blacks who were able to mobilize the black community to fight prejudice and discrimination. This group of challengers had grown impatient with the unwieldy structure of the RCC and the self-serving political behavior exhibited by some of the ministers belonging to it.[26]

After the 1956 referendum, the Richmond Committee to Save Public Schools disbanded, and the Crusade for Voters stepped into the void. Its mission was clear—to empower the city's blacks. The Crusade leadership structure was highly centralized, even though the membership was drawn from each of the black precincts. Its goal was to rally blacks to register and vote in large numbers, a difficult task when one considers the impediments to voting that confronted Richmond blacks. The organization exercised tremendous influence in the black community and was destined to play a major role in Richmond politics during the 1960s and 1970s. Although such an organization eventually might have taken root in Richmond even without such compelling factors as the 1956 referendum and the ineffectiveness of the RCC, surely the roots would not have spread as quickly. The failure to defeat the tuition grant proposal, the passage of the state's interposition resolution, and the Massive Resistance laws that same year, plus the low level of black political participation (the latter due to a combination of voting restrictions and the lack of an assertive political organization in the black community)—all of these ingredients provided fertile ground for the rise of a new organizational force among Richmond African-Americans.

The Crusade quickly set about the task of mounting a voter-registration campaign. Called the "Miracle of Richmond," this drive resurrected an old tradition stemming from the antebellum period when one black taught another how to read and write; the difference in 1958, however, was that each black registered voter was responsible for adding a black non-registrant to the voting roster. The old motto of "each one teach one" now became "each one *reach* one." Relying on a door-to-door canvass of black households, the Crusade's campaign fell short of registering 10,000 new voters, but it did add 3,500 new names to the voting rolls and, in the process, increased black registration by 30 percent. White politicians did not lose sight of the Crusade's ability to mobilize the African-American community. Shortly after the "Miracle of Richmond," Virginia Senator Garland Gray introduced legislation requiring the return of "blank sheet" registration designed to test literacy. In short order, the *Richmond Afro-American* launched a "Boomerang for Bigots" program aimed at educating blacks on how to complete the blank forms. Inasmuch as no white organization was likely to provide similar lessons for white citizens, the *Afro* predicted that the "Boomerang for Bigots" classes would actually work to the benefit of the black community. *The Richmond News Leader*, recognizing the troubling possibilities and clearly disturbed by the recent voter-registration drive in the black community, suggested that when the black community "approaches decisive strength, the only recourse will lie in annexation of white voters from Henrico and Chesterfield."[27]

The 1960 councilmanic election was the first occasion for the Crusade to flex its muscle at the polls. Blacks were urged to drop the practice of "single-shot" voting and to engage in balance-of-power politics. The idea was that those white candidates who garnered solid black support would prevail and, in so doing, acquire debts that could be forgiven only through support of legislation favorable to the black community. If the successful candidate failed to prove responsive as a member of the city council, then the black vote would be denied at the next election and the incumbent would face defeat. The Crusade's Research Committee was responsible for identifying the candidates to endorse. The strategy was to announce the endorsements on the Sunday immediately preceding the Tuesday election. Black churches were important institutions because they reached vast numbers of citizens. Moreover, by waiting until the last hour to announce the endorsements, the Crusade gave little time for the opposition to target the Crusade's endorsees. There was the concern, growing out of the experiences in the early 1900s, that an endorsement of a white by a black organization could be politically lethal to the candidate. A last-minute endorsement also minimized the prospect of dissension within the African-American community. The strategy paid off. Seven of the nine candidates endorsed by the Crusade were elected, and two candidates whom the Crusade had found "unsatisfactory" were defeated. The reward was that, after the new council was installed, a black was appointed to the Richmond Planning Commission.[28]

Just about the time when the Crusade was preparing for the 1960 election, students at Virginia Union University, hearing of the sit-ins staged by students at North Carolina Agricultural and Technical College in Greensboro, initiated a similar protest in Richmond. Charles Sherrod, one of the student organizers of the Richmond protest, was prompted to take direct action by the example set by his North Carolina counterparts. "If they were doing it," he said, "why shouldn't we be doing it?" On February 20, 1960, about 200 Virginia Union students marched down Chamberlayne Avenue to Woolworth's Department Store in downtown Richmond where they sat at the lunch counter, asked to be served, and left only when the counter was closed. Before the end of the day, five other stores, which also had Jim Crow policies of not serving blacks, were the target of student protests. Two days later, when 400 students joined the protest, several students were arrested at Thalhimers Department Store for trespassing, triggering an angry reaction in the African-American community and leading later to a picket line outside Thalhimers urging black shoppers to boycott the store. A mass rally attended by 3,000 was held at Fifth Street Baptist Church, where Oliver Hill, Wyatt Tee Walker, and Charles Sherrod were some of the featured speakers. The rally plus a general leafleting of black neighborhoods calling for a general boycott of all downtown Jim Crow stores produced such support that seven months after the first sit-in the white-owned stores began to desegregate their dining facilities. The student-led protest galvanized the Richmond community, prompting black leaders to join in solidarity with the students. Community power directed at the stores was as effective as electoral power directed at City Hall.[29]

The 1962 city council elections produced another victory for the Crusade for Voters, when, once again, seven of the nine endorsees prevailed. Its ability to determine election outcomes was impressive, and its balance-of-power strategy was proving effective. In fact, even before the 1962 election, the city council passed a fair-employment resolution, a direct response to the Crusade's petition for a fair-employment practices ordinance. Although the resolution did not carry the same weight as an ordinance, it "demonstrated council members' recognition that the Crusade was already a powerful political influence in the city which could not be ignored." By 1964 Richmond Forward (RF), the political voice of the white power structure, decided to endorse a black for city council in an effort to accommodate the Crusade. Given the continued growth of the black population and the Crusade's increasing effectiveness, the time had come, reasoned RF, for reciprocity. The Crusade had been endorsing white candidates, and RF believed that prudent political strategy called for whites to endorse a black. The result was that B.A.

Cephas, an African-American real estate broker who in 1960 had been appointed to the Planning Commission, was elected to city council, becoming the second black to hold the office since 1898. Richmond Forward won the election, but only because of the support from the Crusade. This relationship between the Crusade and the white power structure was an alliance of convenience that made both black and white leaders uneasy. Blacks were looking to the day when they could elect their own candidates without establishment support, and whites desired the same kind of independence.[30]

The 1966 election was a major turning point for the Crusade for Voters. By this time, African-Americans represented 48 percent of the population and 34 percent of all registered voters. Earlier that year, the poll tax for local elections had been declared unconstitutional by the U.S. Supreme Court's *Harper v. Virginia Board of Elections*. The Crusade was becoming strong enough that, with time, blacks could mount a serious challenge to the political status quo. As a consequence, RF proposed to change the manner in which council members were elected by moving away from electing the nine-person council every two years, as was the practice, to a system of staggered terms, so that only five seats would be contested every two years. While RF claimed that the proposed arrangement would provide continuity on the legislative body by having on any single council a combination of newcomers and veterans, the Crusade viewed the tactic as an attempt to maintain the white majority on council. The campaign got ugly, and the surface civility between the Crusade and RF that had characterized the preceding three elections was dropped. Editorials in the white press designed to discredit the Crusade backfired, prompting the black community to redouble its organizing efforts. As a result, election day produced two new council members, one white and one black, whose victory stemmed from the black vote alone. The white newcomer, Howard Carwile, was a populist who attacked big business, the Richmond aristocracy, and the oligarchial power structure of Richmond and who, in his previous eighteen elections, had run and lost for the U.S. Senate, governor, the Virginia House of Delegates, and the Virginia Senate. The black victor was Henry L. Marsh, III, a young civil rights attorney whose law partners were Oliver Hill and Samuel Tucker, and who in 1977 became Richmond's first black mayor. Marsh was reelected in 1968 and remained on the council continuously until 1991 when he was elected to the State Senate. What is also important about the 1968 council election is that the Crusade vote not only elected outright three members of council but also excommunicated two black council members (one of whom was B.A. Cephas) who had lost touch with the African-American community.[31]

One of the ironies of Massive Resistance was that it unwittingly contributed to the emergence of an organization in the Richmond black community that laid the groundwork not simply for the desegregation of the Richmond public schools, but also for the very control of the schools.

Through its ability to marshall the black vote, the Crusade eventually grew in power to the point that in 1977 its endorsees constituted a majority of the Richmond City Council, a majority that, in turn, determined the appointments to and the budget of the Richmond School Board.

Nevertheless, Virginia's actions in the late 1950s were not without serious consequences. Once the mood of defiance to *Brown* had caught hold, massive resistance swept through Virginia with tornadic force. Before the storm had spent its fury, the Warren County High School, one elementary and one high school in Charlottesville, and all six white high schools in Norfolk had been closed. Altogether, 12,000 white students were affected by the closings in order to prevent the enrollment of approximately seventy blacks. Most of the former shifted to private schools. In retaliation for the closing of white schools, the Arlington chapter of the Defenders of State Sovereignty and Individual Liberties unsuccessfully sought to close black schools by encouraging whites to attend the schools and thereby force their closure. It was also not uncommon for students to endure long bus rides, sometimes as long as two hours, in order to avoid integration. There were cases where African-American children were bused out of the state entirely. Even after the state's Massive Resistance laws had been repudiated by the courts, Prince Edward County mounted a resistance campaign of its own. Rather than comply with court orders, the county closed its schools for five years from 1959 to 1964. Over 1,200 white children attended private schools run by the Prince Edward School Foundation. Blacks, on the other hand, received virtually no education until 1963 through the newly established Prince Edward Free School Association. Like the state, however, the County Board of Supervisors finally relented. In 1964, it complied with federal court orders and reopened the public schools.[32]

That the Richmond public schools remained relatively calm during these difficult years was remarkable. After all, Richmond was where Kilpatrick wrote his editorials and where, as the state capital, the Massive Resistance legislation was forged. Not only did the schools stay open, but also the first feeble steps toward desegregation occurred without great commotion, other than some minor jostling that took place when about thirty reporters and photographers crowded around the doors of Chandler Middle School to record the historic arrival of two black children on September 7, 1960. An unassigned *News Leader* editorial written before the school openings that fall and generally thought to have been authored by Kilpatrick typified the thinking of "proper Richmond" when it suggested that, as regrettable as the admission would be, "it would be unthinkable for Richmonders to manifest their distaste in any sort of public display." By the same token, the editorial continued,

nothing in the rule book requires that we burst into joyful song.
The two pupils will be at Chandler when schools open next month, so will

nearly 700 white students. The city's social order will not collapse overnight; the educational level will not be affected perceptibly; the sun will rise in the morning. So two of the city's 20,000 Negro pupils have been integrated. We don't like it, but we don't propose to have hysterics either. What else is news?[33]

Of course, the peaceful transition in Richmond from a Jim Crow system of public education to one where a few blacks began to enroll in formerly all-white schools resulted largely from the controlled nature of desegregation. Lewis F. Powell, Jr., the chairman of the Richmond School Board during the late 1950s (who later became an associate justice of the U.S. Supreme Court), believed that the continuation of public schools required some effort to accommodate the courts, but clearly the effort was to be strictly minimal. In May 1959, less than four months after the state's Massive Resistance laws were declared unconstitutional, Powell spoke before the city council to urge authorization for two new junior-senior high schools. During his presentation he made the following comment: "We foresee no substantial integration in the elementary schools in Richmond. There are, indeed, sound reasons to believe that a majority of the elementary schools will have not more than a negligible percentage of integration for many years." He argued that building the proposed schools, both in white neighborhoods, coupled with the conversion of two older white schools to black schools, would ease pressures for integration. Without these measures, given the growing black school population, space reasons alone might lead to the admission of blacks to white schools. For sure, enrollment pressures were building. Because of overcrowding due to the shortage of black schools and the increase in black enrollments (the percentage of black students in the schools swelled from 37.4% of the total student body in 1943 to 51.1% in 1959), black schools resorted to double shifts. Yet, building new schools for whites and converting older white schools to black schools might not be enough. Powell assured the council, however, "that every proper effort will be made to minimize the extent of integration when it comes."[34]

Richmond's superintendent, H.I. Willett, also spoke in support of the school construction proposals and, in doing so, broached a subject that increasingly was on the minds of many white leaders in the city. He observed that the neighborhood in north Richmond where one of the proposed schools was to be built could become predominantly black if the black population continued to expand. Such an outcome could be avoided, Willett suggested, if Richmond annexed white areas of Henrico County. In fact, either annexation or city-county consolidation was a consideration when the sites of both schools were selected. This concern over the growth of the city's African-American population was also reflected in a 1962 report to the U.S. Civil Rights Commission. University of Virginia law professor Edward A. Mearns, Jr., in a discussion of school desegregation in Virginia noted that the "real problem" in the capital city was not the desegregation of schools nor any type of desegregation. Rather, it was the population issue and its political overtones. "The whites in Richmond fear 'engulfment' and all that that term signifies," Mearns wrote. "Richmond white people fear that the poetry of southern life will soon be gone, if it has not gone already." By the time Mearns had completed his report there had already been in December 1961 an unsuccessful merger effort involving Richmond and Henrico County. Later that same month the Richmond City Council passed two annexation ordinances, one directed at Henrico County and the other at Chesterfield County. As noted by James Ely, the city's growing black population was a concern of the state legislature as well. In 1962 the General Assembly continued its practice of combining Richmond and Henrico into one multimember House of Delegates district with eight representatives.[35]

Once Richmond's desegregation process got under way, Powell's assurance that integration would be minimized was realized. As noted, two blacks enrolled in a white school in 1960 and thirty-seven in 1961. Of the thirty-seven, thirty attended the same school; three attended the biracial Cerebral Palsy Center; and four enrolled in two other schools. Seven years after *Brown* I, only 0.15% of Richmond's black children (37 out of 23,177) attended school with whites. Fifty of the city's fifty-four schools in 1961 remained totally segregated. Nine years after *Brown*, although blacks comprised 58 percent of all children attending Richmond's public schools, only about 2 percent of all blacks attended school with whites. No whites attended black schools. A separate city obviously led to separate schools.[36]

Working to reinforce the minimalist approach to desegregation and Richmond's separate city was the city's pupil placement process, a system not unlike what existed elsewhere in Virginia and throughout the South, including the cities of Atlanta and Memphis. The placement system divided the city into attendance zones for each race. White elementary children were assigned to the school in their neighborhood. Upon completing elementary school, they automatically attended the middle school that served that neighborhood. The middle school, in turn, fed into the high school for that zone. Black children also were assigned to their nearest zoned elementary school. Black children living in Jackson Ward near the central business district or Church Hill in east Richmond did not have far to travel because the black schools were concentrated in their areas. Children living in smaller black residential sections in the more western and southern portions of the city, however, had to travel considerable distances. Moreover, they rode special public buses at reduced rates, albeit this was an expense that poor African-American families could ill afford. If a child, black or white, wished to attend a school other than the zoned elementary school or the appropriate feeder school, the student filed a transfer application with the School Board which, in turn, forwarded the application to the state Pupil Placement Board.

Although legally the Pupil Placement Board was the final authority insofar as student assignment was concerned, in fact, it normally accepted the recommendation of the local school board. Transferring was difficult. For one thing, the grade levels comprising elementary, middle, and high schools varied. In northside Richmond, the black elementary schools contained grades 1 through 6, the black middle schools grades 7 through 9, and the black high school grades 10 through 12. White schools in the same area were configured differently. Elementary school included grades 1 through 5, middle schools grades 6, 7, and 8, and the high school grades 9 through 12. In addition, when considering transfer requests, the state Pupil Placement Board required applicants to meet certain academic criteria not imposed on those already attending the school represented. It also applied a proximity test, so that applicants could transfer only to a school closer to their home than the one to which they would have been automatically assigned in their attendance zones. The proximity test worked against blacks seeking admission to white schools. African-American applicants to white schools would be turned down if they lived closer to black schools. White children living next door, however, would be automatically assigned to the white school.

The application of a proximity test reached absurd limits. In a study of school desegregation in Richmond, historian Robert A. Pratt records one such instance. In 1960 the placement board received an application from Wallace Calloway, a black student who sought to attend a white middle school rather than the assigned black school. The student's father, William C. Calloway, Sr., a prominent black physician in the city, asserted that the distance between the Calloway house and the white school was shorter than that between the house and the black school. Moreover, he argued that the bus stop for the trip to the white school was only a block away; whereas, the stop for the trip to the black school was eight-tenths of a mile. The Placement Board countered with figures from the city traffic engineer showing that, when measured from the house to the intersection nearest each school, the shorter distance was that to the black school. Calloway and his wife, Alice Calloway, contacted Oliver Hill, a well-known civil rights lawyer who chaired the Virginia NAACP legal staff and who in 1941, along with Samuel W. Tucker, had sued the city over the racial disparity of teacher salaries. Hill disputed the city's claims because they were based on measurements from the house to the intersection nearest each school rather than to the schools themselves. The placement board decided to remeasure the distances. An engineering firm was hired to undertake the work. Pratt writes: "Using a surveyor's chain, two engineers, on their hands and knees, measured the distance foot by foot from the home to each of the schools and then, as a double-check from the schools to the home. The measurements showed that the Calloways lived 8,150 feet from Graves [the black school], and 8,530 feet from Chandler [the white school]." Finding that the black school was 380 feet closer, the placement board rejected the application. (Ironically, nine years later Alice Calloway was appointed to the school board.)[37].

This was not the first challenge that the Calloways presented to the Richmond school system. Three years earlier in 1957, Dr. and Mrs. Calloway, together with a few other black parents, had refused to sign the pupil placement form as required by the Virginia Pupil Placement Board on the grounds that the pupil placement process was simply a technique to perpetuate a dual system of education. Board policy required local school officials to submit the names of parents who failed to sign the form to the placement board. Children whose parents did not sign the placement form would not be enrolled in public school. Consequently, when the school year began in the fall of 1957, the children of the protesting parents were denied admission to school. The parents counterattacked by lodging a suit in U.S. District Court against the Virginia Pupil Placement Board, the Richmond School Board, and Superintendent Willett. The parents prevailed in court, and their children were enrolled. In fact, following the suit, the Virginia Pupil Placement Board reissued the forms but in so doing noted that parents of African-American children would no longer be compelled to sign. Pending the outcome of the suit, however, and with the school year already under way, the Calloways and the other parents provided for makeshift schools so their children would not fall behind in their studies. They used space in two churches, acquired books from cooperative teachers, and enlisted the aid of volunteers such as black college-educated postal workers who used their leave time to teach.[38]

Additional legal action by Richmond blacks followed in 1958 after the Pupil Placement Board rejected the first applications from blacks who sought admission to white schools. The federal district court where the suit against the school board and superintendent was filed refused to order the admission of the students. By the same token, Judge Sterling Hutcheson denied the defendants' motion to dismiss the case and allowed the plaintiffs to file an amended complaint directed against the original defendants plus the State Pupil Placement Board. No further action was taken until three years later. By then, all of the black plaintiffs, except Jane Cooper, had withdrawn from the case. But on July 5, 1961, the court ruled in *Warden et al. v. School Board of the City of Richmond* that because the Cooper child had been denied admission to Westhampton School strictly because of her race, the 1958 action of the Pupil Placement Board was unconstitutional. Accordingly, the court ordered the admission of the plaintiff to the school at the beginning of the next school term in September. Having sought admission as a first grader, Daisy Cooper finally got to attend Westhampton as a fourth grade student. The ruling was only a partial victory, however. For one thing, the court order granted relief only to the single plaintiff, not to African-American students as a class. In addition, the judge refrained from declaring Virginia's Pupil Placement Act unconstitutional.[39]

The *Warden* case was only a foretaste of things to come. The same year that Daisy Cooper was admitted to Westhampton School, the parents of ten black children who had been denied admission to white schools filed a class action suit in U.S. district court. Although the case began modestly enough, before all of the litigation growing out of the case was resolved, *Bradley v. School Board of the City of Richmond* was destined not only to challenge the city's sytem of public education but also to approach landmark status. Eleven years later in 1972, the federal district court ordered the consolidation of the city schools with those in the suburbs of Henrico and Chesterfield Counties. The case failed to achieve national distinction when the U.S. Supreme Court affirmed on a four to four vote the decision of the Fourth Circuit to reverse the district court's decree. Consolidation was not to be. Interestingly, the one Supreme Court justice not voting was former Richmond School Board Chairman Lewis F. Powell, Jr.[40]

The plaintiffs in the *Bradley* case were represented, among others, by Oliver W. Hill and Henry L. Marsh, III. While Hill served on the Richmond City Council from 1948 to 1950 and was the first black councilperson since 1898, Marsh was just emerging as a political force. He was first elected to the council in 1966, and in 1977 he became the city's first African-American mayor. The suit focused on the city's use of the feeder system as a devise for avoiding school desegregation. The lower court agreed that the system was discriminatory and ruled in favor of the individual petitioners but failed to award injunctive relief for the class.

The plaintiffs appealed the decision to the Fourth Circuit. Finding "nothing to indicate a desire or intention [by school officials] to use the enrollment or assignment system as a vehicle to desegregate the schools," the appellate court concluded that class injunctive relief was required and that the dual attendance zone and the feeder system had to be replaced with a nondiscriminatory system of enrollments. It stopped short of ordering a unitary system, however, with its comment that "the appellants are not entitled to an order requiring the defendants to effect a general intermixture of the races." What the Fourth Circuit decision seemed to be suggesting, without ordering such a plan, was the creation of a "freedom of choice" plan.[41]

The *Bradley* case was returned to the district court which, in accordance with the directive of the Fourth Circuit, entered an injunction on June 6, 1963, ordering Richmond public school officials to scrap the racially discriminatory pupil assignment and transfer practices. The court ordered the school board to develop a desegregation plan. The plan prepared by the board and given qualified approval by the court was essentially a "freedom of choice" assignment system. Children entering the first grade could attend the school of their choice, although their freedom was conditioned on such factors as proximity to the school, availability of space in each school, the suitability of the school's program for the student, and the "best interest of the student." Other students were to be assigned initially to the schools they had attended the previous year. Parents could request a transfer, but the transfer request was not automatic. Once again, there were conditions, including that most elusive of them all, "the best interest of the student." For students who had completed the last grade in an elementary or junior high school, freedom of choice was to govern where they attended the next school, subject, of course, to certain conditions. In brief, the city's freedom of choice plan still gave school officials considerable discretionary authority in determining pupil assignments.[42]

In giving qualified approval of the plan (the court, for example, retained the case on the docket pending any necessary additional judicial intervention), the court also dissolved the June 1963 injunction. The court decision was a disappointment to the plaintiffs. They appealed the decision to the Fourth Circuit on the grounds that the city's freedom of choice plan contained no provisions for desegregating the faculties and staff in the public schools and that it failed to eliminate conditions governing pupil placement. They also argued that the plan failed to achieve a unitary, nondiscriminatory school system, with no racially identifiable schools. The Fourth Circuit proved unresponsive, however. On a split vote, it upheld the district court decision, ruling that the Richmond freedom of choice plan was an acceptable method for complying with *Brown*. The plaintiffs then petitioned the U.S. Supreme Court to hear the case and to determine whether a nondiscriminatory system of faculty and staff assignments should be included in the city's desegregation plan. The Supreme Court ruled that the plaintiffs were entitled to a hearing on the issue of faculty assignments and ordered the district court to hold the hearings without delay. Hearings proved unnecessary. On March 30, 1966, the district court approved a new desegregation plan for Richmond, one that included the desegregation of faculty and staff as well as an acknowledgment that the school board was responsible for correcting significant imbalances in student enrollment. The plaintiffs reluctantly consented to the plan with the result that the Richmond schools functioned under freedom of choice and without additional court challenges until 1970.[43]

From the first *Brown* decision through the civil rights period of the late 1950s and 1960s, public education in Richmond never experienced disruption. Considering the defiance of desegregation orders by state and local officials, the angry denunciations of the Supreme Court by James Kilpatrick and other opinion leaders, and the legal challenges to school segregation brought by African-American parents and the NAACP, it is significant that the public schools of Virginia's capital never closed and that they functioned in the absence of great public disturbance. Richmond was not Little Rock. Neither were Memphis and Atlanta.

Memphis

That Memphis was subject to neither the relentless diatribes of a James Kilpatrick nor the bellicosity of the Virginia State Assembly meant that the city, insofar as desegregation was concerned, operated in a somewhat more receptive environment than Richmond. The fact that Boss Crump was no longer on the scene also served to ease the tension. For sure, the Tennessee legislature was less belligerent than its Virginia counterpart. Historian Numan Bartley suggests that, with the exception of the Old Dominion, all of the upper South states, although trying to evade the consequences of the court ruling, nevertheless tended to accept the validity of the ruling. On the other hand, Virginia and the Deep South states, including Georgia, refused to grant any legitimacy to the decision. As a consequence, the latter group of states constituted the vanguard of the Massive Resistance movement. Tennessee's legislature adopted a manifesto of protest; however, it refrained from approving interposition resolutions and passing school-closing laws.[44]

Like Virginia, Tennessee passed pupil assignment legislation. Tennessee's Pupil Placement Act passed in 1957, shortly after the Virginia General Assembly in 1956 enacted its pupil placement law. Clearly, the intent of both states' legislation was identical; namely, to prevent or, at least, to minimize desegregation by providing local school boards with a legal framework that would govern pupil assignment to public schools and establish procedures for determining pupil transfers. Tennessee's placement law did not prohibit African-Americans from transferring to white schools, but requests for such transfers were commonly denied and always subject to intense scrutiny. Several factors were considered when transfer requests were made. State law required local school boards in Tennessee to consider such matters as the distance between the school requested and the applicant's residence. Another consideration was the available space in the school where the applicant sought admission. More elusive criteria were the applicant's scholastic aptitude, academic preparation, the suitability of curricula for "particular pupils," and the "psychological qualifications of the pupil for the type of teaching and association involved." If that was not enough, the state code stipulated that a local board regard "any and other factors which the board may consider pertinent, relevant or material in their effect upon the welfare and best interest of the applicant, other pupils of the county, city or special school district as a whole and the inhabitants of the county, city or special school district."[45]

Pupil assignment laws made it easy for localities to circumvent the court decision. Added to an unwillingness by local officials to integrate public schools, the legislation proved to be very effective in maintaining the status quo. The Memphis Board of Education virtually ignored the ruling and took no direct action to desegregate the schools until 1961, one year after the NAACP filed suit against the board. Memphis school officials relied heavily on the state legislation, first in an attempt to thwart desegregation altogether and, when pressed to take action, to slow the pace of desegregation.

One might expect the all-white Memphis school board to have dragged its feet on dismantling the dual school system, but what is particularly interesting is that even the local chapter of the NAACP was slow to respond to *Brown*, applying no pressure to the school board until 1960 when it filed suit against the Memphis school system. Headed by pragmatists who cautiously steered the organization on a moderate course, the Memphis NAACP was hesitant to confront head-on something as sacrosanct as the public schools for fear of triggering a severe white backlash. Fear of white backlash also led the Memphis NAACP to avoid challenges to segregation in other public institutions. The one exception was a suit lodged against Memphis State College in 1955. As far as elementary and secondary education is concerned, six years lapsed before the NAACP finally changed course. On December 10, 1959, the local chapter inquired about the school board's intention to comply with the decision of the Supreme Court. It attached to their letter a petition bearing the signatures of 100 African-American parents of children enrolled in the Memphis school system. When the board issued a statement that it intended to operate the schools according to the law of the state, the NAACP finally initiated legal action in March 1960, the same year and month that the sit-in movement hit Memphis.[46]

Led by black students from LeMoyne and Owen colleges, the sit-ins were directed against segregated public facilities and downtown lunch counters. This student-inspired action differed markedly from the restrained approach to segregation taken by black moderates associated with the local NAACP chapter. The fact that the sit-ins and the filing of the school suit occurred at roughly the same time suggests more than coincidence. The students energized and emboldened the NAACP. Not only did the NAACP finally take direct aim at the public schools, but also, together with black ministers and lawyers, it united behind the students in a highly visible act of solidarity. Unlike what happened in Atlanta, when the sit-ins led to deep divisions between the established black leadership and the student activists, the demonstrations in Memphis unified the African-American community and intraracial conflict was minimized.[47]

Meanwhile, the only person on the school board who supported desegregation was Frances Coe, a Vassar-educated woman who fourteen years before *Brown* had persuaded the YWCA to integrate. She had been elected to the school board in 1955, the same year that reformer Edmund Orgill was elected mayor. Shortly after Coe joined the board, she began to press for school desegregation but found that she was alone in her views and unable to exercise any influence over school policy, at least as it pertained to race.

"Our superintendent at the time," Coe remarked, "was an open segregation-ist though not a member of a Citizens Council or anything like that. He simply believed in and enforced second class citizenship for the Negro pupils, teachers and principals in the system."[48]

The 1955 election that brought Coe to the school board and Orgill to the mayorship was the first electoral contest between the reformers and those associated with the political machine since Boss Crump's death a year earlier. By 1955 black registered voters numbered more than 39,000 and represented approximately one-fourth of all registered voters in the city. The numbers of black registrants had increased by 77 percent since the last local election in 1951. Lieutenant George Lee, the leader of Memphis black Republicans, and Dr. Joseph E. Walker, the leader of black Democrats, deserve much of the credit for that increase.[49]

Actually, Lee and Walker figured in an even larger proportional increase in black voter registrations (roughly 280%) in the 1951 election. Then, too, they had worked together by serving as co-chairmen of the newly formed Non-Partisan Voters Committee (see Chapter 2). A major incentive to regis-ter blacks and an important reason for the big jump in black registrations was that Walker himself was a candidate for the school board. In addition to his being the only African-American in the election and the first black in over three decades to run for a major public office in Memphis, he was also the only candidate to oppose the Crump slate. Crump tried to force Walker out of the race by sending black minister Blair T. Hunt as an emissary to advise that he withdraw from the race or be run out of the city. Walker, however, refused to be intimidated by Crump's machine and forged ahead whith his campaign.[50]

Walker's campaign involved an extensive grass roots effort that was managed by a young black attorney, Benjamin Hooks, who several years later, along with other younger blacks, would lead a move to establish black political independence from whites. African-Americans certainly were not in that position in 1951. To make even a good showing, least of all to win an election, blacks had to get white support as well as to vote as a bloc. In a radio appeal to white voters, Walker declared that "since the boys of Memphis are permitted to serve and even cheered for service on the battlefield, would it be a righteous act to permit a capable Negro to serve on the School Board of Memphis where these same boys are trained." Walker's white support was minimal, although he received endorsements from several prominent white members of the Civic Research Committee (CRC), a civic reform group to which Walker belonged. Included among the endorsers was the chairman of the CRC, Edmund Orgill. Although supportive, Orgill also was mindful of the fears that most whites had about integrated education and, therefore, tried to allay their anxiety. "I really believe that it would be good . . . for Dr. Walker to be elected," Orgill said, "It would give the Negroes a feeling that they were having a part in the operation of the schools. This might lessen to some extent their insistence upon their children attending the same school."[51]

Although almost two-thirds of the black registered voters stayed at home on election day, blacks who did vote failed to unite solidly behind Walker. The Crump machine could still count on enough black support to carry the day. Some black leaders, because of "personal connections," had already committed to Crump and, therefore, did not vote for Walker. Some black school teachers feared that a vote for Walker would lead to reprisals. In the twenty-three black precincts, Walker got less than half the vote. The consequence of the low turnout and of the defections was that Walker lost the election, receiving only 7,433 votes compared to the successful white school board candidates who each averaged 21,000 votes.[52]

With Crump gone and no heir apparent, Lee and Walker closed ranks in the 1955 election and mounted a united front to increase black political participation. Although they favored different mayoral candidates (Lee endorsed incumbent Mayor Frank Tobey and Walker backed businessman Edmund Orgill), they and many other black leaders made common cause in their support for Reverend Roy Love, pastor of Mt. Nebo Baptist Church and head of the Baptist Ministers Alliance, for an at-large position on the school board. Walker and other black Democrats also supported Frances Coe for another of the four elected school board positions. Love was a popular minister whose congregation exceeded 1,000 members and whose politics embraced Democrats and Republicans alike. "I kind of hold hands with both," he once remarked when explaining his party loyalties. Love's role as a minister was important because Lee and Walker estimated that upwards of 90 percent of the African-American adults in Memphis were members in at least one of the 250 local churches. As a result of Lee and Walker's appeal on Love's behalf to the ministers and other well-known blacks in the community, the largest gathering of local black leaders in twenty-five years occurred in August 1955. Admonished to put aside denominational rivalries and political differences, those attending the meeting formed the Ministers and Citizens League whose purpose was to mount a voter- registration drive and push the total number of black registrants to 60,000. The subsequent campaign, however, fell considerably short of its goal but added about 5,000 names to the registration lists and expanded the total number of black registrants to 39,000.[53]

The election produced mixed results. Love lost the election, coming in fifth in a field of sixteen candidates and falling 5,000 votes behind the fourth-place winner. Frances Coe finished third and, thus, won a seat on the school board. Among her 29,185 votes were those of African-Americans who had also supported Love. Some blacks believed that if single-shot voting had been employed, thereby concentrating all the black school board votes on Roy Love, that Love would have been elected. For sure, if black turnout had been greater, Love's chances of election would have vastly increased and, perhaps, the seating on the board of two persons supportive of integration, Love and Coe, might have been possible. Only one-half of the black registered voters showed up at the polls. Nevertheless, one has to keep these results in perspective. After all, in 1951, only about one-third of all registered blacks voted. Walker in 1951 also received 7,433 votes. In contrast, Love received 20,082 votes, over two and a half times the number of Walker's total in 1951. Finally, black and white leaders attributed the African-American vote as being decisive in the mayoral election. Orgill's 19,000 vote margin over Watkins Overton was due also to Orgill's strong support from labor and the business establishment, but blacks played a major role. In the black wards, support for Orgill was overwhelming. In Orange Mound, for example, Orgill's support swamped Overton's by a margin of six to one. Much the same happened in the LeMoyne Gardens area.[54]

Irrespective of Love's failure to gain a position on the school board, the 1955 election signified increasing involvement of blacks in the local political process. One observer of Memphis politics claimed that the campaign "was the greatest effort that Memphis Negroes had made in a local election . . . and marked the beginning of white leaders' concern about the Negro vote." The election, for sure, caught the attention of the state legislature. After 1955 the legislature, by special act, changed the method for selecting members to the Memphis Board of Education. Until the change, the five-member board consisted of four at-large elected persons plus the president of the board who was appointed by the mayor. After 1955 the legislature required that persons seeking election to the board had to run at-large for four different slots on the board. Jesse H. Turner, the president of the local branch of the NAACP, stated in hearings conducted in Memphis by the U.S. Commission on Civil Rights that the new method of election made it more difficult for blacks to get elected to the school board. "In fact," he went on to say, "the political history of this community will show that, in every instance when the Negro unity and voting strength materialized to such an extent that the chance for electing a Negro to an important post became better than average, rules for election to that post were changed in subsequent elections."[55]

The Orgill Administration represented a marked departure from the old Crump regime. In the past, as historian David Tucker notes, Crump garnered black support through such tactics as patronage, persuasion, and fear. Whatever relationship existed between the black community and the white power structure was based almost exclusively on terms established by the latter. Those days were over. Orgill and his white allies rejected Crump's methods and sought to establish new relationships with blacks. Such efforts were particularly important given the Supreme Court's ruling and the anxiety and fear over desegregation that now gripped the Memphis white community.[56]

As Mayor, Orgill appointed the school board president. Thus, shortly after Orgill's election, Roy Love, the defeated black school board candidate, wrote the new mayor seeking the post. Orgill questioned the timing of such a controversial appointment but indicated in a reply to Love that should an advisory committee be established to study the school integration issue, blacks would be represented on the committee. Orgill wanted to nominate a black to the board of John Gaston Hospital as African-Americans represented about 85 percent of the patients. His candidate was Orgill ally and former school board candidate Dr. Joseph E. Walker. But, once again, a black appointment was not to be. Walker's nomination triggered strong opposition from the other four members of the City Commission. That reaction, plus a cross burning in Orgill's front yard, midnight phone calls, and false fire alarms made by angry white citizens, led Orgill to withdraw the nomination. Both the Love and the Walker incidents were major disappointments for the Memphis black community and were some of the first indications that dependency on white liberals was frustrating for blacks, particularly for those who were growing restive with the sluggishness of change and the strategy of moderation that guided the efforts of white reformers.[57]

One major area where change proved to be elusive during the Orgill years was public schools. Some movement, albeit small, occurred in other areas. For example, at Mayor Orgill's urging, and in the face of white segregationist opposition, the Memphis City Commission voted unanimously to honor former mayor Frank Tobey's promise to allow a black golfing association to use a "white-only" municipal golf course (whites had five courses; African-Americans had one nine–hole course). Another small step was taken in 1956 when the owner of the airport limousine service announced that from then on the transit operation would be available to members of both races. When it came to such issues as public education, "gradualism" was the guiding principle that for many whites was an excuse for delay and, in effect, for doing nothing. Fearful of the growing extremism of white segregationists, some members of the black establishment also subscribed to the gradualism principle. They assumed, nonetheless, that gradualism meant that, gradually, something would be done. Dr. Hollis Price, the president of LeMoyne College, observed, "I suggest more Negroes here are quite content with a gradual approach to integration," conceding that he was willing to wait five to ten years for integration. Republican leader Lee was also a "gradualist," and although he refused to commit to a time table he did say, "I won't wait too long."[58]

The new mayor, however, had to maintain a delicate political balance. His electoral majority included a large contingent of blacks who expected a far different reception than what they had encountered before. Knowing these expectations and moved by his own moral commitments, Orgill opened new channnels of communication with blacks and pleaded for reason and tolerance in race relations, even suggesting that "integration would not be the end of the world," all of which earned Orgill the 1956 Merit Award from the *Tri-State Defender*, one of the two black-owned newspapers in Memphis. Yet, realizing the strong segregationist sentiment in the city, he knew where to draw the line.[83] He was careful never, either publicly or privately, to advocate school integration. In his public statements, Orgill unequivocally embraced segregation: "Now about segregation. Memphis has enjoyed the best race relations of any Southern city. This is undoubtedly due to sensible policies followed in Memphis over a long period of years. I, along with the other members of the present City Commission, am on record as being in favor of continued segregation. The policy of the present City Commission, in which there has been unanimous agreement, has been to use all legal means to preserve segregation." On another occasion, this time in a personal letter, he said, "I want to again emphasize the fact that I am not for integration of the schools, and I wish we did not have this problem."[59]

Above all else, Orgill wanted to avoid violence and preserve social stability. At the same time, he advocated fairness and mutual respect between the races and, therefore, was equally concerned about cases of police brutality against blacks and harrassment of black passengers by white bus drivers. City image was clearly uppermost in Orgill's mind, and, if race baiting and other forms of crude behavior were damaging to an image of progressive race relations, so, too, would any insistence by blacks on sudden and dramatic change in the educational status quo.[60]

In order to foster biracial communication as a means of reducing racial tension and delaying desegegation, allies of Mayor Orgill formed the Greater Memphis Race Relations Committee (GMRRC) in March 1956. Inclusive of moderates from both races as well as white segregationists, the GMRRC was the first such organization to emerge in the city since 1940, when the Memphis Commission on Interracial Cooperation was created to "promote harmony and justice between all races and creeds." The commission proved ineffective and disappeared after 1942. The GMRRC fared no better. The major problem, ironically, was that some of the white members of the group refused to meet with the African-American members. Consequently, two separate committees were formed, one for blacks and one for whites, with communication between the committees occurring through delegates. Even advocating interracial meetings was taboo, as a prominent white banker who chaired the GMRRC discovered when his bank board threatened to dismiss him from the bank for making such recommendations. Obviously, an organization designed to promote black/white dialogue but that foundered over the very effort to engage in such dialogue was destined to be short-lived and ineffective.[61]

Out of the ashes of GMRRC arose another organization, the Memphis Committee on Community Relations (MCCR), this one truly biracial and far more effective in stimulating interracial dialogue. The new effort was spearheaded by Lucius E. Burch, Jr., a white liberal attorney, who, along with Orgill and Edward Meeman, the editor of the *Memphis Press-Scimitar*, was an active figure in the group of anti-Crump reformers that defeated the old guard in the 1955 mayoral election. Incorporated in January 1959, the MCCR sought to open channels of communication between the black and white communities and was animated by a genuine desire to negotiate remedies to racial problems in Memphis in order to head off the black demonstrations and white violence that had broken out in other southern cities in the fall of 1958. In constructing the white contingent of the organization, Burch generally avoided ministers and professors and opted instead for businessmen who could exercise some political muscle in developing community decisions. African-Americans who asked to participate included George Lee, Joseph Walker's son, A. Maceo Walker (Joseph Walker died a few months before the creation of MCCR), and NAACP officials such as Russell Sugarmon, Jr., Jesse H. Turner, Dr. Vasco Smith, and A.W. Willis, Jr.[62]

In order to prevent racial disturbances, the MCCR knew that some action directed against unequal treatment of blacks was essential, that talk alone was not enough. The kind of action taken, however, was also important. The MCCR sought voluntary responses, believing that quiet persuasion was preferable to waiting for court orders that would mandate change and possibly create more disruption. One of the arguments that white members of the group used when negotiating with more conservative leaders in the city was that voluntary desegregation could defuse the power of the NAACP. Any pressure applied by blacks simply added to their arguments. In March of 1960, for example, forty-one students from LeMoyne and Owen colleges entered two white public libraries and were arrested, setting off a series of NAACP-sponsored sit-ins and boycotts. In the fall of the same year, the City Commission reluctantly agreed to end segregation on a gradual basis, beginning with buses (which were desegregated in September) and then focusing on libraries and the municipal zoo (which were desegregated in October and December, respectively). The MCCR also developed a list of blacks that the organization believed were qualified to serve on city boards and agencies. The list was submitted to the City Commission, and the result was that in 1961 A. Maceo Walker was appointed to the Memphis Transit Authority.

The MCCR operated outside of public scrunity and preferred publicity after the fact rather than during the discussions leading up to any agreements. This was possible since the editors of the *Memphis Press-Scimitar* and of the *Commercial Appeal* were active members of the MCCR. The committee was successful in negotiating voluntary desegregation in some areas. Its great disappointment was in public education. The board of education spurned the committee's offer of assistance in developing desegregation plans. As a rule, white members of MCCR remained optimistic about the state of race relations in Memphis, more so than the younger black members. The former took pride in the fact that blacks and whites had come together out of a mutual concern for the city and that peaceful change was occurring. Younger blacks, on the other hand, were becoming restive with the slowness of change and the whole policy of gradualism. Neither MCCR nor the Orgill Administration provided the breakthrough in racial justice that they expected after *Brown*[63].

The turning point in racial politics in the post-Crump years was the 1959 election. The year before, the leading black Democrat, Dr. Joseph E. Walker, had been murdered by one of the founders of Universal Life Insurance Company and a Memphis coal yard operator, Judge W. Hamilton. Hamilton never forgave Walker for foreclosing on his business in 1949 and vowed that one day he would kill Walker. Walker's death left a vacuum in the African-American power structure that was filled quickly by blacks, who, unlike both Walker and Lieutenant Lee, were less willing to work in coalition with white liberals and who sought more political independence and direct action against segregation. In addition to Walker's death in 1958, Orgill's health problems (a blocked artery and two operations) forced the mayor out of the reelection campaign. Quite suddenly, the road was clear for an independent, bipartisan black ticket.[64]

Once again, a black ran for the school board. Five years had passed since *Brown* and there had been no movement whatsoever to comply with the order. Memphis schools remained totally segregated. Henry Clay Bunton, minister of Memphis's largest Christian Methodist Episcopal church and who headed the Ministers and Citizens League during the 1955 election when Roy Love was a school board candidate, decided in 1959 to run for the school board and, this time, to be more insistent on desegregation. He joined other candidates on a unified African-American ticket that also included Love, who ran for another at-large slot on the school board; Russell Sugarmon, a candidate for public works commissioner; and Benjamin L. Hooks, who ran for juvenile court judge. Sugarmon and Hooks were young attorneys, who, as leaders in the Shelby County Democratic and Republican parties, respectively, symbolized the bipartisan nature of the campaign. Sugarmon, the son of a prominent black realtor and a graduate of Rutgers University and Harvard Law School, returned to Memphis in 1956 at the age of 27 to practice law after attending a year of graduate school at Boston University and doing a stint in the U.S. Army. In 1958 he helped to organize the Shelby County Democratic Club, a cohesive, precinct-based organization in the black community, and served as its executive director. Hooks, who years later served as the executive director of the national NAACP, graduated from DePaul University Law School in Chicago and returned to Memphis as one of Sugarmon's law partners. Hooks was also a Baptist minister whose family was comfortably established in the Memphis African-American community. In addition, he was allied with Republican leader George Lee and worked for the party as the vice-chair of the Shelby County Executive Committee.[65]

Two other blacks announced their candidacies, but they were independents who refused an offer to join the black unity slate known as the "Volunteer Ticket." One of the candidates, O.Z. Evers, a postal employee who earlier had filed a desegretation suit against the Memphis bus company, failed to qualify. The second, Elihue Stanback, a public accountant and operator of a printing shop, did qualify and ran for tax assessor. Altogether five blacks ran for office in the 1959 municipal election.[66]

The election proved to be the most racially confrontational of any political contest in Memphis history. The sides were clearly drawn. The fact that several white candidates for each of two posts, the public works commissioner and the juvenile court judgeship, faced only one black candidate and that state law then made no provision for a run-off vastly increased the possibilities of a black victory. By this time 57,151 blacks were registerd to vote with black registrants representing one-third of all registered voters. Only four years earlier in 1955, African-Americans constituted only one-fourth of all registrants. The growth of black voting potential did not escape the attention of whites. A solid black vote for either Russell Sugarmon or Benjamin Hooks could lead to the election of the first black officeholder in Memphis since 1879. Of the two races involving multiple white candidates, the one that received the most attention, both locally and nationally, was the contest for public works commissioner, partly because of the greater significance of the city commission post but mostly because there were, at least initially, as many as six white challengers.[67]

Even before the election, many blacks had become disenchanted with white civic reformers because of their lackluster record on civil rights. During the campaign, however, the disenchantment mounted as these allegedly erstwhile allies of Memphis blacks took steps to limit the field of white contenders for the public works position as a way to prevent Sugarmon's election. Blacks expected strong opposition from avowed white supremacists and they were not disappointed. Even forces from outside the state applied pressure. In one instance, the executive secretary of the Assocation of Citizens Councils of Mississippi orchestrated a postcard campaign threatening white business leaders in Memphis with an economic boycott of city stores if a black were elected to the city commission. What was particularly distressing and what destroyed any vestiges of goodwill between blacks and white liberals and moderates was the role played in the campaign by the reform group that had supported Orgill in the 1955 mayoralty campaign.[68]

Two years into his term and on the insistence of liberal U.S. Senator Estes Kefauver, Orgill had run unsuccessfully for governor in 1958, making an impressive statewide showing, yet losing Shelby County because of the race issue. With Little Rock having just integrated its schools a year earlier, southern moderates such as Orgill who urged compliance with the law were unpopular among whites in the Memphis area. Consequently, during the 1959 municipal election, reformers were skittish about any position on the race question that would alienate white support. Once Orgill's illness forced him to withdraw from the mayoral reelection bid, the members of his campaign committee convened and decided to continue their involvement in the election by endorsing those candidates who were committed to the same civic reform objectives as Orgill. Known as the "Dedicated Citizens Committee" (DCC), Orgill's associates asked the candidates to state their position on nine points including such items as annexation, consolidation of duplicate city-county services, and countywide comprehensive planning. The last point was the maintenance of "community patterns of segregation by all legal means." The ninth point drew fire from blacks and led to such dissension within the DCC itself that it was dropped from the list of principles when the DCC reorganized as the Citizens Association following the election. But during the election, the segregation principle was part of all the DCC ads. The chairman of the DCC, Dr. Stanley Buckman (the head of a Memphis chemical firm whom reformers had recruited as a move to enlist DCC support from conservatives), claimed that the ads simply reflected the candidates' position, not the position of the organization. That distinction might have made sense to Buckman and a few other members of the DCC, but not to blacks. The truth of the DCC, black leaders argued, was to be found in the organization's endorsements—all white (including two incumbent commissioners allied with the old Crump machine)—and in the editorials praising the work of the DCC and supporting its endorsements. Meeman, the liberal editor of the *Press-Scimitar* and close friend of Orgill, lauded the DCC for its continued participation in the election and for its role in developing the "Unity Ticket" as a strategy for preventing the election of a black. Electing a black, according to Meeman, would not promote good race relations nor would it lead to the political progress of blacks. Meeman's advocacy of a white unity ticket was typical of the position taken by several other white moderates and liberals. Historian Tucker suggests that reformers such as Orgill and Meeman divorced their support for desegregation (albeit gradual desegregation through voluntary efforts), which they pursued through the MCCR, from their support for white candidates, which they channeled through the DCC and, after 1959, the Citizens Association.[69]

The *Commercial Appeal*, under the editorship of Frank Ahlgren, also endorsed the DCC's Unity Ticket. That both daily newspapers endorsed the same candidates was unusual as the *Commercial Appeal* was the voice of conservative Memphis and the *Press-Scimitar* spoke for the reformers. Given the stakes in the election, however, the sentiment was to close ranks and support a common slate in an effort to prevent the election of an African-

American. On August 2, 1959, the *Commercial Appeal* urged one of the stronger white public works candidates to withdraw from the campaign so as to minimize a splintered white vote. The editorial pandered to white hysteria by pointing out the possible consequences of a black victory, noting the following: "Whether a successful Negro commissioner would upset the department with wholesale replacements or a Negro judge exercise close supervisory powers over broken white families becomes a real fear in the hearts of many in the white community. The avowed determination of the Negro candidates for the school board to insist on immediate integration causes uneasiness and is contrary to the wishes of the majority group in this area."[70]

Such editorials and, generally, the whole siege mentality of the white community simply emboldened the black community. A highly visible grass roots campaign in support of the Volunteer Ticket was mounted by a coalition of African-American leaders. By election day, 1,200 people had been recruited to work for the slate, and the $17,500 campaign budget was exceeded by over $2,000 when $20,000 was raised, practically all of which came from within the black community. Mass rallies were held, with the largest one featuring Dr. Martin Luther King, Jr., who exhorted the 5,000 blacks in attendance to bloc vote for the black candidates. On another occasion, when word was circulating that a few black ministers had accepted money from white politicians, juvenile court judge candidate and fellow minister Benjamin Hooks condemned their action and threatened to go public with their names. "There are a lot of traitorous Negro ministers in Memphis," Hooks charged. "I know a lot of you. Some of you are seated in this very audience. And if you start your traitorous selling the Negro out during this election, I am going to buy radio time and reveal your names."[71]

The African-American campaign ran very smoothly. The only dissension, other than that sparked briefly by the independent candidacies of O.Z. Evers and Elihue Stanback, was the concern expressed by some blacks of running Henry Bunton for the school board slot held by Frances Coe, the sole integrationist on the all-white Memphis Board of Education. Although one black leader continued his support for Coe, his decision did not lead to a serious split in the black community. The incident over Frances Coe, however, reflected the extent to which blacks were willing to go in running a campaign independent of whites.[72]

On election day, a record 129,870 voters cast their ballot—a 50 percent increase over the previous record established in 1955! Contributing to the high turnout was the unprecedented number of African-American voters. Sixty-three percent of all black registrants showed up at the polls. The highest proportion of blacks to vote in a local election prior to 1959 was estimated to be 41 percent. In addition, the vote was evidence of black solidarity as each of the black candidates garnered at least 90 percent of the ballots in all-black precincts. But as remarkable as were the size and unity of the black vote, they were insufficient to elect a single candidate. The reason was simple, namely, the even larger number of white voters. Two-thirds of the registered voters in Memphis were white, and not only did 63 percent of them cast a vote, but white voters were as united in their opposition to blacks as blacks were to whites. In the closely watched race for public works commissioner, even a 100 percent black turnout would not have been enough to elect Sugarmon inasmuch as the victorious white candidate received more votes than the sum total of black registered voters. The white victory was aided by the heavy editorializing of the two daily papers that contributed to the withdrawal of one of Sugarmon's opponents, thereby reducing the field of white candidates and to the unusually heavy and solid white vote. In any previous contest, Sugarmon's 35,000 votes would have elected him.[73]

The 1959 election was not a complete disappointment for African-Americans. Although failing to register a victory, every black candidate, interestingly enough, placed second, including school board candidates Henry Bunton and Roy Love. Commenting on the solidarity of the black vote and the significance of the 1959 election, Sugarmon said, "We won everything but the election." The level of black electoral involvement also was a testament to the ability of organizational leaders from all quarters of the black community to work in coalition and their effectiveness in mobilizing their community. Moreover, if the black vote alone in 1959 was not strong enough in the face of massive white opposition to elect a black, it was sufficiently potent that in future elections black support of a white candidate could be decisive. It was the recognition of such a fact that, following the election, led blacks to reassess their political strategy.[74]

The lessons of 1959 were clear. On one hand, given the unwillingness of white reformers to support a single black candidate and, generally, given the lack of significant desegregation during the Orgill Administration, any permanent association with whites would be unproductive. On the other hand, however, it was just as unproductive for African-Amercians to operate autonomously. By becoming less ideological and more pragmatic, they could form temporary alliances with whatever white politician was willing to exchange substantive concessions for black support. But unlike the machine days when blacks occupied a position of subservience and traded votes for small favors from boss Crump, this time blacks occupied a position of independence and could bargain out of strength, giving or withdrawing support at will.

Still, in the final analysis, as important as the 1959 election was to the growth of black political independence, black electoral power had not developed to the point of seating blacks on the school board or moving the school board away from its segregationist policies. The black vote had proved ineffectual just as had coalition policies prior to 1959 and biracial dialogue both before and after 1959. Direct action was now the order of the day.

In March 31, 1960, the NAACP filed a desegregation suit on behalf of eighteen black children against the Memphis public schools. As noted, the frontal assault on the schools was a long time in coming, but the combination of the suit and the student-led sit-in movement that had gotten under way thirteen days earlier on March 18 accomplished what 1955 reform politics and 1959 black independent electoral politics had failed to achieve. It was only after the lawsuit that the school board made preparations for desegregation, minimal though they were.[75]

The suit contended that the city operated a dual system of education through its use of separate attendance zones and feeder patterns, procedures similar to those used in Richmond. It also charged that the state's pupil assignment laws provided no effective remedy to segregation. Obviously, the ultimate objective of the suit was the creation of a unitary, nonracial school system. The case was not heard until one year later, in April 1961. On May 2, 1961, the U.S. district court ruled in favor of the defendants, prompting the NAACP to appeal the case to the Sixth Circuit. [76]

The case pending before the appellate court weighed heavily on the school board. Adding to the concerns of board members and other white officials were the numerous protests organized by black students and non-students that had taken place over an eighteen-month period at downtown stores and municipal facilities. In addition, there was the economic boycott of downtown merchants organized by black ministers, representatives of the NAACP, and other leaders in Memphis's black community. These events had a cumulative effect on the Memphis power structure with the result that white resistance to school desegregation eased. In a report he prepared on Memphis for the Southern Regional Council (SRC), Benjamin Muse commented that "the demonstrations were larger and more disruptive than many realized—owing to the policy of the Memphis press of minimizing publicity. Some say that Memphis had more sit-ins than any other city." The protests not only brought pressure to bear on white business and political leaders, but also they galvanized the African-American community. When asked during hearings before the U.S. Civil Rights Commission about the effects of direct action, Sugarmon, one of the attorneys who provided legal assistance to students arrested for their participation in the sit-ins, made a telling comment. He observed that before the protests social change in Memphis was slow because "the Negro citizens in a city like this grew up and were taught accommodation of things that they shouldn't have to accept. I think the impact of the sit-in movement had as profound an effect on the attitude and the insight of Negroes as it did on the attitude and insights of the whites in the community about what is involved in civil rights."[77]

Working with the NAACP, the City Commion, the MCCR, and the

chamber of commerce, the Memphis Board of Education announced a sur-
prise school desegration plan on September 30, 1961. Thirteen black children
were to be reassigned to four previously all-white elementary schools.
Unlike Atlanta, where elaborate preparations were made to prepare the city
for desegreation, Memphis acted without mounting any educational campaign. In fact, even the teachers at the schools where the African-American
children were to be enrolled did not know about the decision until the
evening before the desegregation was to begin. Appearing before the faculty
on Monday evening, October 2, School Superintendent E.C. Stimbert announced: "Now tomorrow morning you are going to have some new pupils
and there is nothing different about them from all the pupils you have
already had. You are professional people; they are going to be your children
and their parents are going to be your parents, and I know that you are going
to do the good job with them that you have done with your other pupils all
over the years.[78]

The lack of planning was due to several factors. One was the fact that the
accelerated pace of events in September 1961 simply did not allow for any
careful preparation. Only a month earlier, in mid-August, leaders in both the
black and the white communities assumed that no school desegregation
would occur in 1961. Yet, shortly afterward, blacks began a recruiting drive
to locate parents of first-graders willing to request reassignment to white
elementary schools. Operating under the Tennessee pupil placement law,
the Memphis school board assigned students to the designated zone or
feeder school, although students had the right to appeal the decision and
request a transfer. As a result of the campaign, parents of about fifty first-
graders in late August sought transfers from all-black elementary (their
initial assignment) to white elementary schools. At the hearings held to
consider the transfer requests, however, only thirty-nine of the fifty appellants appeared, and, of those, thirteen were granted transfers. Until the
transfer requests were submitted, the school board had thought little about
assigning black children to white schools, but suddenly in late August, the
school board had to come to grips with the issue. That the school board was
unprepared to begin desegregation in the fall of 1961 might have been reason
for it to have denied all thirty-nine transfer requests during the hearings. But,
as G.W. Foster, Jr., pointed out in his report to the U.S. Civil Rights Commission, "Tactically . . . such a decision would have wrecked the board's position
in the school case which was pending on appeal at the time in the U.S. Court
of Appeals for the Sixth Circuit at Cincinnati."[79]

Memphis school officials were pressed for time and that largely accounts
for the absence of a community-wide program to prepare the city for desegregation. Another factor was the desire to confine information about desegregation plans only to those who needed to know, thereby keeping public
awareness to a minimum. During September, when the board worked on the

appeals, it issued only cryptic announcements that intimated that some desegregation was possible in the near future. Nothing more specific was said. City officials did not want the general public to have advance knowledge that at the beginning of the academic year African-American children would be attending formerly all-white elementary schools. Advance publicity could activate strong resistance from white supremacists. The Memphis power structure desperately wanted to avoid the kind of ugly confrontations that had occurred in Little Rock and New Orleans. There was also concern that, with advance notice, the national press would descend on Memphis, making the delicate process of desegregation much more difficult and giving a forum for those who would seek to disrupt the process. In an effort to enroll the thirteen children with as little fanfare as possible, the president of the school board, W.D. "Billy" Galbreath, met with members of the local press the day before the "desegregation day" and requested that they delay any announcement of the event until after the children entered their schools. The press honored the request by withholding news reports until the next morning.[80]

While the board refrained from developing plans to prepare the public, it developed for itself some general guidelines regarding the desegregation process. One guideline was that no fewer than three black children should attend a particular school lest a single child have to face alone all of the pressure associated with this new experience. Another objective was to place the students in the most receptive schools. One of the problems in New Orleans was that both of the white elementary schools selected for desegregation were located in city's lowest-income white neighborhoods where hostility toward integration was greatest. Cognizant of the New Orleans experience and wanting a broader geographic spread of the schools targeted at desegregation, Memphis school authorities selected four elementary schools in several different areas, none of which were located in low-income white neighborhoods. The problem was that the black children lived long distances from their new schools, and transportation, therefore, became an added burden for them and their parents. Still another factor that the school board considered was security. The Memphis police recommended twenty-four-hour surveillance at each school. As it turned out, 200 police officers guarded the four schools.[81]

The first day of desegregation was relatively calm, in spite of the swarm of reporters and spectators that had engulfed the schools. Also, on learning that black children were attending formerly all-white schools, fifteen white students were withdrawn by their parents from the four elementary schools. News stories suggested that some of these angry white parents were newcomers who had moved to Memphis from Mississippi. The Associated Press carried quotes from two of the parents. "We will either transfer him or move plumb out of the city," said one parent who had withdrawn her fourth-grade son out of one of the schools. "We may go back to Mississippi where they don't let them go to school with whites." "Yeah," said another, "I'd rather be dumb than go to school with them."[82]

As the year wore on, the internal operation of the four schools also was stable, and all but one of the thirteen children performed well, some extremely so, and passed to the second grade. White faculty members, who had never taught black children, had to adjust as did black and white students alike. The lack of any prior contact between white teachers and black children was also evident. In one of the progress reports that the teachers were required to submit as part of the school board's academic evaluation of the thirteen first-graders, one teacher reported: "Dwania's art work is unusual. She colors the faces of all characters brown."[83]

Both Memphis and Richmond avoided violence when school desegregation got underway. Both cities were very image conscious and wanted to distance themselves from other southern localities where the school issue led to severe civil disruption, school closings, or other forms of state intervention. Yet, in both cities, desegregation progressed slowly and involved only a few children. Although pleased that the process had started, blacks were not content with the desegregation. In Memphis, legal pressure continued to be applied to what African-Americans regarded as a segregated system. In response, the school board attempted to have the school case dismissed based on the enrollment of the thirteen black children. The board reasoned that the admittance of blacks into white schools made the issues raised in the appeal moot. The appeals court refused to dismiss the suit and on March 23, 1962, reversed the lower court decision. Finding that the Memphis Board of Education operated a dual system of public schools, the Sixth Circuit ordered the board to submit a plan for reorganizing the schools in accordance with federal law.[84]

The school board, after losing a second round with the Sixth Circuit when the court refused to rehear the case, also failed in its attempt to get the U.S. Supreme Court to accept the case on appeal. Facing a court order to prepare a desegregation plan, the board finally complied and developed a plan calling for new attendance zones and a method of gradual integration. Grades 1 through 3 were to be desegregated by September 1962, and one additional grade each year thereafter. Under the plan it would have taken nine years to desegregate the Memphis public schools, hardly the response that the NAACP was seeking. The district court, however, approved the plan. In short order the NAACP appealed to the Sixth Circuit. Once again, the appellate court took the district court to task by noting that the school board's new attendance zones were designed to preserve "a maximum amount of segregation" and that the grade-a-year approach did "not now comply with the Supreme Court's current interpretation of desegregation with all deliberate speed [*Brown II*]." Finding for the NAACP, the Sixth

Circuit ordered in 1964 that the school board accelerate its action so that all grade levels be desegregated by 1966.[85]

Legal battles continued beyond 1966 when the NAACP became impatient with the board's lack of progress and sought further judicial relief. The court never ruled on the motion, and in the now-familiar cycle of action/reaction the NAACP filed another motion. Among other things, the new motion sought to desegregate the faculty and to force the board to develop unitary school zones. Again, the court proved recalcitrant. The case moved back and forth from the district court to the Sixth Circuit when, finally on January 12, 1970, the appeals court ruled that Memphis was no longer operating a dual system of education. The U.S. Supreme Court, having accepted the NAACP's appeal, called for further examination by the trial court. Following a seven-day hearing, the district court on May 1, 1970, found that, although Memphis school officials had revised the school zones, the educational system would not be classified as "unitary" until the board had complied with court orders such as the one requiring the desegregation of the faculty.[86]

Clearly, the legal machinery moved slowly, too slowly. Moreover, it did not produce the fundamental changes in the Memphis school system that blacks sought. Just as student protests in 1960 had been instrumental in getting the NAACP to become more aggressive, so direct action by blacks nine years later was instrumental in bringing about a more responsive school board. A combination of events in 1969, including school boycotts by over 40,000 black students, boycotts of downtown stores by black shoppers, picketing, and mass marches, culminated in negotiations between the NAACP and the school board and a series of commitments from the board that included appointing two non-voting black advisors to the board; filling the next two board vacancies due to resignation, death, or increase in the size of the board with blacks; restructuring the board so that blacks would stand a better chance of getting elected; and appointing a black assistant superintendent and a black coordinator. As its part of the agreement, the NAACP suspended direct action against the schools.[87]

It took fifteen years following *Brown* I to arrive at this point. Yet, in the face of incessant delays over school desegregation, Memphis schools, like those in Richmond, never closed and never experienced the wrenching disorder that occurred elsewhere in the South. At the same time segregated schools surged as a central political issue in the African-American community of both cities, contributing to the rise of organizational politics in Richmond through the creation of the Crusade of Voters and independent electoral politics in Memphis through the bipartisan efforts of younger black professionals who had grown impatient with white reformers.

Atlanta

Atlanta was to Georgia as Richmond was to Virginia insofar as school desegregation was concerned. Capital cities, yes, but, more particularly, status-conscious cities with reputations for progressive race relations set in the midst of reactionary state governments. Like Virginia, Georgia was fully involved in the Massive Resistance campaign and passed resolutions of interposition. In fact, some historians credit the state's chief power broker, Governor Herman Talmadge, with unearthing the antebellum doctrine of interposition that Richmond's James Kilpatrick later popularized through his editorials. Unlike Virginia, however, Georgia actually declared the Supreme Court's *Brown* decision null and void. When in 1956 Georgia governor Marvin Griffin invited his counterparts in Virginia, Mississippi, and South Carolina to take similar action, they all refused. The year before Georgia passed its interposition resolution, the state legislature in 1955 ruled that spending money on integrated schools by either state or local officials constituted a felony. Two years later in 1957 the Georgia attorney general officially announced that black football teams were not allowed to play on fields reserved for whites, adding that "for segregation to remain an integral part of Georgia's social customs and traditions, it must and will be practiced twenty-four hours a day, seven days a week, and three hundred and sixty-five days a year." The Georgia Board of Education, that same year, adopted a resolution directed at the state's public schools that disallowed any student organization from participating in any integrated activity.[88]

Even prior to the *Brown* decision, Georgia had begun to erect barriers to protect the classroom from "corrupting" influences. As early as 1935, for example, in an effort to eliminate "subversive" teachers, the state legislature adopted a "Teachers Oath" requiring instructors to "refrain from directly or indirectly subscribing to or teaching any theory of government or economics or of social relations which is inconsistent with the fundamental principles of patriotism and high ideals of Americanism." Espousing integration, of course, was considered subversive. This oath remained part of the contract for all Georgia teachers until the 1966–1967 school year. A particularly powerful state institution created just months before *Brown* and whose purpose was to ensure the continuation of school segregation was the Georgia Education Commission. Comprised of prominent private citizens and state officials, it exercised significant influence with Georgia lawmakers as was evident when the legislature approved the Commission-sponsored measure that made it a felony to fund integrated schools. The Commission was perhaps best known for its nationwide dissemination of white supremacy proposals, an activity that the state legislature officially sanctioned and supported financially through state appropriations. In addition, the Commission conducted surreptitious investigations of organizations and individuals believed to be supportive of integration—investigations carried out not only in Georgia, but also in two neighboring states, Florida and Tennessee. In support of these activities, the Commission's executive director acquired the governor's approval to spend several thousand dollars to purchase wiretapping equipment. The Atlanta press brought these activities to light, prompting the state's lieutenant governor to stop the agency from becoming "a state gestapo where intrigue and dangerous tactics are substituted for sincerity, sound thinking, and legal procedure."[89]

Atlanta was a political oasis in the Georgia desert. As the state's pre-eminent urban area, Atlanta was always at odds with Georgia's rural-dominated legislature. The city's cosmopolitanism stood in stark contrast to the parochialism so evident in the less populated areas of the state. Atlanta reveled in its uniqueness and, like Memphis and Richmond, jealously guarded its image. Atlanta's white leaders, indeed the national press, extolled Atlanta as "a city too busy to hate," a clever slogan concocted by longtime Mayor William B. Hartsfield. On one occasion, Hartsfield proclaimed: "What happened in Little Rock won't happen here. We're going to ride herd on these damn rabble rousers. . . . We've had men from our [police] force in Little Rock and New Orleans studying what they did wrong . . . when racists come in this town, they know they're going to get their heads knocked together." Such statements made great press and contributed, as did the editorials to the national and even international attention given to Georgia's capital city.[90]

The New South leadership of Atlanta was influential in breaking the grip of Georgia's Old South leadership on Massive Resistance. The change was dramatic, but it was not sudden. Atlanta itself was completely segregated, and racial discrimination was rampant for years after the *Brown* decision. Notwithstanding that the African-American middle class of Atlanta escaped much of the barbarism that blacks elsewhere experienced, that the city's white power structure relied on the support of black leaders, and that since 1948 Atlanta had employed black police officers (albeit officers confined strictly to black neighborhoods), the city held fast to its Jim Crow system. By 1960 Atlanta had desegregated its buses and golf courses, but nothing else. As noted by Alton Hornsby, six years after *Brown*, not a single black attended school with whites. Pressure to desegregate was mounting, however, particularly as it applied to education.[91]

In 1958 the NAACP lodged a suit against the Atlanta Board of Education in an effort to challenge the Georgia statute prohibiting the use of state funds for integrated schools, the first such test case filed in the state. The plaintiffs prevailed. As a consequence, the court ordered the Atlanta school board to develop a desegregation plan by the end of 1959, with the effective date of the plan to be September 1960. School officials responded with a gradual grade-a-year desegregation plan. The federal court accepted the plan in January 1960 but delayed implementation of the plan until the fall of 1961 "to enable the people of Georgia and its legislators . . . [to] prevent the closing of the schools."[92]

Mindful of the city's progressive reputation and of the economic conse-quences of racial unrest, moderate and liberal Atlantans were becoming increasingly concerned about the volatility of the school issue. They were anxious to avoid the chaos and near-mob rule that desegregation produced in Little Rock and New Orleans and the racial hysteria that led to school closings in Virginia. They feared that unless something constructive was done, Atlanta's reputation would be seriously damaged.

Initially, Atlanta's most influential business leaders remained aloof, saying and doing nothing as the local debate over school desegregation began to grow more heated. One of the first groups within the city's white community to urge restraint and to counter the resistance appeals of state officials was an assemblage of eighty Protestant ministers. In November 1957 they signed a major statement on race relations in which they urged all citizens, irrespective of their views regarding the *Brown* decision, to obey the law until such time as it might be changed through constitutional methods. The ministers also asserted that whatever else happened, the Atlanta public schools must not close. The United Churchwomen of Atlanta and the execu-tive committee of the United Churchwomen of Georgia circulated thousands of copies of the statement. Although the declaration failed to dislodge the state from its position of massive resistance, it did embolden a lay leader in one of Atlanta's Baptist churches, Mayor William Hartsfield. The year fol-lowing the ministers' pronouncement, Hartsfield locked horns with both Governor Marvin Griffin and Governor-elect Ernest Vandiver. The gover-nors were determined, if necessary, to enforce the state's resistance legisla-tion and close public schools rather than integrate them. Hartsfield, on the other hand, argued that Atlantans should be allowed to determine for themselves whether or not to desegregate the city's schools. Fearing that the city would integrate its schools rather than close them, Griffin blasted Hartsfield, telling a reporter for the *Atlanta Journal*, "He can't throw in the towel for me." By no means was Hartsfield an integrationist, as Hartsfield made clear in his response to Griffin, but the mayor did believe that each community should decide for itself what course its schools should take. Hartsfield's battles with Griffin and Vandiver wedded the mayor even closer to those in the city wanting open schools as evidenced by a 1958 race relations statement that garnered the support of 311 ministers, 231 more than en-dorsed the statement issued only a year earlier.[93]

Another group that advocated an "open-schools" policy was formed by eighteen white parents. Quickly, this new organization, which operated under the banner HOPE (Help Our Public Education), became the leading voice of white open-school advocates. Its efforts, bolstered through the editori-alizing of Ralph McGill, eventually expanded to the point that its leadership claimed a membership of 30,000 citizens. Of course, the group did not speak for all white Atlantans. Many whites were staunch defenders of Massive Resistance whose sentiments coincided with those of Georgia's most reactionary politicians. Chief among Atlanta's segregationists was Lester Maddox, the colorful restaurant owner who twice sought the mayorship (once in 1957 in a race against Hartsfield and again in 1961 in a contest involving Ivan Allen, Jr.), who ran for lieutenant governor in 1962 and lost, but who won the gubernatorial election in 1966. Throughout his political career Maddox capitalized on the racial fears of working-class whites. This was no less true when he spearheaded two prosegregation organizations, GUTS (Georgians Unwilling to Surrender) and MASE (Metropolitan Association for Segregated Education). The names of these competing forces within the white community could not have reflected a sharper contrast. The choice was HOPE or a combination of GUTS and MASE.[94]

As important as HOPE and other groups such as the PTA, civic associations, religious and professional organizations were in mobilizing support for the schools, they were not as powerful as the business community. As noted, Atlanta's key business leaders initally were uninvolved, at least until Ivan Allen, Jr., was elected president of the Atlanta Chamber of Commerce. Allen was an aggressive leader who led the Chamber to adopt a plan of action known as the Six-Point Program. This served not only as a guide to the work of the Chamber but also later as a set of objectives for the city during the 1960s under Allen's mayorship. The first point of the program dealt with schools. The action plan called for the Chamber to exercise leadership in keeping the schools open and, in so doing, to "clearly set forth to the public at large and the business community in particular the full implications of the Little Rock, Norfolk, and New Orleans stories."[95]

The school action plan of the Six-Point Program also called for the Chamber to endorse the creation of a blue-ribbon panel of citizens by the 1960 Georgia General Assembly to restudy the issue of school segregation. The Committee on Schools was popularly known as the Sibley Commission because it was headed by John Sibley, a leading Atlanta banker, lawyer, and chief counsel to the Coca-Cola Company. The pupose of the study committee was to find a way out of a legal bind. If the Atlanta schools complied with the federal court order to desegregate, they would violate state laws, lose state funding, and, thus, would have to close. Even though rural areas still controlled the state legislature, the prospect of closing the schools of the capital city created unease among the members of the General Assembly. After sponsoring hearings in all of the state's congressional districts and receiving testimony from more than 1,800 people, the Sibley Commission issued a report calling for the repeal of Massive Resistance legislation and replacing it with local option provisions that would make it possible for jurisdictions such as Atlanta to keep its school open.[96]

The 1961 session of the Georgia General Assembly braced for what many observers assumed would be a raucous debate over the Sibley Commission recommendations, a debate that would center on the Atlanta schools. Yet, only three days before the legislature was to convene, an unexpected federal court order diverted attention from Atlanta's public schools to one of the oldest universities in the nation and the alma mater of large numbers of Georgia politicians, the University of Georgia. On January 6, 1961, the court ordered the immediate admission of two African-Americans to the university. The events triggered by that decision were highlighted in an address that Ralph McGill delivered at Harvard University later that year. McGill noted that the fast-moving legal drama in Georgia had all of the elements of a chase scene in an old movie. Upon hearing the decision, the lawyers representing the university's board of regents got in a car and raced the 100 miles from Athens to the federal district court in Macon to seek a stay in the ruling. Following them in another car was a lawyer representing the two students. The university lawyers prevailed, at least for the moment. The court granted the stay, but the plaintiffs appealed, and the chase was on again. As McGill observed, "back to the highway went the two cars. They drove another one hundred miles to Atlanta's Federal Building [which housed the Fifth Circuit Court of Appeals] where the students' attorney argued the delay was invalid because previous rulings had covered, and denied, the grounds for it. The appeals judge, in a written decision, agreed." On January 10 the two students entered the university, thus marking the first tentative move toward desegregation of any public educational institution in the state's history. The event triggered both a riot on the Athens campus and anguish in the halls of the state legislature. Segregationist legislators now had to consider the reality of the Massive Resistance laws that, if implemented, would force the closing of the venerable academy. Such a prospect was unsettling even for the most reactionary members of the General Assembly.[97]

Although the University of Georgia had displaced the Atlanta public schools as the top item on the state legislative agenda, Atlanta's leaders knew that the state's response to the university issue would have direct bearing on the fate of the city's schools. Governor Vandiver had been elected to office after having vowed that "no, not one" black would enter a white school. Faced with the closing of the university, Vandiver issued contradictory statements, noting on the opening day of the General Assembly that the state could not afford to abandon public education and assuring the legislators that no funds had been withheld from the university, but then declaring only two days later on January 11 that schools that desegregated would lose state aid.[98]

Public reaction to the questionable status of the university came swiftly. Letters, telegrams, and telephone calls to the governor's office as well as the legislature urged the state not to close the university. Of the 600 letters directed to the floor leader of the House, only 12 supported the shut down of the school. Many of those contacting state officials were parents, but equally concerned about the university and public schools in general were educators and ministers. All 175 Methodist ministers in the Atlanta metropolitan area endorsed a petition calling for "continued uninterrupted operation of the University system and the public schools of Georgia." The United Churchwomen of Georgia, an ecumenical assembly meeting in Atlanta, took a similar position. Another voice for open schools came from business leaders in the state. Some individuals in the business community had grappled with the school issue as members of the Sibley Commission, but business as a group had been largely silent about school desegregation until the university was on the verge of closing. When they finally decided to speak, however, Georgia's business leaders constituted a potent force. The first business group to endorse limited desegregation and whose action triggered similar response from business leaders throughout the state was the Atlanta Chamber of Commerce. Shortly after the Chamber's executive committee (headed by Allen and including the presidents of Georgia's two largest banks and one of the state's largest utilities) wired the governor, nearly 1,000 Georgia businesspeople contacted state officials to express their support for open schools. In a resolution sponsored by 26 economic notables and carrying the support of an additional 960 signatories, all drawn from the business community, the private sector leaders argued that school closings would cripple the economy and that "immediate legislation action" was needed to avert tragedy and to ensure the "uninterrupted operation" of the state's public schools.[99]

The consequence of the pressure brought to bear on the governor and the state legislature was that within twenty days after the University of Georgia court order, the state legislature scuttled its Massive Resistance laws. In addition, the General Assembly adopted the recommendations of the Sibley Commission that included local option measures and provisions governing pupil assignment. The new legislation mirrored acts adopted in Tennessee and in post-resistance Virginia. It made desegregation permissible, but it was to be kept to a minimum. The significance of this legislation for Atlanta was that the city could move ahead with its plan for token desegregation without fear of state intervention. As political scientist Alton Hornsby noted in his study of school desegregation in Atlanta, "it is certainly no exaggeration to conclude, as others did at the time, that the university crisis saved the Atlanta public schools; for until that crisis erupted, Georgia's political leaders were adamant in their view that desegregation would be eternally resisted, even if public education had to be sacrificed."[100]

Massive Resistance constituted only one roadblock to desegregation. Its removal was critical, but other obstacles remained, obstacles that constituted an even greater challenge to Atlanta's white political elite and a threat to its carefully cultivated image of a city "too busy to hate." A series of civil rights protests in the city in 1961 led by black students angry about the slow pace of change in Atlanta was one. The protests actually started about a year earlier shortly after students in Greensboro sat at a white-only lunch counter. Word of the sit-in spread quickly, and soon black college students in localities across the South, including Richmond and Memphis, engaged in direct protests against segregation. The student protests in Atlanta also produced a new political dynamic within the city's African-American community. A new generation, less patient than the older generation, not only challenged white segregationists but also protested the city's long-standing relationship between the black bourgeoisie and the white economic and political elite.

The student protests in Atlanta over desegregation introduced a distinctive element in African-American politics that differed from that in Richmond and Memphis. All three cities experienced sit-ins, but in Atlanta the protests over segregated schools, downtown lunch counters, restaurants, and department stores also led to *intraracial* conflict and factional politics. Although they prompted some conflict within the black community, student protests in Memphis were far less divisive than those in Atlanta. The distinctive feature of African-American politics in Memphis was not factional politics but the widespread involvement of blacks in school board elections and the emergence of black political independence. Even less intraracial conflict was apparent in Richmond's African-American community. If factional politics characterized Atlanta and electoral politics characterized Memphis, then organizational politics characterized African-American politics in Richmond. The school issue in Richmond led to the formation of the Crusade for Voters, an organization with a broad-based membership but whose leadership was highly centralized, and whose efforts at voter education and registration solidified the black community.

For over ten years prior to the student-led protests of 1961, Atlanta's image as a progressive southern city was fostered by a coalition between white patricians in the corporate and political worlds and middle-class black professionals and business leaders. The national press made much of this biracial relationship as an example of the city's forward-thinking leadership, but the fact is that the partnership was the product of old-fashioned brokerage politics. The white elite and the black bourgeoisie each exercised some leverage over the other and the result was an arrangement which proved mutually beneficial. Even prior to the 1940s, blacks occasionally experienced success in using their vote to wrest concessions from white-controlled government (see Chapter 2); however, it was not until the mid- to late 1940s that black participation in the political process increased to the point that the African-American vote was actually courted and became essential to the electoral base of an Atlanta mayor.

What brought about the dramatic increase in black political influence was a combination of factors including the state's repeal of the poll tax in 1945 and the 1946 U.S. Supreme Court ruling in *Chapman v. King* that abolished the state's white primary. The poll tax repeal, together with the legislative decision to lower the voting age from 21 to 18, resulted largely from the leadership of Ellis Arnall, a reformist Governor who won the 1942 election after having defeated Eugene Talmadge in the Democratic primary. The *Chapman* decision was even more far-reaching than the action of the state legislature because it enabled blacks to participate in primary elections that, given the one-party system operating in Georgia and other southern states, were tantamount to general elections. With access to the nominating process, blacks now could begin to exercise some leverage within the party itself.[101]

The *Chapman* ruling was a major blow to segregationists, doubly so as just prior to the decision they had witnessed a stunning upset largely as a result of the black vote in a special congressional election. Robert Remspeck, representing Atlanta and two suburban jurisdictions in the Fifth Congressional District, resigned his seat in January of 1946, and a special general election was called in February to select someone to serve out his term. Inasmuch as the election did not involve a primary, blacks were able to vote. The black community quickly mobilized a voter-registration campaign under the leadership of the NAACP, the Atlanta Civic and Political League, and the *Atlanta Daily World*. The campaign succeeded in more than doubling the number of black registrants from what it was the previous year, from 3,000 in 1945 to 6,876 in February 1946. The additional numbers also doubled the proportion of black registrants among the total, from 4 percent to 8.3 percent.[102]

The election attracted a large field of candidates. Among the nineteen contenders was Helen Douglas Mankin, a former state legislator, a progressive who was aligned with organized labor and one of only a few candidates who sought the black vote. Given her qualifications and her record in the legislature, she received the support of African-Americans, although without any black organizational endorsement. She was not expected to win and, based on the vast majority of precinct returns after the polls had closed, it appeared that the pre-election forecasts that called for the election of Tom Camp were accurate. He was leading Mankin by 146 votes. The lone precinct that had not reported, however, was the largest black precinct in Atlanta, Precinct 3–B of the Third Ward. When the results of the vote in Precinct 3–B were reported later that evening, and the final tally was completed, not only had Mankin won the election, but she had done so with an 810-vote margin. Atlanta's blacks had cast the decisive ballots.[103]

The election was both a shock to white supremacists and an incentive for Mayor Hartsfield and his supporters in the city's business community to broaden their electoral base by forging an alliance with blacks. Segregationists quickly organized a counterattack. Through their control of the local party committee of the Fifth Congressional District, they placed the district under the county unit system to dilute the city's influence. Mankin sought a full two-year term and entered the Democratic primary in July 1946. Because the *Chapman* decision had been rendered in April of that year, blacks could now vote in the July primary. The problem, however, was the county unit system. Mankin received the majority of popular votes, actually 3,200 votes more than her two opponents, but James Davis received more unit votes. Mankin took Fulton County's six unit votes, but Davis got the six unit votes from DeKalb and the two from Rockdale.[104]

Mankin's loss notwithstanding, the 1946 congressional contests, plus Eugene Talmadge's gubernatorial campaign that same year fueled the voter-registration drives in the Atlanta black precincts. Heartened by Mankin's victory in February and alarmed by Eugene Talmadge's racist appeals in his bid for governor that same year, Atlanta blacks redoubled their efforts. The registration drives mounted by the Atlanta Civic and Political League, the NAACP, and other organizations had increased the number of registered voters, but they failed to reach the black masses. As a consequence, black organizational leaders decided to pool their efforts under the banner of the All Citizens Registration Committee. It embarked on a campaign to identify all areas in the city where African-Americans resided and to recruit ward and precinct captains, census tract workers, and block workers (a total of 870 volunteers) to contact all persons of voting age in each of the 1,162 blocks. Churches, labor unions, employers, university professors, college fraternities, public housing project managers, and youth groups each did their part by distributing 50,000 leaflets and 20,000 posters and sponsoring a continuous series of sermons, mass meetings, and social get-togethers. Mayor Hartsfield added an incentive when he told a group of African-American leaders that he would discuss their requests for improved public services in black neighborhoods once there were 10,000 registered black voters. At the Butler Street YMCA, he told an assembly of blacks "your vote will buy you a ticket to any place you want to sit." The registration campaign was a stunning success and represented a major turning point in Atlanta political history. In a short fifty-one-day period, the number of black registered voters increased over 320 percent from 6,876 registrants to 21,244. Blacks now represented just over 27 percent of the total number of all registered voters.[105]

The significance of the drive was that it vastly increased the political clout of Atlanta's black community and gave added reason for white politicians such as Mayor Hartsfield to build alliances with this growing force of voters. Given the mayor's comment during the 1946 voter-registration drive, black leaders were ready to bargain and to hold Hartsfield to his word. One of their major concerns was the absence of black police officers. The concern had been raised before, even prior to Hartsfield's election as mayor in 1936, but no action had been taken. Included in the police ranks during those days were active members of the Ku Klux Klan, and Hartsfield's predecessor, James L. Key, was unwilling to move against them. Mayor Hartsfield, however, was not intimidated by the Klan. Working with his police chief, Herbert Jenkins, Hartsfield purged the Atlanta police of Klan influence. But the police remained an all-white organization. Not until the sudden increase in black voting power in 1946 did Hartsfield address the composition of the police force. In the spring of 1948, he appointed eight black officers. The new recruits were not allowed to arrest white lawbreakers or to change into their uniforms at the Decatur Street police station (only at the Butler Street YMCA). Still, their presence on the force symbolized a new era in race relations. Hartsfield used every opportunity to remind African-American voters of his action by parading the new officers in front of black audiences during election campaigns. Meanwhile, black leaders could point to tangible evidence that increased voting power captured the attention of white politicians.[106]

By 1949 black Democrats headed by A.T. Walden and black Republicans led by John Wesley Dobbs (the maternal grandfather of Maynard Jackson, who twenty-four years later would become Atlanta's first black mayor) decided to join forces to prepare for the fall nonpartisan elections. The product of the union, the Atlanta Negro Voters League, became the most powerful political institution in the city's African-American community. Whereas the All Citizens Registration Committee concentrated on expanding the electorate (in 1949, blacks represented almost 40 percent of the total number of registered voters!), the Voters League used the vote as leverage to secure additional policy changes and public services favorable to the black community. Black votes alone were insufficient to elect anyone, black or white, but if used in a bloc they constituted the margin of difference among competing white candidates. The League evaluated white candidates and endorsed the person most likely to act favorably on matters important to the black community. League endorsees were rewarded with solid support amounting to 95 percent of the black vote. William Hartsfield was the major beneficiary of League-generated support. In return for the vote, Hartsfield and his allies in the business community, in city government, and in middle- to upper-income white neighborhoods worked together to maintain racial harmony and to keep white reactionaries at bay. In 1951, for example, Hartsfield welcomed the NAACP to Atlanta for its national convention. He reviewed the racial progress that the city had made "under a city administration which believes in fairness and justice for all of our citizens" and asked the conferees "to look us over thoroughly with kindly and understanding hearts and minds . . . and go away with a happy and pleasant impression of our great and friendly City of Atlanta." Hartsfield's embrace of the NAACP contrasted with his attitude seven years earlier when he urged

Martin Dies, chairman of the U.S. House Committee on Un-American Activities, to investigate whether the NAACP was surreptitiously supporting
"professional white agitators . . . who were . . . stirring up racial questions in
the South, especially among educators, church people, and women's
groups." In 1952 Hartsfield established the city's first biracial planning
committee, the West Side Mutual Development Committee. The committee
concentrated on issues related to black population growth and neighborhood change and tried to stabilize white neighborhoods located near areas
of black growth (see Chapter 4).[107]

The alliance between the Negro Voters League and the city's white
political and economic elite was also the critical factor in the 1953 election of
Atlanta University President Dr. Rufus Clement to the Atlanta Board of
Education. He became the first black since 1870 to win a citywide office. His
margin of victory was substantial (10,000 more votes than his white oppo-
nent) and included strong support from whites. Commenting on the election,
McGill observed in the *Atlanta Constitution* that "editorialists about the
country found the news good, chiefly because the new school board member
was not elected by Negro votes, but did, in fact, receive a big majority of the
white votes cast, carrying 40 of the 58 precincts and losing none by a wide
margin."[108]

Many of Clement's white votes came from citizens who the year before
had been annexed to the city as part of Hartsfield's grandiose Plan of
Improvement. In addition to its call for expanding the municipal boundaries
of Atlanta, the Plan of Improvement also called for a smaller, at-large elected
city council and a redefinition of responsibilities between the city and the
county. Overall, however, the purpose of the plan was to maintain white
upper-class control of the city. For years Hartsfield had sought to annex
Buckhead, an affluent white neighborhood northwest of the city in Fulton
County. As early as 1942 Hartsfield made his case for the annexation of
Buckhead in a letter that he sent to several hundred people. The letter read
in part:

> The most important thing to remember cannot be publicized in the press or made
> the subject of public speeches. Our Negro population is growing by leaps and
> bounds. They stay right in the city limits and grow by taking more white territory
> inside Atlanta. Out-migration is good, white, homeowning citizens. With the
> federal government insisting on political recognition of Negroes in local affairs,
> the time is not far distant when they will become a potent political force in
> Atlanta if our white citizens are just going to move out and give it to them. This
> is not intended to stir race prejudice because all of us want to deal fairly with
> them; but do you want to hand them political control of Atlanta?

The letter was not convincing enough for the white suburban residents in
1942 to support annexation. Ten years later, however, Hartsfield achieved

his objective. What is particularly noteworthy is that the Atlanta Negro Voters League supported the 1952 annexation even though it meant the addition of approximately 100,000 white citizens. Hartsfield convinced the League that the interests of the black community would be served by the annexation of upper-class suburbanites inasmuch as the latter supported racial harmony and opposed the reactionary forces that controlled the state and that enjoyed a large following among Atlanta's white working-class population.[109]

The Voters League never pushed for measures that would disrupt the relationship that existed between Hartsfield and big business. As a consequence, the League remained a status quo organization and the black community remained in a subservient position. Hartsfield's biographer, Harold H. Martin, noted that the mayor made sure that blacks made sufficient progress "to keep them quiet for the moment, while not moving so fast as to stir up the violent anti-Negro element." Hartsfield was reported to have said after he left public life that he knew how to "use" the black vote without putting himself in a position where blacks could "use" him.[110]

It was the unwillingness of the organization's leadership to push for significant alternatives to the status quo by confronting such issues as school segregation that caused a major rift between the black power brokers and black students at Atlanta University. Throughout the South, including Richmond and Memphis, students became restive with the sluggishness of change and organized protests to undermine gradualist desegregation policies common to all cities. Protests took the form of boycotts and walking picket lines outside businesses that refused service to blacks or required them to use separate entrances or maintained "colored" areas. The most common and most effective protest, however, was the sit-in. Blacks would deliberately violate Jim Crow laws by sitting at department store lunch counters or other white-only areas in restaurants and refuse to move when ordered to do so. In Memphis and Richmond, the sit-in movement did not lead to serious splits in the black community but, in fact, tended to elicit support from established black leadership. The protest campaign in Atlanta, on the other hand, fostered deep divisions.

The first sit-in in the South occurred on February 1, 1960, at Greensboro, North Carolina. Four African-American students at North Carolina A&T College went to Woolworth's Department Store and requested service at the lunch counter. They were denied service, asked to leave, and when they refused, the city police arrested them. This simple act of protest by the students received national press attention and sparked a chain of similar events in cities throughout the South. Only four days after the Greensboro sit-in, several students at Morehouse College, one of six black educational institutions comprising the Atlanta University Center, got together to talk about the protest in North Carolina and plan similar action in Atlanta. One

of the students was Lonnie King, who later would become president of The
Onyx Corporation, run for Congress, and head the Atlanta chapter of the
NAACP. Another student, Julian Bond, eventually became a member of the
Georgia Senate and assumed national prominence as a civil rights leader.
Benjamin Mays, who was still president of Morehouse College in 1960,
recounted in his autobiography, *Born to Rebel*, that Lonnie King and a
delegation of students met with him and the other five presidents of Atlanta
University Center to prepare for the Atlanta sit-ins. All six presidents supported the students, although they asked the students to keep them informed
of their plans. As a result, the students and the Council of Presidents began
meeting twice a week. During those meetings the students briefed the
administrators, and the latter offered suggestions and made sure that the
students understood the implications of civil disobedience. At a meeting in
early March one of the college presidents suggested that the students prepare
a manifesto that would provide a rationale for the demonstrations. The
students agreed with the suggestion and, as a consequence, formed the
Committee on the Appeal for Human Rights and drafted a statement. The
product was a declaration entitled "An Appeal for Human Rights" in which
the students of Atlanta University made common cause with those in
Greensboro. The declaration addressed grievances related to inequalities in
education, public accommodations, housing, health care, law enforcement,
voting, and entertainment. Evident in the statement was the students' impatience with the slow pace of change: "We do not intend to wait placidly for
those rights which are already legally and morally ours to be meted out to
us one at a time. Today's youth will not sit by submissively, while being
denied all of the rights, privileges, and joys of life. We want to state clearly
and unequivocally that we cannot tolerate, in a nation professing democracy
and among people professing Christianity, the discriminatory conditions
under which the Negro is living today in Atlanta, Georgia—supposedly one
of the most progressive cities in the South.[111]

Appealing to government officials, civic leaders, and people of good will
to abolish racial injustice, the students resolved "to use every legal and
nonviolent means at our disposal to secure full citizenship rights as members
of this great Democracy of ours." The students asked Rufus Clement, the
president of both Atlanta University and the Council of Presidents, as well
as the lone black on the Atlanta School Board, to convey the Appeal to the
press on their behalf. On March 9, 1960, the *Atlanta Constitution*, the *Atlanta
Daily World*, and the *Atlanta Journal* carried the statement by the students. It
also appeared in the *New York Times*. Mayor Hartsfield noted that the
declaration was "of the greatest importance to Atlanta" and expressed "the
legitimate aspirations of young people throughout the nation and the entire
world."[112]

Faculty members at the Atlanta University Center formed the Atlanta

Committee on Cooperative Action (ACCA) to support the students. The leadership for ACCA included individuals such as Whitney Young, the dean of the school and later president of the National Urban League; Vernon Jordan, who also later served as president of the National Urban League and in 1992 was a major figure in the transition team of President Bill Clinton; M. Carl Holman Clark, who later headed the National Urban Coalition; and Sam Westerfield, dean of the School of Business and who later served as U.S. ambassador to Liberia. The ACCA published its own statement, "A Second Look," that discussed the consequences of segregation on the city. It also sparked the formation of the Atlanta Summit Leadership Conference, a coalition of civil rights organizations devoted to supporting student demonstrations and negotiating with downtown businesses to desegregate voluntarily.[113]

Sit-ins began in downtown Atlanta on March 15, 1960, with 200 students participating in the demonstrations. Seventy-seven students were arrested under a state trespass law that the Georgia General Assembly quickly passed (less than three weeks after the Greensboro protests) in anticipation that sit-ins would soon spread to Georgia. The arrests emboldened the students and, while court cases of those arrested were pending, additional protests were mounted and larger numbers of blacks, including many older blacks, participated. Sit-ins were supplemented with mass meetings, marches, pickets, and boycotts. Students spoke at black churches to explain why they had resorted to direct action and sought support from other members of the African-American community. In April demonstrators began to picket white-owned stores that discriminated against black customers or refused to hire blacks or else employed blacks only in menial positions. On May 17, 1960, the sixth anniversary of the *Brown* decision, 1,400 students took part in a march on the state capitol. Before they reached their destination, however, Atlanta Police Chief Herbert Jenkins diverted them in order to avoid a confrontation with a large group of whites who were waiting at the capitol. That same month civil rights activists targeted the City Auditorium where segregated seating was the norm. After sit-ins at Rich's Department Store, Atlanta's preeminent department store and the largest store in the Southeast, and after negotiations with Rich's executives failed to produce results, economic boycotts of both Rich's and Davison-Paxon, another leading Atlanta department store, commenced. The boycotts of these and other white-owned stores with large African-American clientele were particularly effective. The stores experienced a sharp drop-off of black customers and total sales dropped by 22 percent. One study based on a survey of 594 African-American households revealed that, after the boycott began the number of non-shoppers at the targeted stores increased 278 percent.[114]

Even with the initial demonstrations of black units, the civil rights demonstrations during the spring of 1960 produced deep splits within the black community. On one side were those who endorsed direct action; on the other were those who, although subscribing to the same goals of the demonstrators, questioned the tactics. The latter group was comprised largely of older black leaders associated with the Atlanta Negro Voters League. The conservative black elite opposed the use of boycotts and sit-ins to bring about racial justice, believing that such direct assaults on white businesses threatened the long-standing biracial alliance that kept reactionary whites at bay, but they did not want to be viewed as unsupportive of the students' goals and face the prospect of losing support within the black community. As a consequence, they, too, joined the boycotts. The message was clear, however. The black community no longer spoke to the Atlanta power structure exclusively through the Negro Voters League. Of course, such a reality had implications for the white community as well. Gone were the days when the white business and political elite could set the agenda. With the Negro Voters League unable to control the students, and with larger numbers of blacks joining the ranks of student protesters, the white power structure had to contend with an increasingly independent and less predictable black community leadership.[115]

During the summer months protests slackened somewhat but picked up again at the beginning of the new academic year. The Fall Campaign, as the civil rights action came to be known, led to additional arrests of student demonstrators. In October students protestors were joined in a sit-in at Rich's Department Store by Martin Luther King, Jr., who had moved back to Atlanta following the Montgomery bus boycotts to lead the Southern Christian Leadership Conference. When the demonstrators were refused service in the store's restaurant, they remained in their seats, thus precipitating an angry reaction from a group of whites. Concerned about the disruption to their business, the store management again told the students to leave, but the students stood their ground. Losing patience, store officials called the police who then proceeded to arrest the protestors, including King.[116]

King's arrest made headlines across the country and presented Mayor Hartsfield with another opportunity to demonstrate his political acumen. Hartsfield later recalled the telegrams from all over the country that poured into his office from black organizations and individuals to register their support of King and of the students. The national press also converged on Atlanta. The 1960 presidential election was less than a month away and the race between Senator John Kennedy and Vice-President Richard Nixon was shaping into a very close contest. Hartsfield and Morris Abram, an Atlanta attorney who was one of Hartsfield's close advisers, were struck by the spontaneous and impressive display of support for King and the civil rights demonstrators and realized that Kennedy could tap that support for his own election interests by personally intervening and seeking King's release from jail. Hartsfield's own words best described what happened:

So we looked at that gigantic pile of telegrams and my political instincts began to assert themselves. Morris looked at them; I looked at them. And I said, "Great Goodness, this presidential race is close. None of us knows which way New York's going; none of us knows which way Illinois is going and the Negro vote counts heavily." Morris said to me, "Gee whiz, Mayor, if Kennedy had this (we were both for Kennedy, you know) if Kennedy had this and could grab this wouldn't it be wonderful?" and I said, "It sure would." He said, "Let's call the National Committee and see if we can't get Kennedy to take a hand. It'll help. It'll be national publicity and it will throw the Negro vote on his side, without any question." I said, "Let's do it."[117]

Hartsfield talked by phone with officials at the National Democratic Committee headquarters to explain his plan and to find out how to reach Kennedy. The problem was that the candidate was campaigning in Kansas, and his heavy travel schedule called for him to stop at several places during the day, thus making it very difficult for the mayor to reach the senator. In spite of several frantic efforts to reach the senator, Hartsfield never got to talk with Kennedy. That did not stop the mayor, however, from moving ahead with his plan. Acting on the assumption that Kennedy would approve, Hartsfield proceeded first to tell the city's black leaders and moments later the national press that the senator "had called" Hartsfield to express support for King and to urge King's immediate release. Hartsfield's gamble paid off inasmuch as Kennedy, having learned of the incident later that day, immediately contacted Mrs. King to convey his sentiments. King was released on bail, although the very next day a DeKalb County judge had the civil rights leader jailed again on a traffic charge. The rejailing of King triggered a fire storm of protest across the nation. That Kennedy had already expressed support for King worked to the candidate's advantage, particularly as Nixon had refused to take any action in spite of pleas by the vice-chairman of the Georgia Republican Party, John C. Calhoun. Calhoun was a member of the black delegation whom Hartsfield had informed about Kennedy's intervention. Upon hearing the mayor's claim about Kennedy, Calhoun slipped out of the meeting to call the Nixon headquarters. Nixon campaign officials, however, expressed no interest, concerned that any sympathy for King would not play well with white southerners.[118]

At the same meeting when Hartsfield informed the black leaders about Kennedy's "intervention," he also indicated his intent to seek a peaceful settlement to the conflict between the student protestors and the downtown businesses. In exchange for a thirty-day truce in the demonstrations, Hartsfield promised to contact the owners of the downtown businesses and attempt to persuade them to accept black customers on the same basis as whites. A truce was arranged, giving time for the mayor to negotiate with the owners. Many of the larger merchants, however, refused even to discuss the issue, and the result was that the Jim Crow practices remained in place.

The students who in October had been arrested continued their protest by refusing to seek bail. They remained in jail through Thanksgiving and December, and when the new year arrived with the students still in jail and with demonstrations back in full swing, Atlanta suffered a major blow to its carefully cultivated image of "a city too busy to hate." The politics of protest proved too difficult for the adroit Hartsfield to negotiate.[119]

It was at this juncture that the older, more conservative black leaders, whose close ties with the white establishment had been ridiculed by student protestors, used their ties to the Atlanta's political and economic elite to explore a solution to the crisis. Ivan Allen recalls in his autobiography that while he was still president of the chamber of commerce, A.T. Walden and Robert Troutman, the attorney representing Rich's Department Store, came by Allen's office supply firm to talk. Over the next few days, the three men continued to meet. Allen and Troutman decided to call together all of the owners and managers of Atlanta's major downtown stores to review the most recent events and to determine what the next step should be. When the all-white group convened, the discussion centered on the havoc created by the protests and whether the time had come for the stores to reverse their discriminatory policies. The conversations centered largely on the negative effect of the demonstrations on Atlanta business. Unless business practices changed, downtown would continue to be the target of civil rights activity and the stores would continue to lose money either through boycotts or because they had closed to prevent students from staging sit-ins. Even the most ardent segregationists among the assembled grudgingly acknowledged that the loss of business warranted some give among the owners. For the moderate businessmen, the primary concern was the city's image and how the picketing, sit-ins, and the jailing of civil rights demonstrators had affected Atlanta's reputation as a progressive southern city. As reporter Fred Powledge observed about Atlanta during this period, "an image, to Atlanta, was what raw steel was to Birmingham. Without it, no one would come to the new airport. Without it, there would be no decent whites to annex."[120]

When the meeting adjourned, all twenty-five businessmen unanimously agreed that a settlement to the conflict should be worked out immediately with the African-American community and that biracial talks involving leaders of both communities should get under way. A resolution to the controversy was important because in addition to the disruption that the protests were causing downtown businesses, there was growing concern in the city that the protests could complicate the Fall 1961 implementation of the federal court's school desegregation order. Some Atlantans feared that the tensions triggered over the downtown stores would only worsen with the desegregation of schools and that violence was not out of the question. Very quickly a summit conference was called, and negotiations once again got under way. Allen was one of the white business representatives, and included among the contingent of black leaders were Walden, Clement, and Martin Luther King, Sr., the pastor of Ebenezer Baptist Church. Some student leaders, including Lonnie King, also participated, although they were out-numbered by the older, more tradition-bound leaders of the African-American community. For a five-week period during which meetings were held almost every day, an agreement was reached. The agreement called for desegregating downtown stores thirty days after the beginning of school desegregation. Students who had been jailed would also be released with all charges dropped. In return, all protests directed against the downtown stores would cease.[121]

Clement wrote out the agreement and presented it to the city's estab-lished black leadership, and Allen's job was to sell it to the downtown business community. With support from the leadership of both communi-ties, Walden released the agreement to the press. Once public, however, the agreement met fierce opposition. Some white reactionaries dropped their accounts with downtown stores. Lester Maddox resigned from the chamber of commerce. Reaction from student protestors was also negative. Even though African-American student leaders attended the summit and agreed to the settlement, others criticized the agreement because it failed to call for the immediate desegregation of the stores. Meetings held in the African-American community to discuss the agreement turned into interracial con-flicts when younger blacks accused their elders of placing a higher value on safeguarding their relationships with the white economic elite than on social justice. Allen attended one of the meetings that got out of hand. It was only after Martin Luther King, Jr., walked into the room and expressed confidence in the negotiating committee and support of the agreement itself that order was restored.[122]

Political scientist Jack Walker examined the split in the African-Ameri-can community over the sit-in movement. He observed that the student leaders played an important role in focusing public attention on the barriers that excluded Atlanta blacks from full participation in the life of the city. Notwithstanding the disunity within the African-American community that the student protest engendered, the sit-in movement led to a quickened pace of change in race relations. Yet, Walker also suggests that the protests were quelled and that the initial steps toward desegregation were taken only because of the relationships that the older conservative blacks had developed with the white power structure. In short, Walker argues that black disunity, not solidarity, was the important ingredient that forced Atlanta to live up to its reputation as a city "too busy to hate."[123]

On August 30, 1961, school desegregation began in Atlanta with the enrollment of nine black students in four white high schools. Seven years after the *Brown* decision the first small step toward compliance with the court order was taken. Atlanta, like Memphis and Richmond, avoided the violence that gripped other southern cities when blacks enrolled in white schools. Unlike Memphis and Richmond, however, Atlanta got international attention for its efforts, in spite of the fact that Memphis began school desegregation the same year and that Richmond, the former capital of the Confederacy, actually began desegregating its schools a year earlier. Also, unlike Memphis, Atlanta carefully orchestrated the desegregation process and used the months between the negotiated settlement reached in March and the start of school in August to prepare an elaborate public relations campaign, including the printing and distribution of materials for reporters who would be writing news stories about the desegregation of city schools. The deliberate cultivation of the press paid handsome dividends. Articles in *Newsweek*, the *New York Times, Life, Look,* and *Good Housekeeping* lavished praise on Atlanta for its progressive leadership and the quiet manner in which its schools had desegregated. On the same day that the four white high schools enrolled the nine African-American students, President Kennedy began a press conference by congratulating Atlanta and urging "all communities which face this difficult transition . . . to look closely at what Atlanta has done." Contributing to Atlanta's reputation as a progressive southern city was the editorial writings of McGill. His editorials and his speeches were widely quoted, and his reputation as a voice for reason and racial harmony in the South was interrelated with the reputation of the city itself. In an address to Harvard Law School graduates shortly before the Atlanta schools desegregated, McGill excoriated the legal community in the South for its failure to urge compliance with the Supreme Court's school desegregation order. In a reference to Atlanta, McGill noted that "only one city Bar association in the South had made a public statement affirming the validity of court orders as they apply to schools."[124]

City elections followed the desegregation of schools. William Hartsfield, having served twenty-four years as Atlanta's mayor, announced that he would not seek another term. Ivan Allen, who led the business community through the sit-in movement and whose social and professional life placed him at the epicenter of Atlanta's corporate elite, became the heir apparent, particularly so as he was Hartsfield's choice as well as that of the black political establishment, the Atlanta Negro Voters League. Among the candidates running against Allen was Lester Maddox, the segregationist whose fight against school integration led to the creation of such groups as GUTS and MASE. Two other opponents, both white, were Charlie Brown, who on two occasions had run against Hartsfield, and M.M. "Mugsy" Smith. Having failed to win the endorsement of the Voters League, Smith capitalized on the split in the black community to gain support from black students still angry over the March agreement and resentful of Allen's role in shaping the agreement. The election was a test of the old biracial coalition formed during the Hartsfield era. The coalition held, with Allen beating Smith by a two to one margin in the black precincts. Still, with Smith siphoning 4,000 black votes from Allen and with the white vote split three ways, Allen was denied a majority, and a run-off election was held that pitted Allen against Maddox. On this occasion, faced with no alternative but to support Allen, the black community supplied a solid bloc of votes. Coupled with the support of the white upper class, Allen easily carried the day.[125]

The coalition also returned Clement to the school board for a third term but broke apart in elections to the Board of Aldermen. For one thing, the Voters League was not able to deliver a solid vote for its candidate because two other blacks also declared their candidacies. The consequence was that League-endorsed candidate Q.V. Williamson received fewer black votes than did Ivan Allen. Furthermore, upper-income whites, in spite of Williamson's endorsement by the two white daily newspapers, were not as enthusiastic about Williamson's bid for the Board of Aldermen as they were for Clement's reelection bid to the school board.[126]

Williamson lost the election and with it the tight grip that the old coalition had on city politics since the late 1940s. Atlanta's reputation as a racially progressive southern city was cultivated with great care. The reality, however, was quite different. Although the city's elite kept the race baiters at bay, the fact remains that Atlanta did not move any more aggressively in desegregating the city than did Memphis and Richmond. All three approached school desegregation in much the same way, very gradually. Local elites controlled the pace of change and engaged in just enough reform to provide justification for the courts but not enough to alter fundamentally the status quo. Atlanta's first year of desegregation involved only nine students in four white high schools whose total white enrollment approximated 6,000. In Memphis, the same year, four white elementary schools enrolled thirteen black youngsters. Richmond began desegregating its schools in 1960 with the enrollment of two African-American middle-school students. Each year thereafter the number of black students attending predominately white schools increased. In 1962, for example, Atlanta school officials added the tenth grade to the grade levels targeted for desegregation and the total number of blacks enrolled in white schools increased from nine to forty-four.[127]

All three cities resorted to complicated pupil placement procedures designed to minimize integration. Like the other two cities, Atlanta required a student desiring to transfer to a school other than the one initially assigned to be screened and tested. The burden of complying with the policy fell on African-American students. The nine students who had enrolled in the four white high schools in 1961 had been drawn from a pool of 130 applicants. In 1962 the forty-four black enrollees were drawn from a pool of 266 applicants. As one NAACP official observed, "We've got a saying around here that it's easier to go to Yale than to transfer from one public school to another in

Atlanta." This obstructionist procedure, plus the one-grade-a-year desegregation plan, were finally scuttled as a result of a controversy during Allen's administration over the proposed demolition of a black elementary school for an exhibition hall adjoining the new civic center auditorium. The proposed closing of C.W. Hill Elementary School located in Buttermilk Bottom, a low-income African-American neighborhood east of the central business district, generated an angry response, and Mayor Allen, in an effort to diffuse the tension, appointed a biracial negotiating committee to resolve the conflict. The committee, which included three members of the school board and three representatives selected by the black community, succeeded in persuading the school board to accelerate the pace of school desegregation and to build another school to replace the one slated to be razed as part of the redevelopment project. The new desegregation plan, adopted in 1965, substituted the slower grade-a-year approach with a "freedom-of-choice" approach applicable to all grades. Nevertheless, five years after the institution of "freedom of choice" (a plan similar to those also adopted by the Memphis and Richmond public schools), 80 percent of Atlanta's public school students still attended totally segregated schools.[128]

In 1970 the U.S. Supreme Court in *Green v. New Kent County, Virginia,* ruled that freedom of choice plans were insufficient. Consequently, Atlanta adopted a new plan under court order that contained several provisions. Larger attendance zones were designed to bring about a larger number of integrated schools. Faculty transfers were mandated in order to attain a more equitable racial mix of faculty in each school. The 1970 order also permitted majority-to-minority transfers; that is, students of the majority race in one school could enroll in schools where they would constitute the minority race. Blacks students in majority black schools, for example, could enroll in majority white schools and white students in majority white schools could enroll in majority black schools. In addition, the 1970 court order also created a biracial committee to advise the school board in the development of future desegregation plans. Atlanta's school board was becoming more serious about desegregation. This new attitude was due in part to the fact that the ten-member board now included three blacks. Clement, who had served on the board for fifteen years, died in 1968 but was replaced by Dr. Benjamin Mays, one of the most influential members of the black community. Another factor contributing to the responsiveness of the school board was the growing recognition among the city's economic elite that economic development and education were tied together and that economic growth could not proceed without the resolution of the school issue. [129]

In 1971 the U.S. Supreme Court sanctioned cross-town busing as a means of desegregating public schools in *Swann v. Charlotte-Mecklenburg.* Rather than wait for a court order, however, Atlanta, unlike Memphis and Richmond, decided to negotiate a biracial settlement to school desegregation and to activate the committee created by the 1970 court order. The settlement reached by the committee and adopted by the court in 1973 did not include busing as a remedy, as urged by the NAACP. Lonnie King, one of the student leaders during the sit-in movement of the early 1960s and who was the president of the local chapter of the NAACP, served as a member of the biracial committee and supported the settlement. As a consequence of his role in negotiating the settlement, he was ousted from the presidency of the local NAACP by the national organization. King's position, like that of other black leaders in Atlanta, was that the city schools in 1973 were already 83 percent black and that busing would only contribute to greater white flight out of the city into the suburbs. Furthermore, many blacks were placing more emphasis on their own neighborhood schools and did not wish those schools to be disrupted by massive busing schemes. The settlement included an expanded majority-to-minority transfer plan, new student assignments such that no school would have less than a 30 percent black enrollment, additional staff desegregation, and a major effort to desegregate the school administration by reconfiguring the administrative structure and the appointment of a black superintendent, the latter occurring in July 1973 with the appointment of Harvard graduate Dr. Alonzo Crim.[130]

As was typical of Atlanta, negotiations involving black and white leaders led to a resolution of the school crisis. Large-scale busing was eschewed, and a metropolitan solution to school segregation was also rejected by both the biracial committee and white business supporters of the Metropolitan Atlanta Rapid Transit Authority (MARTA) who sought to expand transit lines into additional political jurisdictions and, therefore, did not want discussions of a metropolitanwide school district concept to disrupt the negotiations. The settlement of 1973, however, was negotiated by leaders who, like those who preceded them, understood the art of compromise and the demands of political reality. On one hand, white leaders, always conscious of the city's image, did not want a school problem to tarnish the city's reputation as the South's most progressive city or to stymie the city's economic development efforts. On the other hand, black leaders, always the pragmatists, saw little to be gained by pressing desegregation strategies that would disrupt their own neighborhood schools, contribute to additional white flight, and diminish their ability to negotiate for a more significant voice in educational decision making. In Atlanta, one set of elites needed the other.

Perhaps no other issue galvanized as effectively as did school segregation the residents of the separate city into a social and political movement that challenged the racial status quo. And, of course, what brought the school issue to bear on the politics of Atlanta, Memphis, and Richmond (indeed the politics of the South) was the U.S. Supreme Court's *Brown v. Board of Educa-*

tion decision of 1954. With the decision and the Massive Resistance laws that followed in quick succession, new forces were unleashed in the black community. In the case of Richmond, these forces led to the emergence of Virginia's premier black voter-registration group, the Crusade for Voters, an organization that forever changed the contours of Richmond politics. In the case of Memphis, these forces gave rise to bipartisan coalitions involving young black professionals disillusioned with white reformers who, in spite of being elected with solid black support, failed to keep their commitments to the black community. In the case of Atlanta, these forces led to a new group of black reformers impatient with older, more conservative black leaders more intent on maintaining their ties to the white power structure than on demanding social change.

Although the separate city was a visible reminder of the entrenched racial divisions endemic to the urban South and a physical manifestation of the social and economic disadvantages that befell black citizens, in all three localities it served an important function. Through the concentration of African-American citizens in a racially defined geographic area, the separate city provided the institutional networks and communication systems necessary for mobilizing an aggrieved people. The *Brown* decision was but a triggering device. It was not the only impetus for change, but it surely was one of the most important as increasingly during the postwar years blacks struggled to surmount the barriers that had been so tightly constructed around their separate cities. The barriers were many, and among them, as the next chapter points out, community planning policy, including urban renewal, slum clearance, and public housing, were particularly pernicious.

4

Neighborhood Restructuring

From the early 1900s through the early 1940s the social geography of Atlanta, Memphis, and Richmond constituted an amalgam of separate neighborhood units differentiated by age, architecture, social class, and, of course, race. The neighborhood-formation process was essentially an organic one, in that there was in all three cities continuous change in the social composition of most sections. At the same time the impetus of Jim Crowism in the urban South engendered concerted efforts to take chance out of neighborhood change and to engage in racially motivated social engineering. The most popular strategies to plan for racial separation were zoning and the use of private real estate covenants to control and segregate the growing urban black population. The absence of explicit public legal controls over racial change in neighborhoods, owing to the Supreme Court's decision in *Buchanan v. Warley* (1917), placed the highly sensitive issue of where the growing black population would live in the hands of real estate brokers, housing developers, and individual consumers in the 1920s and 1930s. In all three cities expansion of the public planning function in the 1940s aimed both at stabilizing an increasingly volatile social situation and at speeding the process of neighborhood separation by class and race. The public planning activities that had a direct bearing on the process of neighborhood separation by race included the siting of public housing projects, neighborhood planning, urban renewal, and various public improvement projects, especially highway construction. Whereas real estate brokers, housing developers, and consumers prevented uncontrolled expansion of black neighborhoods prior to 1940, urban planners and the civic and political leaders who helped to prepare their agenda successfully engineered the separate black city between the 1940s and the 1960s. In the process of fashioning the modern metropolis, Atlanta, Memphis, and Richmond relied on planning policies to institutionalize the separateness of the class and race worlds that had been sustained loosely in the unplanned city of the early 1900s.[1]

The planning approach employed in Atlanta, Memphis, and Richmond after 1940 proved remarkably similar, in large part because all three relied heavily on federal programs to finance their urban reconstruction initiatives.

Public housing constructed in Richmond in the 1940s looked identical to the complexes already constructed in Atlanta and Memphis. By the 1950s all three possessed a public housing inventory that numbered in the thousands of units and that by location reinforced the segregation of low-income black neighborhoods. Likewise, urban renewal efforts in all three cities adhered to a common set of federal guidelines and produced similar processes of neighborhood clearance and rebuilding. Unlike in public housing, the federal government granted broad discretion to cities from the 1940s through the 1960s in the use of urban renewal funds. Cities controlled the level and timing of their participation in housing and urban renewal, and the local political culture played a major role in articulating the objectives of its replanning efforts. Owing to the influence of local political culture, there were differences, as well as expected similarities, in reconstruction of the southern city through neighborhood planning after 1940.[2]

A common and important concern of planners in all three cities was to contain the expanding black community while eliminating the blighting influence of substandard housing from their neighborhoods. Memphis and Richmond adopted a similar approach, in part because nationally renowned planning consultant Harland Bartholomew prepared master plans for both cities in the early 1940s. Bartholomew offered both clients a prescription for urban improvement centered around neighborhood rebuilding and preservation philosophy that ensured strict separation between the classes and the races. The sort of neighborhood planning that Bartholomew recommended coincided with the prevailing local attitudes toward the proper social division in cities. Through vigorous slum clearance, rebuilding of neighborhoods, careful site selection for new low-income housing, and preservation of established middle-income neighborhoods, Bartholomew suggested that the southern city could have change, reordering, and maintenance of the status quo all at the same time. Only a few critics, such as Chicago planner and community activist Reginald Issacs, regarded neighborhood planning as an insidious "instrumentation for segregation of ethnic and economic groups." For most urban leaders, especially those in Memphis and Richmond, Bartholomew offered a planning remedy to a enduring social problem that seemed to be getting worse.[3]

Although Atlanta relied essentially on planning strategies similar to those suggested by Bartholomew for Memphis and Richmond, it experimented with a novel approach to neighborhood planning that seems to have been wholly homegrown. Late in 1952 Atlanta's mayor, William Hartsfield, appointed a special committee, known as the West Side Mutual Development Committee (WSMDC) "to consider the various living, building, and development problems of the west side of our city." What his December memorandum did not, and could not, state explicitly was that the primary purpose of the group was to safeguard the sort of racial segregation in neighborhoods that had been the intent of racial zoning. The unique feature of the WSMDC was its biracial composition. Historian Robert B. Fairbanks noted in a study of Dallas that mayor Woodall Rodgers responded to violence against blacks moving into white neighborhoods between September 1940 and April 1941 by creating an "interracial committee" made up only of white members. The committee urged the city to buy out blacks who already lived in the South Dallas neighborhood and declare it and other areas "white only." Although the city council endorsed the idea, it rescinded their resolution when reminded that it probably violated the 1917 Supreme Court decision against racial zoning.[4]

The WSMDC got around the restrictions set forth in *Buchanan* by using private negotiation between black real estate brokers and community leaders rather than official designation of either white or black neighborhoods as the way to determine where blacks would be shown residential properties. The charge to the WSMDC included preserving racial homogeneity in existing neighborhoods by fighting blockbusting, identifying white neighborhoods where transition to black occupancy should be encouraged, planning for new black residential areas, and advising on public improvements, particularly road construction, to promote clear and unbreachable boundaries between white and black neighborhoods. It sought to dissuade black real estate brokers from showing black clients properties in neighborhoods where whites preferred to remain, even if it was adjacent to a black neighborhood. For their part, community leaders in white West Side neighborhoods were obliged to organize residents to resist the temptation to sell out either from fear or avarice. Given the voluntary, nonbinding nature of the agreements drawn up between blacks and whites, the WSMDC, Hartsfield, and the director of the Metropolitan Planning Commission consistently maintained that they did not engage in racial zoning but rather in promoting neighborhood stability and peaceful neighborhood transition in the best interest of Atlanta's citizens. Even if it technically skirted the forbidden practice of racial zoning, the link between the WSMCD and the Metropolitan Planning Commission ensured that planning for the city as a whole would be coordinated with an eye toward creating a separate black city in Atlanta's West Side. Maybe the short-term successes of the WSMDC in guiding racial change in the West Side neighborhoods actually facilitated the wholesale transformation that occurred in the 1960s when the negotiation process broke down. Rather than preventing neighborhood change, as will be discussed, the WSMDC actually worked to reduce resistance to the westward migration of blacks, a migratory flow that increased quite dramatically in the early 1960s. It is both ironic and important to note that a major impetus for the westward movement by African-Americans in Atlanta was massive displacement in the center city owing to urban renewal, highway construction, and other related private and public developments.[5]

The replanning of Atlanta, Memphis, and Richmond, beginning with the public housing initiatives of the 1930s and early 1940s and through the urban renewal and highway construction boom of the 1950s and 1960s, represents a significant factor in the changing pattern of race relations in the urban South. By the end of the public housing construction era in the 1960s, not only the black community but also the very nature of all three cities themselves were permanently altered. What began in an atmosphere of confidence regarding the ability of urban leaders to use public policy to resolve urban problems within the framework of a racially segregated society became a series of last-ditch efforts to prevent these cities from shifting to a black majority, a process that many white leaders regarded as a sign of the demise of the city itself. The replanning process that so many blacks resisted in an attempt to preserve some semblance of community in the 1940s through the 1960s served to undermine the prevailing power structure. It also served as a springboard for African-American political dominance after 1968. For that reason, it is necessary to examine the replanning of the southern city from the 1940s through the 1960s to understand not only how the separate city emerged but also how this process inspired rather drastic changes in black community leadership.

Public Housing and Early Slum Clearance

Atlanta

Altanta's national leadership in the public housing and slum-clearance efforts owed to two major factors, the initiative and political influence provided by Charles F. Palmer, a local business executive and self-proclaimed "slum fighter," and the abysmal condition of neighborhoods surrounding the city's core. A 1934 survey of blighted areas in central Atlanta conducted by Raymond W. Torras, secretary to the Atlanta City Planning Commission, disclosed that 43,000 residents lived in dilapidated housing, many lacking running water and toilets, and most otherwise in need of major repairs. Palmer's influential coalition of local housing reformers drafted a plan to clear a section of blighted flats adjacent to Georgia Tech and then added, at the request of Dr. John Hope of Atlanta University, a comparable clearance scheme for low-income black housing adjacent to Spelman College. The condition of the area designated for slum clearance was one of marked contrasts. "Along with two of these valleys lay the districts which now include Techwood and University Homes. In each, there was the anomalous situation of a university devoted to enlightenment overlooking the unenlightened hovels in the City" (John Lear, 1935, quoted in Arnold, p. 6). The initial plan called for 557 units in Techwood Homes for white occupancy and 800 units in University Homes for black families, with the federal government covering $3.4 million in primary costs. The limited dividend corporation (Techwood, Incorporated) set up by Palmer provided an additional $550,000 for secondary costs. When the Federal Emergency Housing Corporation took over slum-clearance and low-income housing projects in March 1934, the funds for the Atlanta projects increased to $5.1 million, and Palmer's group assumed an advisory role rather than participating directly in the development.[6]

Palmer's plan to secure federal backing for slum clearance in Atlanta had the support of Clark Howell, Sr., publisher of the *Atlanta Constitution* and a personal friend of Franklin Roosevelt, as well as Mayor James L. Key and Dr. M. L. Brittain, President of Georgia Tech. In their appeals to Washington to approve the project under the Limited Dividend Housing Program, the Atlanta group stressed the employment potential as well as the slum-clearance and housing implications of the Techwood proposal. Yet another significant feature of the Atlanta proposal was the inclusion of the black housing project in conjunction with a project for whites. As one federal official noted, it was known from the outset that "we would encounter considerable difficulty in endeavoring to develop a white project, and a colored project in the same community." The transfer of the Atlanta project to the Federal Emergency Housing Corporation in early 1934 and a subsequent ruling by U.S. Comptroller General J.R. McCarl that the corporation was unconstitutional jeopardized the initiative and, in effect, delayed construction for several years. It took until May 1935 for the low-income housing program to get under way, even though Secretary of Interior Harold Ickes came to Atlanta on September 29, 1934, to "personally dynamite the first shack to be removed in the deserted slum" that was to become Techwood Homes. Once land acquisition began in May 1935, however, the project moved quickly toward completion. On November 29, 1935, President Roosevelt came to Atlanta to dedicate the nation's first New Deal public housing project. Yet, a subsequent ruling by McCarl required that rents at Techwood had to cover the entire cost of land, buildings, as well as operating expenses and that no part of the rental fees could be used to reimburse Atlanta (as originally agreed to). These provisions delayed the opening for another year. Although Georgia's senate delegation secured passage of a bill in May 1936 to correct the problem, the Techwood experience led directly to a new housing program under the Wagner-Steagall Housing Act of 1937 that decentralized administration of low-income housing while unifying financing, management, and construction practices and that served as a permanent public housing program.[7]

Palmer and his public housing and slum-clearance allies initially found the city's new mayor, William Hartsfield, resistant to the idea of creating a local housing authority. Under the 1937 Housing Act, cities that wanted to participate in the low-income housing program needed to establish a local housing authority. Atlanta's city council passed a resolution to establish a five-member local housing authority. Hartsfield vetoed the resolution on September 24, 1937, on the grounds that "Atlanta is not going to be a guinea pig in this matter." Palmer and the chamber of commerce continued to press for a local housing authority, although it was the near loss of Grady Hospital because of a huge fire in an adjacent slum in March 1938 that galvanized support for a housing authority so that Atlanta could get additional federal assistance under the 1937 Housing Act. On May 19, the Atlanta City Council passed an ordinance to create the Atlanta Housing Authority, and this time Hartsfield gave his consent.[8]

Opposition to Atlanta's initial foray into public housing, slum clearance, and the creation of a permanent local housing authority came from a number of sources, including property owners in the two areas. Through the Atlanta Apartment House Owners Association, property-owners challenged public housing as deleterious to their investments, given the city's 25 percent vacancy rate in rental housing. Another local opposition group, the Citizens Committee led by attorney Phil C. McDuffie, chimed in that "what Atlanta needs is slum clearance, *not more apartments.*" He called for spot clearance in the Techwood and Spelman areas and construction of one- or two-family houses for sale to the working class. "Then spend the balance of the money cleaning up Atlanta slums—they're lousing and unfit for hogs to live in." Certain black leaders also criticized the Techwood and Spelman projects for overlooking much worse areas such as the Butler Street area known as Darktown, which "for twenty-five years has been a veritable 'hell-hole' of squalor, degradation, sickness, crime and misery polluting the entire stream of Atlanta's community life." An interracial group, the Home Improvement League, applied to Washington early in 1934 for funds to clear and rebuild the Darktown area. Although it seemed set that the Techwood and University homes projects would be carried out, the Darktown project backers, including Atlanta's eminent African-American attorney, A.T. Walden, and Harvey W. Cox, president of Emory University, argued that additional federal funds should be found to make a more direct impact on black slums as "nothing of this character has ever been done for the negroes of this city."[9]

What made the Techwood and University home sites so attractive to federal officials was that they were not the worst areas. They wanted a foolproof initial slum-clearance and housing project in Atlanta, and all of the criticism of the initial sites as not constituting a true slum only served to strengthen federal resolve. As early as January 1934 a four-day site visit by Federal Emergency Housing Corporation officials M. Drew Carrel and N. Max Dunning solidified support for the original sites. Both the Butler Street and Capitol Avenue areas were dismissed "because the slum areas are so great in extent that any housing development would be submerged in its surrounding, and would accomplish nothing in an important way in clearing out or changing the general characteristics of large slum areas." These areas were, in the opinion of several local officials, including Mayor Key, located in the "dying" part of Atlanta. Key stated that "the south side of Atlanta is dead—growth is toward the north—[and] no residences have been built on the south side for ten years." The transition of the south side from residential to commercial and industrial uses was already under way, and local and federal officials seemed content with "forecasts" of "continuing and increasing 'blight,' which would make a housing development hazardous." Assistant Director of Housing Dunning, who prepared the Atlanta evaluation, summed up the strength of the Techwood site as follows: "There is no area in Atlanta where a white housing project could be placed with more assurance of success." The University Homes site was even more advantageous given that it was in the "favored neighborhood" in Atlanta for blacks but was adjacent to a "large colored housing development" where houses were sold in the $3,500 to $20,000 range. "The general appearance of this colored subdivision," Dunning noted, "compares favorably with any white subdivision."[10]

The success of the Techwood and University projects had a mushrooming effect on Atlanta's low-income housing and slum-clearance initiatives, especially after the creation of the Atlanta Housing Authority (AHA). Almost as soon as the city had acquired the necessary conduit to receive federal funds, the money began to pour in. Within the next two years, Atlanta launched six additional public housing projects that gave the city 4,924 units and removed 1,621 sub-standard housing units at a cost of slightly over $16 million. Both the University and Techwood sites were expanded while public housing also went into the area adjacent to Grady Hospital that had burned down in 1938. There was a clear pattern in the siting of public housing to remove deteriorated sections to the east of the downtown in the Old Fourth Ward as well as to guide migration of low-income blacks in a westwardly direction. The Egan, Herndon, and Hope Homes projects accomplished that objective. Only the addition to the Techwood project, known as Clark Howell Homes (602 units) and the Capitol Homes project (635 units) were for white occupancy. By the early 1940s over 60 percent of the city's public housing units were for black occupancy. Although the city maintained the balance between white and black communities that had been so carefully orchestrated with the original Techwood and University projects, public policy shifted decidedly toward restructuring the black community through the intensified public housing program.[11]

Memphis

Blacks in Memphis had little opportunity for the sort of participatory role played by blacks in the creation of Atlanta's public housing program. Under the autocratic rule of Crump, Memphis initiated a public housing and slum-clearance program under the Public Works Administration (PWA) in

1934. By 1938 the city had cleared a few hundred dilapidated dwellings to provide space for 1,124 new public housing units in separate complexes, one for whites and the other for blacks. Within three years, under the leadership of Joseph A. Fowler, executive director of the Memphis Housing Authority (MHA), it completed three additional projects to increase the city's housing stock to 3,337 units by 1941. As in Atlanta, more than one-half of these units were for black occupancy. And as in Atlanta, there was a rather broad-based coalition supporting public housing and slum clearance in Memphis because of an increasing awareness of the severity of blighted conditions in the city's older neighborhoods. A 1940 survey of local housing conditions financed by the Works Progress Administration (WPA), disclosed that 46,753 of the city's 83,540 homes (56%) were substandard. The city eschewed intensive clearance activities during the 1930s in favor of renewal of sparsely populated areas of blight adjacent to the central business district. For the time being, the public housing and slum-clearance programs posed no direct threat either to white or black neighborhoods.[12]

Public housing construction in Memphis during the late 1930s brought relief to some African-Americans who lived in substandard housing, but there was opposition among others less needy that foreshadowed future battles over where low-income housing would be built. One of the city's first two projects, the white-occupied Lauderdale Homes, sprang up on the site of a black neighborhood recently cleared. In the case of another project, Foote Homes, the Memphis black community protested the clearance of a black middle-class neighborhood. The area selected for the Foote Homes was in a once-affluent white neighborhood north of the central business district that had become a black middle-class area. The protest from black property owners included Reverend T.O. Fuller, the prominent black Baptist minister and Crump ally whose church was one of the "slums" to be torn down. Despite a vigorous letter-writing campaign to Mayor Watkins Overton, the MHA stuck to its original site selection. According to historian Roger Biles, "the callous disregard for the misfortunes of uprooted slum dwellers confirmed what many black leaders had adduced—that the primary function of public housing was not only to maintain existing patterns of racial segregation, but also to further concentrate blacks in designated sections of the city increasingly being vacated by suburban-bound whites."[13]

The aggressive prewar construction boom in public housing for African-Americans was complemented by a postwar campaign by white and black developers to satisfy the enormous demand for new houses by black Memphians. A.L. Thompson, a race relations advisor for the Federal Housing Administration (FHA) and a former school teacher in Memphis, urged black developers to construct new housing, but to do so in consultation with city officials to ensure compliance with local preferences regarding the direction of black residential expansion. White builders took the lead, however, and constructed the 170–unit Vandalia Homes in the Binghampton neighborhood in 1948. The necessary rezoning for the project initially prompted protest by white residents. The neighborhood accepted the rezoning with assurances from the city that Cyprus Creek would remain a buffer between the new project and the adjacent white neighborhood. The Vandalia project was followed in 1951 by the construction of a 426–unit apartment complex in Southeast Memphis under the FHA mortgage insurance program. In 1951 black businessman and community leader Dr. Joseph E. Walker also participated with three other black financiers in development of a subdivision of 207 two-bedroom homes selling in the $6,000 range. Walker initiated an even bolder project the following year when he began the 1,500-unit subdivision known as the Walker Homes. In 1955 he added a 165–house subdivision for middle-income blacks named after another black Memphian, George W. Lee.[14]

The construction of such a substantial amount of new housing for African-Americans in Memphis occurred almost exclusively along the southeastern edge of the city. Given that there was relatively little new public housing built during the late 1940s and early 1950s and no large-scale urban renewal projects until after Edmund Orgill became mayor in 1955, conflict over neighborhoods between whites and blacks flared up only occasionally and did not engender widespread concern among local officials. One minor flareup occurred in 1952 when blacks began inquiring about houses in a white North Memphis neighborhood. The A.P. Hill Civic Club posted signs in the area informing real estate agents that houses in the neighborhood were "not for sale to Negroes" and warned the city commissioners that violence would ensue if blacks attempted to move into the neighborhood. The commissioners responded by barring further black subdivisions in the area and requiring developers to erect a steel fence to separate already constructed black and white residential sections. For their part, black neighborhoods sought protection from the disruptions that accompanied public improvements. In 1952 a confederation of more than two dozen black neighborhood civic clubs, known as the Bluff City and Shelby County Council of Civic Clubs, formed to give blacks a unified voice over neighborhood concerns. One of its member groups, the Eleventh Ward Civic Club, openly criticized an MHA proposed urban renewal project in the Railroad Avenue area on the grounds that neighborhood residents there recently spent money to remodel homes slated for demolition. Tensions also flared in the Fordhurst subdivision near Riverside Park when real estate agents began to show blacks houses following a ruling by a Chancery Court judge that restrictive covenants on property in the subdivision that forbid whites to sell to blacks were illegal. A committee of prominent Memphis blacks, led by Dr. Walker, appealed to Mayor Frank Tobey for protection in the transitional neighborhoods—the "twilight areas"—following a bombing on East Olive Street in 1953.[15]

Memphis attempted to preserve the prevailing neighborhood balance by encouraging housing rehabilitation in substandard areas. Modeled after the so-called Baltimore Plan, the city's neighborhood-rehabilitation program (known locally as the "Memphis Plan") involved code inspections in deteriorated areas and voluntary compliance by property owners regarding needed repairs. In the first year of the program in 1954 the city issued 1,911 repair permits. The next year saw a significant increase in permits to 4,911. According to Public Service Commissioner John T. "Buddy" Dwyer who headed the program, efforts to rehabilitate concentrated only on "redeemable" areas to prevent further deterioration rather than trying to tackle the most dilapidated neighborhoods. The city claimed that between 1954 and 1956, the number of substandard units declined from 47,000 to 25,000. Ironically, one black neighborhood, Douglas Park, which pushed the home repair effort "with amazing resolution" also reminded city officials that this middle-income neighborhood still lacked paved streets. The Memphis *Commercial Appeal* tried to encourage continued neighborhood rehabilitation by providing a grant of $1,000 to assist the residents. The growing interest in housing rehabilitation represented one alternative to the construction of additional public housing in Memphis. By 1957 there was a concerted move to prevent any further public housing by seeking an amendment to the state's housing law to require a referendum for any new projects. To secure local backing for urban renewal, Mayor Edmund Orgill assured Memphians in 1958 that the MHA would not "expect a nickel's worth of additional public housing in any of the urban renewal areas," only private housing development. As city and community leaders quickly discovered, however, Memphis's ambitious program of urban renewal and highway construction generated an equally significant degree of residential displacement, especially in black neighborhoods. By early 1958 the Memphis *Press-Scimitar* noted that the "$70 million urban renewal program for Memphis is endangered by the community's slowness in providing new housing for negroes." Obviously in the twenty years since the MHA completed its first public housing projects, local attitudes toward federally assisted housing had changed markedly. Indeed, by the late 1950s black neighborhoods joined their white counterparts to challenge key portions of the city's restructuring efforts, especially construction of additional public housing units.[16]

Richmond

Richmond's public housing and slum-clearance efforts began later than those of Atlanta and Memphis, were far more modest in scale, and boasted precious few accomplishments. The failure of the limited dividend "Sunshine Apartment" project in the mid-1930s, coupled with Mayor Bright's success in preventing the establishment of a housing authority until 1940, put Richmond well behind its southern urban counterparts in the provision of new low-income housing. Unlike Atlanta and Memphis, Richmond never attempted to nurture a biracial coalition in support of public housing by pursuing a balanced program of attention to white and black residents. The city's initial project, Gilpin Court, as well as three of its next four complexes, were for black occupancy from the outset. Until construction of separate public housing for the elderly in the 1970s, only one project, Hillside Court in South Richmond, ever accommodated white residents. From its inception, public housing in Richmond was black housing and designed to achieve the objectives of slum removal and elimination of a public health hazard and maintenance of residential segregation.[17]

The mayoralty race of 1940 brought the issue of public housing and slum-clearance directly into the political arena. Gordon B. Ambler opposed Bright's quest for a fifth consecutive term on a platform that emphasized the incumbent's inattention to slum problems. Ambler called for creation of a housing authority and an aggressive slum-clearance initiative. The increasing political strength of Richmond's progressive coalition not only aided in Ambler's surprisingly easy victory over Bright but also helped to secure the establishment of the Richmond Housing Authority (RHA) in October 1940. By February 1941 the city secured a commitment of $3,191,000 from the U.S. Housing Authority (USHA) to launch its first slum-clearance and public housing project, Gilpin Court. The RHA selected for the 297–unit complex an eight-block area in "Apostle town," the same area identified in the late 1930s as an appropriate site to begin slum clearance. This was also the same area opposed by the black community six years earlier when a local group proposed a low-rent project. This time, however, RHA did not consult black residents until *after* they selected and secured control of the site for Gilpin Court. Because the black community was represented on the RHA board of commissioners by Dr. Henry J. McGuinn of Virginia Union College, it could not be argued that the black community was entirely excluded from the site decision for the project. By locating it in a section of Jackson Ward, there was less chance of white opposition because it reinforced established black neighborhood boundaries. When the city resumed public housing construction in the mid-1950s, it merely extended the original Gilpin Court by 388 units. Although Richmond's conservative city council was not enamored with the idea of additional public housing in the 1950s, it was acceptable as a substitute for slum housing in areas already relegated to poor blacks.[18]

The negative experience of African-Americans in planning for residential development, especially public housing siting, carried over into a generally critical posture toward the city's overall planning agenda. The black response in Richmond to neighborhood planning from the 1940s through the 1970s is best characterized as a critical and defensive posture. More often than not, blacks opposed the housing and neighborhood programs devised for them by well-meaning but misguided white reformers. Ironically, black opposition to an array of neighborhood rebuilding schemes and related planning ventures required them to join forces with whites whose antiplanning sentiments were complemented by an equally intense desire to maintain the racial status quo. Blacks and conservative whites not only opposed slum clearance and public housing in the 1930s and 1940s but also teamed up to fight highway development in the early 1950s and urban renewal throughout the 1950s and 1960s. Not until the late 1960s did blacks in Richmond possess sufficient voting strength to form an independent political bloc capable of offering its own planning agenda. Yet, by the late 1960s, the transition of Richmond from a city of diverse neighborhoods to one bifurcated along racial lines was nearly complete. Whereas blacks and whites had competed for neighborhood space in various parts of the city in the 1940s, a racially defined Maginot line had nearly obliterated the traditional neighborhood configuration by 1970.[19]

Planning Racial Change in Neighborhoods: Atlanta

When Atlanta Mayor William Hartsfield quietly created the West Side Mutual Development Committee late in 1952, the city had not yet launched the massive urban renewal program that, in concert with housing code enforcements and public housing development, displaced approximately 75,000 persons, most of whom were black, between 1959 and 1968. The problem of sufficient housing for displaced, low-income families was so critical, noted outgoing mayor, Ivan Allen, Jr., in 1968 that "unless the city can promote tremendous amounts of subsidized housing in some form which will produce 4,300 units of low income housing . . . the city will have to delay or cut back federal programs such as urban renewal." In the early 1950s the WSMDC faced a situation of relative calm compared to the 1960s, but one in which many neighborhoods in the city's rapidly changing West Side threatened to resist in any way necessary the seemingly inevitable in-migration of African-Americans. Five new black subdivisions sprang up in the West Side between 1945 and 1949, two of which abutted all-white neighborhoods. The WSMDC represented an effort to facilitate a smooth transition rather than resist change so that the city's growing black community would not seek outlets for new housing in any other direction. Even before the WSMDC began its work, the plan for a separate black world in the West Side (and southwestern area) and exclusion from everywhere else was already established as the basis for future planning in the city. In the WSMDC Hartsfield fashioned one of the nation's first neighborhood planning organizations whose principal purpose was to partition further Atlanta's communities along racial lines.[20]

The work of the WSMDC focused initially on the Mozeley Park neighborhood and park, both of which had been a battleground for racial occupancy in Atlanta's West Side since the 1930s. Mozeley Park was one of the city's older suburbs that lay in the path of Heman Perry's black housing development in the 1920s. In 1937 an African-American physician who owned three lots in the neighborhood attempted to build a house but was dissuaded by threats from white residents. Another potential African-American resident met a hooded welcoming party the following year, and he, too, chose not to cross the color line in Mozeley Park. The conflict came to a head when the son of a black publisher in Atlanta decided to build a house in the neighborhood on lots inherited from his father. White residents tried unsuccessfully to have the city revoke his building permit and then reverted to threats of violence. In this case, however, the black World War II veteran refused to alter his plans and moved into the new house in 1949. What followed, in addition to his continued harassment, was an increasingly volatile situation in 1949 when some Mozeley Park residents realized that demand by affluent blacks for new housing in the neighborhood brought inflated sales prices. In this pre-blockbusting era, white owners (and real estate brokers) slowly recognized that neighborhood transition was a way to secure higher sales prices on houses. Soon thereafter, three houses were sold through African-American brokers. In response, approximately 100 Mozeley Park residents stormed city hall and demanded protection against in-migration. Mayor Hartsfield created a temporary committee that agreed on Mozeley Drive (Hunter Road) as the dividing line between black and white areas. As the compromise was being hammered out in city hall, Georgia Governor Herman Talmadge urged that "the State Real Estate Commission revoke the license of any real estate broker who sells residential property in a white neighborhood to a Negro." Mozeley Park avoided violence through a process of having entire blocks listed and sold to blacks, with "the understanding that the white seller would continue to occupy the house until conditions permitted the Negro to move in." This process went on from 1949 until the transition was complete in 1954, at which time the park and the neighborhood school, long coveted by blacks, officially became available for their use.[21]

Even though the WSMDC formed long after the Mozeley Park transition process had already begun, the details of the unofficial agreement between the Empire Real Estate Board (EREB), the organization of black real estate brokers, and the neighborhood became the standard formula used by the group throughout the 1950s. Clearly, the Mozeley Park problem convinced Hartsfield that negotiations between whites and blacks was an effective strategy and that a permanent rather than an ad hoc group needed to oversee the process throughout the West Side. The main feature of the Mozeley Park agreement was to maintain Westview Drive as the southernmost boundary of the black section of the neighborhood. The September 1952 agreement noted specifically that the "Board [EREB] is not setting up any property boundary line or zoning area for Negro expansion" but "in the spirit of good will" promised not to accept listings south of the Westview Drive boundary on condition that white brokers also not try to "bust" beyond that line. The EREB claimed that it had not agreed to any permanent racial dividing line but merely to a temporary demarcation between white and black sections of the community.[22]

Following establishment of the WSMDC in December, similar agreements were worked out over the next eight years in the Center Hill, Grove Park, Cascade Heights, Collier Heights, and Adamsville neighborhoods in the West Side. Overall, the WSMDC was involved in sixteen neighborhoods during its ten-year life. In addition, it expanded the range of tools available to preserve neighborhood stability as it sought to deal with other places undergoing racial change. For example, it experimented with the idea of a neighborhood corporation purchasing properties that, if sold directly to blacks, would violate existing agreements about racial boundaries. It created the West Side Corporation in 1954 to purchase marginal properties in the Center Hill and Grove Park neighborhoods. The intent was to "give assurances that the area was not going Negro" as under existing laws "the private property owner can sell his property . . . to whomever he wants to . . . [but] under the present circumstances people who need to sell have no choice but to sell to Negroes."[23]

The Corporation set forth a six-point program to control the real estate market in affected neighborhoods that included getting people to take down for-sale signs; encouraging sellers "not to show to Negroes"; informing the Corporation before agreeing to a sale; raising capital to allow for the purchase of critical properties, which included repurchasing properties already sold to blacks so they could be remarketed to whites; and organizing residents in affected areas to ensure conformity with the goals of the Corporation. Robert C. Stuart, director of the Atlanta Metropolitan Planning Commission and technical advisor to the WSMDC, stressed that this program was not a subterfuge for illegal racial zoning but that "the course of action being pursued by the Corporation represents a legal and constructive procedure." The WSMDC believed that "if the line [between white and black sections of Center Hill-Grove Park] can be stabilized," especially by construction of a new access road to serve as a buffer, "a potentially explosive situation will have been prevented." Mayor Hartsfield urged the city's chief of construction to establish the right-of-way for the access road as a "voluntary racial boundary" for the area. Hartsfield remarked that "the people are becoming very much upset and threatening to sell out, which would, in turn, make extension of the access road rather useless." Once the line was drawn, it would be the role of the Corporation to purchase properties along the racial divide to ensure that their future use conformed to the overall plan of racial occupancy for the neighborhood.[24]

It was not just the manner in which the WSMDC served the interests of

white neighborhoods that accounts for its initial successes in fostering peaceful neighborhood change in the West Side but also the fact that it enabled
African-Americans to press quietly, but often effectively, their claims on
better neighborhoods. This function of the WSMDC had its origins in the
immediate postwar era in Atlanta as black leaders searched for ways to meet
the housing needs of the growing black community. In 1948 the Atlanta
Urban League (AUL) created a Temporary Coordinating Committee on
Housing (TCCH) to address what had become a black housing crisis precipitated by numerous factors, such as increased demand by veterans for housing, the loss of several thousand housing units due to the city's expressway
construction program, and dilapidated conditions owing to neglect and
poverty. Already, according to an Urban League report, there was evidence
that black migration into "white neighborhoods" would evoke a harsh
response, including "mob violence, the dynamiting of homes of negroes and
general confusion and frustration in the Atlanta community."[25]

According to the TCCH, which was headed by black developer W.H.
Aiken, the city needed 4,500 new housing units for returning black veterans
and their families alone. Fellow black real estate broker T.M. Alexander
headed a "land committee" to investigate ways to secure areas for black
residential expansion. The TCCH also formed a committee of black business
executives, headed by J.P. Whitaker of the Atlanta Mutual Building and Loan
Association, to explore ways to finance housing construction. Given the
generally positive response to the group by local planners, the Atlanta
Chamber of Commerce, and key government officials, the group became a
permanent black housing organization, the Atlanta Housing Council, and
began to plan specific housing developments. Under the sponsorship of the
Urban League, it began the 153 single-family house Fair Haven subdivision
in 1948. A second project proposed in 1949, the High Point Apartments, met
immediate opposition from white livings in nearby Lakewood Heights who
"objected to any further Negro occupancy in the South Atlanta area." The
willingness of the developers to set aside 27 acres to serve as a buffer between
the project and Lakewood Heights failed to assuage the concerns of whites.
The creation of an industrial zone satisfied the Fulton County Commissioners that the neighborhood's integrity would not be sacrificed, however, and
they gave the project their unanimous approval in February 1950.[26]

Aiken's role in the WSMDC from its inception ensured that it would give
attention not only to protecting white areas but also to finding additional
areas in Atlanta's West Side for new black housing. This also was an objective
of the Atlanta Metropolitan Planning Commission that provided technical
support to the WSMDC. As Stuart noted in a confidential memorandum to
Hartsfield in 1957, one of the key objectives of the WSMDC was to "locate a
new Negro expansion area to take the pressure off of existing white communities." A further elaboration of this view became a part of the 1958 WSMCD

policy statement drafted by Stuart. It pointed out that the largest increases in black housing have resulted from new construction targeted toward that market rather than through black occupancy in the "white market." It went on to note that "the need for new housing for both white and Negro will continue to grow" and that "the land in the Negro corridor to the West can only provide for part of the new housing." Consequently, Stuart suggested that "all parts of the metropolitan area will have to take their share of both white and Negro development."[27]

To create new black neighborhoods and, at the same time, to minimize the difficulties of neighborhood transition, Stuart called for extending the WSMDC approach to the entire metropolitan area. Although it was a goal of the WSMDC to reduce the incidence of "transition of housing from white to Negro markets," the WSMDC approach presumed the inevitability, indeed the necessity, of racial change in certain Atlanta neighborhoods. The 1958 policy statement noted that "transition is an essential adjustment mechanism, enabling the real estate market to meet the housing needs of different racial and income groups. We would be in bad shape if we had to do without it," Stuart continued. To accomplish a metropolitanwide neighborhood planning program, Stuart proposed that the WSMDC be given funds for permanent staff to map the racial occupancy of all neighborhoods in Atlanta as a way to forecast transitions based on "expressed intentions and indicated trends."[28]

Both in matters of neighborhood transition and support for new housing, the WSMDC offered a unique way for black leaders to influence urban development policy in a period when blacks otherwise had no say in the process. In the Collier Heights neighborhood, for example, the EREB used the WSMDC in 1955 to pressure Hartsfield and the Atlanta City Council to provide a number of public improvements, such as street widening, paving, drainage, lighting, and the construction of a park and a golf course. To black leaders, the park, golf course, and public improvements represented compensation for a 1954 agreement that kept the neighborhood outside the corridor of black residential expansion. The legally unenforceable Collier Heights agreement, which preserved black residential development to the west of a predetermined line, received support from the National Development Company, a black housing development firm, the Southwest Citizens Association, the Collier Heights Civic Club, the Metropolitan Planning Commission, as well as the WSMDC. Not only did the city agree (unofficially) to the public improvements, but also it assured black developers that their housing project would be approved by the City Planning Commission, the Zoning Board, and the Board of Zoning Appeal so long as they did not encroach on the racial boundary.[29]

The Collier Heights agreement demonstrated the willingness of black leaders to accept residential segregation as the price of community improvements. In turn, public improvements, highway construction, and housing projects were the building blocks of a separate black world in Atlanta. The success of the WSMDC neighborhood planning process relied on the will-ingness of the community to accept or collectively resist change. In Collier Heights, the WSMDC surveyed white households early in 1954 to determine whether the community should remain white, how much interest there was in selling homes, and whether individuals would abide by the will of a majority of residents. A slim majority of the ninety-eight responses favored preservation of Collier Heights as a white neighborhood, and twenty-eight "preferred to sell to colored." Only thirty-five favored "selling as soon as possible," but a mere twenty-six preferred to stay in the neighborhood. Even with such an equivocal response, the WSMDC interpreted the survey results as favoring preservation of Collier Heights as a white neighborhood. It informed the residents that the "Empire Real Estate Board of Negro business-men reaffirms its position that it is not interested NOW, or in the near future, in securing or purchasing property in Collier Heights for Negro occupancy, and will continue to respect the wishes of the community." In a notice to residents, the WSMDC noted that the neighborhood would not be entirely "surrounded," but that it would be "tied on" at the northeast corner to an adjacent white community and that it still possessed "considerable room to expand eastward." Finally, the Southwest Citizens Association appealed to the "sense of fair play" of white real estate brokers to "refuse to have anything to do with sales of white-occupied homes in Collier Heights to colored."[30].

The transition process in the Adamsville community operated much like that in Collier Heights; a highway buffer separated the remaining white section from areas designated for future black occupancy. Unlike in Collier Heights, however, there was no single developer of black housing in Adamsville. That made it more difficult to ensure that the boundaries would be respected. Delmar Lane was the center of controversy because it had been put in the black area by the WSMDC, but the Adamsville Civic Club, with the backing of Hartsfield, wanted "to maintain a white market on Delmar if at all possible. The mayor "ordered" Stuart to fix the problem. The real problems, apparent in 1958, was that property owners holding vacant lots on the street let it be known that they were willing to sell to developers of black housing *even if it violated the agreement*. As Stuart pointed out to Hartsfield, "disregard of the Committee's agreement with Adamsville by developers in Land Lot 16 raises serious questions concerning the future effectiveness of the West Side Mutual Development Committee." Despite efforts by the Adamsville Civic Club to combat redlining through the use of a neighborhood corporation to purchase disputed property, the Adamsville agreement broke down. The Adamsville situation demonstrated the tenu-ousness of the WSMDC's voluntary agreements to achieve racial stabiliza-tion at the community level.[31]

Throughout the existence of the WSMDC, Stuart sought to transform it from an unofficial community group to an official and more comprehensive neighborhood planning organization to connect citizens throughout Atlanta, both black and white, to the policy process. As early as 1953, he proposed the creation of what he called the "West Atlanta Planning Council" to serve as an "advisory citizens' group" so that "the people of West Atlanta might intelligently participate in the planning of their community" not only on the issue of racial occupancy but also regarding "major streets, highways, residential areas, industrial areas, parks, schools, shopping and business centers, utilities and other physical facilities." While restricting the role of the West Atlanta Planning Council to providing advice, Stuart's goal was to formalize connections between neighborhood residents and the planning process to handle the "growing pains" of this rapidly changing section of the city. It is significant that Stuart cited the "lack of opportunities at present for responsible Negro leadership to participate in community activities and decisions" in his rationale for such a planning council. It was obvious to Stuart after only a year of work with the WSMDC that the success of neighborhood planning for community stability in Atlanta required direct participation by African-Americans.[32]

In the view of George Goodwin, executive director of the Central Atlanta Improvement Association, "there should be similar groups in many areas around Atlanta," although "all need not be bi-racial." Although he agreed that "there should be some voice of which the people of any community can speak to the planners and tell them what they want," he was not convinced that a planning council would be able to control neighborhood change in West Atlanta. "The situation is moving so swiftly out there that the council may have only limited value in the present situation." Indeed, Stuart and the WSMDC were so enmeshed in the "present situation" that it was not until nine months after it was initially proposed that there was an opportunity to discuss a possible planning council. As late as 1958, Stuart still attempted to broaden the focus of the WSMDC through the creation of an ad hoc citizen planning organization that would work directly with various planning and public bodies. Stuart wanted the activities of West Atlanta neighborhoods to involve comprehensive planning to overcome the "misconception that 'WSMDC zones for race,' which is illegal." To overcome this perception, Stuart suggested that either the WSMDC or some new citizen group develop a citywide "Plan for Race Relations" (which, in fact, he had drafted already) to address issues such as housing, neighborhood transition, police relations, service delivery, economic opportunities, political participation, transportation, public employment, and access to public facilities.[33]

The difficulty with the WSMDC moving discussions of neighborhood change into the broader context of civil rights for black Atlantans was that the WSMDC process itself lacked legitimacy. By 1960, for example, the agreement covering Grove Park, once considered a model of neighborhood stabilization, broke down. Through the West Side Development Corporation thirty houses in Grove Park had been purchased to create a buffer between white and black areas. Yet, keeping these houses for white occupancy ran contrary to the prevailing market, according to the newly appointed housing coordinator, Jim Parham, of the Metropolitan Planning Commission. He found little demand by whites for housing available along the "lengthy" fringes of the neighborhood and yet a "critical demand for Negro housing, which makes it profitable to sell to Negroes." That was what happened in 1959 when two black families violated the Grove Park covenant. This was followed immediately by news that a 112–unit apartment project would be built in the white area and marketed to blacks. Despite community efforts to block the necessary zoning for the apartments, the Georgia State Supreme Court reversed a local injunction that had temporarily halted the project. Hartsfield tried to convince the developer to rent the units to whites but was told that it was not economically feasible. There simply was no demand for rental housing among whites in that area. Consequently, the Simpson Road line was "broken" when blacks moved into the apartments. Although the Grove Park Civic Club still possessed some "financial resources" to use in controlling property transfers, Parham felt that it was "doubtful it could withstand a widespread desire to sell." More significant, in the view of the Housing Coordinator was that "many Negro homebuyers want to live in a close-in, west side community. The existing Negro community in that vicinity contains practically no vacancies. Negroes will be alerted to any opportunity to convert sections of that area."[34]

In the case of the Moreland Heights neighborhood, a biracial committee formed in late 1954. For two years, the Moreland Heights Civic Club maintained the status quo despite the inability of their own biracial group or the WSMDC to find "a boundary that can be generally agreed upon." By late 1956, acting on rumors that blacks had begun to move in, approximately twenty property owners listed their homes for sale to blacks. Although swift action by the local civic club and the WSMDC resulted in the removal of "most" of the houses from the market, "some sales" ensued, leading to the demise of the biracial committee and the addition of Moreland Heights to what was becoming a growing list of failed attempts to control neighborhood change in the West Side.[35]

The failures did not dampen Stuart's ardor for a metropolitanwide neighborhood planning and improvement program, however. Throughout 1957 he and staff member Bob Allen developed a general outline of the functions that could be fulfilled by such a program. In essence, Stuart saw neighborhood planning as a process of linking the comprehensive plan to specific actions affecting neighborhoods, such as highway locations. He also emphasized the function of "community management," which embraced studies of housing and land use trends and a citizen-participation process to handle "particular strains/fires as they develop" around matters such as housing, land use, utilities and highways. This sort of planning was far more inclusive than the WSMDC approach, although it would involve efforts to "relieve pressing immediate problems of minority housing, expansion areas, mortgage vacuums." Allen stressed the importance of using the neighborhood improvement program as "a mechanism that would consolidate the various neighborhood and civic groups into a powerful and vocal community force." In addition, he proposed a demonstration project that would make use of "all existing tools and forces to rehabilitate and conserve one or more neighborhoods." He agreed that a third component of neighborhood planning involved the prevailing "fire-fighting approach to neighborhood tensions" as well as the need to "promote more extensive development of minority housing."[36]

By 1958 the neighborhood improvement program had boiled down to its essence: the creation of a staff position to carry out neighborhood analysis and planning to assist in the location of sites for housing for blacks displaced from the recently launched urban renewal program areas (that is, to "develop procedures which will minimize neighborhood frictions before they occur") and to collect and analyze data on race and housing in existing neighborhoods to "facilitate the orderly and harmonious transfer of housing from white to Negro, and from Negro to white." It was not to be the grander vision of neighborhood planning proposed by Stuart in 1957 but, rather, a data-gathering exercise required by Atlanta to participate in the federal urban renewal program. Even though the WSMDC continued to operate into the early 1960s, by 1958 and continuing on throughout the 1960s and early 1970s the city's massive urban renewal program, rather than neighborhood improvement, guided planning initiatives in Atlanta.[37]

Anti-Neighborhood Planning: Memphis and Richmond

In June 1957 Memphis mayor Edmund Orgill floated the idea of encouraging two local independent race relations committees, one representing whites and other blacks, to merge into a single group similar in form and function to the WSMDC in Atlanta. He had written to Hartsfield to learn more about Atlanta' s unique attempt to regulate neighborhood change and had discussed the idea with the Memphis Real Estate Board. Orgill must have recognized that a formal dialogue between blacks and whites over an issue as sensitive as the racial makeup of neighborhoods would not work in Memphis. Yet, Orgill also recognized that his ambitious plans for urban renewal in Memphis required that areas be designed for new black housing to absorb displacees and the anticipated natural black population increases. Rather than regulating change in existing white or mixed-race neighborhoods, Memphis opted simply to expand its boundaries to provide new areas for development. Through annexation, the city recaptured whites who had fled to the suburbs and, at the same time, secured additional space in which to locate new black residential developments. In a lengthy memorandum to the Memphis city commissioners in July 1957, Orgill outlined several annexation options, all of which centered around the problem of finding new areas for black residences within the city boundaries. He urged the annexation in South Memphis because it was where "Negro subdivisions can be developed without causing a controversy. I do not see how anybody could ever complain about Negro housing in this area." Although Orgill favored a sweeping annexation that would take the Memphis city boundaries all the way to the Mississippi state line (and bring in remote white subdivisions), the pressing need was enough space to address the current black housing problem. The city annexed the white North Memphis community of Frayser in 1958, but Orgill failed in his attempt to secure additional space in the predominantly black areas of South Memphis. Overall, between 1951 and 1960 the city added 25 square miles by expanding eastward and northward. Between 1961 and 1967 Memphis added much of the southside that Orgill had hoped to secure earlier to provide space for the expanding black community. (See Map 8)[38]

The lack of an organization such as Atlanta's WSMDC may be explained by Memphis's less conciliatory stance toward neighborhood change. Even though there had been scattered incidents of conflict between whites and blacks over neighborhoods in the 1940s and early 1950s, the issue of where to *allow* new black housing became a subject of intense debate by 1957. In February the MHA proposed a site on Crump Boulevard for a new public housing project and immediately ran into stiff opposition from the Real Estate Board, the Home Builders' Association, and residents of the adjacent neighborhood. According to opponents of the project, which included approximately fifty black homeowners, the neighborhood's recent investment in repairs through the city code enforcement program would be lost if the MHA built a public housing project nearby. The controversy raged on for more than a year, and, although the 320–unit public housing project was built, it proved to be one of the last in Memphis for over a decade.[39]

The Crump Boulevard controversy was part of the broader issue of finding additional areas for low-income black housing in Memphis. When Mayor Frank Tobey first declared "war" on Memphis slums in 1953, the ten–year plan involving approximately 37,000 substandard housing units stressed code enforcement and rehabilitation rather than clearance. By early 1955, however, and after only four months of rehabilitation under the Memphis plan, the city received a commitment of $3.4 million "for clearing slums." By 1957, as the slum-clearance program got under way, the effects of wholesale removal of black neighborhoods focused attention on the issue of "what to do with the Negro families." In a five-part series in the *Commercial*

Appeal in July, reporter Mike McGee examined the social impact of the city's proposed urban renewal, highway construction, and housing code enforcement programs. He estimated that approximately 20,000 persons, most of whom were poor blacks, would be displaced within the next three years. The city needed to find ways to alleviate the housing shortage while minimizing the impact of black residential change on white neighborhoods. McGee noted that one approach would be to annex the southeast suburbs, including the site of the black-occupied Walker Homes, to secure additional areas for new black housing. At the same time, Orgill and the Real Estate Board were exploring ways to regulate racial transition in existing city neighborhoods. According to McGee, however, there were strong sentiments within the city that "transition [had] gone far enough and should be stopped." The city's commitment to massive slum clearance through urban renewal and highway development, coupled with white intransigence toward neighborhood change, made annexation the most appropriate strategy. Annexation would provide space for new black housing without disturbing existing neighborhoods, although it could not completely eliminate the possibility of neighborhood tension. As noted in a *Commercial Appeal* editorial, "the changing situation has resulted principally in extension of Negro areas by purchases of old homes along the fringes. This process finances some white removals to the suburbs but also produces some intense neighborhood tensions without more than postponing the search for more space."[40]

The search for more space led Orgill to criticize the allocation of land uses in the city's zoning plan that had been prepared by Harland Bartholomew. In a letter to the Memphis Planning Commission chairman, William "Billy" Galbreath, Jr., Orgill contended that the zoning plan overzoned existing black neighborhoods to industrial uses at the very time "when we need residential Negro areas pretty bad." In his view, the planning commission should address seriously "the need for additional areas in which Negro subdivisions can be developed without controversy." In response to the city's needs, the Shelby County Commission noted that it was planning for "new residential areas outside the city limits, particularly for Negro citizens who will be displaced by expressways and other projects." Yet, neither Orgill nor the County Commission could contend effectively with the vehement opposition to new black housing when it occurred anywhere near white neighborhoods. When MHA Executive Director Walter Simmons suggested that a large South Memphis tract "be set aside for Negro families forced to move because of expressways, urban renewal and other public improvements," residents of three adjacent white subdivisions "vowed to resist efforts to build a proposed Negro subdivision near their neighborhoods." Despite Simmons's warning that the city's $70 million urban renewal program was in jeopardy of being cut by the federal government unless housing for 4,800 displaced black families appeared soon, the city refused to push for additional public housing units or to sanction large-scale private development. To real estate interests, who consistently opposed more public housing, to most neighborhood groups, and to the post-Orgill administrations, black neighborhoods should not expand but remain within their existing boundaries. Memphis showed no interest in neighborhood planning over the next decade, at least not until the shattering events following the King assassination in 1968 made clear the price of white recalcitrance to neighborhood change.[41]

Richmond seemed poised to launch a major neighborhood revitalization effort in the late 1940s. The cornerstone of the process was the Master Plan of 1946 prepared by Harland Bartholomew that offered a vision of a centralized city held together by strong, revitalized neighborhood units. Bartholomew's plan for Richmond devoted considerable attention to housing and neighborhood upgrading in an effort to reorient the planning process from its tendency to encourage rapid decentralization. Bartholomew believed that "slums, blighted districts and excessive decentralization" were "by-products of unbalanced design of the city." He suggested that various planning controls be used to restrict future population growth "so that it will be confined to the area allotted to future growth rather than scattered over unnecessarily large areas." Bartholomew desired to protect existing neighborhoods "so that they will continue to be desirable places in which to live and thus prevent further shifting of their population." As a consultant to the National Association of Real Estate Boards in 1938, Bartholomew devised a model "Neighborhood Improvement Act," under which owners of property in deteriorated neighborhoods could form improvement associations that would develop a neighborhood plan, submit it to the city planning commission, and then work with the city in carrying it out. His target group was white middle-class neighborhoods because he desired to make city areas "fully as attractive as the suburbs" so as to slow down the outmigration. His neighborhood planning formula embraced slum clearance, but he preferred rehabilitation to demolition. "Slum areas must be rebuilt, good districts protected, blighted areas restored," he noted. "The city can no longer afford the vast processes of abandonment and decay, of speculation and dispersion, which have produced its present chaotic situation. . . . The ownership of slums must be made unprofitable, large-scale operations encouraged," Bartholomew concluded.[42]

The 1946 plan included an evaluation of deteriorated neighborhoods based on a survey of housing conditions conducted by Bartholomew under a Public Works Administration (PWA) grant in 1938. Approximately one-third of the city's 43,000 housing units lacked indoor toilets. Nearly one-half had only cold water, and 2,635 units had no water at all. Except for the demolition of a few hundred units in Apostle Town to provide space for the Gilpin Court public housing project, little had changed between the 1930s and 1940s apart from further deterioration of city's old housing. The detailed maps in the 1946 Master Plan indicated that the worst housing conditions were concentrated in black neighborhoods and that these neighborhoods had been spreading gradually since the 1920s. Other than selective data on housing and income in Richmond neighborhoods, the 1946 Master Plan failed to address certain key questions such as racial change in neighborhoods or the way that rehabilitation and new construction might address black housing problems. Its greatest failing, however, was the lack of integration between key proposals regarding public improvements, especially highway construction and street widening, development of a civic center, and zoning, and neighborhood preservation. Implementation of Bartholomew's public improvement strategy destroyed vast sections of the city's black community throughout the 1950s. New housing for blacks accommodated only a small proportion of the displacees. As a result there was substantial racial transition in Richmond neighborhoods between 1950 and 1960.[43]

There was a point in the early 1950s (and prior to the initiation of major public improvement projects) when it appeared that Richmond might experiment with the neighborhood-preservation program outlined by Bartholomew in the 1946 Master Plan. The Richmond Redevelopment and Housing Authority (RRHA) secured federal funds to conduct a slum-clearance study involving all of Jackson Ward in 1950. The study pointed to severely blighted housing conditions throughout the area but also showed that there was a potentially strong market for new housing in the Jackson Ward area and that existing residents, including many black families, had incomes sufficient to purchase new housing valued at $5,000 or more. Bolstered by the market data from the Jackson Ward study, the Central Richmond Association proposed the redevelopment of an 11-acre tract on the other side of the central business district in the once-fashionable Gamble Hill neighborhood overlooking the James River. The Central Richmond Association's Gamble Hill project conformed to the model for neighborhood redevelopment outlined by Bartholomew in the 1946 Master Plan. It combined clearance of deteriorated structures with new construction of apartments as well as preservation of many of the historically and architecturally significant buildings in this downtown neighborhood. Although many civic leaders hailed the Gamble Hill scheme as a prototype for neighborhood planning in deteriorated center city areas, it became a target of those seeking to derail the urban renewal program before it got started. *Richmond News Leader* editor James J. Kilpatrick was "dead against it" on grounds that urban renewal should be used only to clear areas completely unfit for habitation rather than in a neighborhood such as Gamble Hill where some houses were capable of rehabilitation. Kilpatrick warned his readers of "The Shadow of Marx on Gamble Hill" and secured enough support on City Council to secure defeat of a motion to study the Gamble Hill neighborhood for possible redevelopment. The demise of the Gamble Hill project was a major blow to the city's nascent neighborhood-preservation movement and shifted attention back to the slum-clearance initiative previously considered for Jackson Ward. Whereas the *News Leader* vehemently denounced the Gamble Hill proposal as immoral and illegal, when the planners shifted attention from a poor white neighborhood to the black neighborhood of Jackson Ward, it maintained that "the Carver plan [for Jackson Ward] merits close and sympathetic study. It begins where slum-clearance programs ought properly to begin—with some genuine slum conditions." When black residents of the Carver area of Jackson Ward protested the categorization of their neighborhood as a slum, much like the white residents of Gamble Hill, the *News Leader* offered no commensurate attack on urban renewal.[44]

The Carver Displacement League, headed by African-American mortician Oliver P. Chiles, opposed the clearance strategy and proposed a program combining spot demolition and extensive rehabilitation. Chiles stressed that not all homes slated for demolition were slums and that pictures of the area published in the newspaper to verify the level of deterioration were misleading, because they focused on rental properties. Elderly persons who owned modest homes in the area would not be able to find substitute housing elsewhere given the meager compensation for their dwellings. Chiles argued that the neighborhood favored housing improvement, but not at the cost of neighborhood displacement. "We would not have you believe we are against progress or against the city being made more beautiful," he noted, "but we are gravely concerned with one factor and this is, that, this progress and beauty not be purchased by those persons who are least able to do so."[45]

Although the RRHA officially rejected as unfeasible the suggestion that rehabilitation be substituted for total clearance, the idea of rehabilitation caught on with the Richmond Home Builders and the City Health Department, which were looking for an area to implement code enforcement under the newly enacted (1950) Housing Code. The city would do the inspections, and the Home Builders' Rehabilitation Corporation would provide loans to owner-occupants to finance the necessary improvements. The city selected a section of Carver adjacent to the designated clearance site, and between 1954 and 1959 nearly 900 units had some form of rehabilitation carried out. The residents thought that active participation in the code enforcement and rehabilitation would forestall redevelopment, but the city and the RRHA maintained their interest in Carver as the initial urban renewal site in Richmond as well as the location for a major new north-south feeder street and expressway that would further dismantle the community. Throughout the 1950s residents continued to speak out against the redevelopment plan that called for removal of 400 residences and the displacement of approximately 500 families. When Harland Bartholomew testified before the City Planning Commission in 1955 that the Carver plan was consistent with the Master Plan, he not only sealed the fate of the neighborhood but also effectively undermined the whole basis of the neighborhood-preservation strategy that he outlined in that same plan. With the greater portion of the renewed Carver area to be converted to industrial and highway uses, even the rehabilitated section stood in jeopardy. In seeking to eliminate one slum, the urban redevelopment process that Bartholomew posited as the preserver of center-city residential areas seemed in practice to work much differently.[46]

Although Carver's clearance did not begin until the early 1960s, it was already obvious that Richmond's rejection of neighborhood planning was having a profound effect on the social makeup of the city. Largely as the result of demolition caused by highway and street construction, nearly 20,000 persons, most of whom were blacks, had to find other places to live. During the 1950s, unlike in previous decades, Richmond's black population migrated not only into other blighted inner-city neighborhoods but also "into attractive neighborhoods farther from the core city." Between 1950 and 1960 there was a net increase of 20,000 blacks that added further pressures on existing black residential areas to expand. What was most devastating was the loss of housing units in black neighborhoods. According to census data, the city lost more than 4,700 housing units during the decade in census tracts where African-Americans represented more than 20 percent of the population in 1960. These housing units would have been enough to accommodate at least two-thirds of the population growth among blacks in the city. The RRHA constructed 1,736 units of public housing for blacks during the decade to assist many who had been displaced. Yet, the concentration of public housing in the Gilpin Court area and, especially, in the East End, further undermined the stability of neighborhoods where whites and blacks previously coexisted. Except for the Eastview subdivision of more than 100 moderately priced homes located less than 1 mile from downtown (and adjacent to a high concentration of public housing) and for the public housing units, displaced blacks in Richmond secured new homes during the 1950s only by moving into areas abandoned by whites.[47]

In a detailed assessment of Richmond's social and economic problems in 1957, Richmond *Times-Dispatch* reporters Ed Grimsley and Larry Weekly explored "the chain reaction of problems" confronting an increasingly blighted city. While noting the lure of the suburbs, they stressed that the spreading blight of center city must be regarded as a repulsing factor. They warned the largely white readership of the *Times-Dispatch* that the rapid outmigration of whites hastened by the dispersal of black families posed a grave threat to the perpetuation of white supremacy. They cited the failure of past planning studies to anticipate the racial shifts in the city's neighborhoods and pointed to the combined impact of public improvements and the failure to build new housing, particularly for low- and moderate-income African-Americans, as principal causes for the rapid transition in white neighborhoods and the extensive degree of white flight to the suburbs. Two years later, Grimsley returned to the same theme of the changing character of central Richmond and reasserted that the destruction of the residential fabric of the city, especially because of highway construction, and "the shortage of housing for those residents of slums and blighted areas who could afford to purchase or rent modest homes," explained the city's crisis, a crisis that whites defined almost exclusively in terms of race. Rather than depart from strategically rebuilding the city outlined in the 1946 Master Plan (alongside the neighborhood planning elements), Richmond chose to follow a path similar to that of Memphis, namely, to deal with the race problem through the politics of annexation. There were differences between Richmond and Memphis, however. Where Memphis sought to resist further racial change in its neighborhoods by securing space for new black developments along the periphery, Richmond seemed content to allow the East End, where a sizable white working-class population still resided in 1960, to become exclusively black. In the context of Richmond's revitalization efforts, annexation was simply a device to recapture white residents and to secure space for new white neighborhoods to dilute the voting strength of blacks. When Grimsley and Weekly had discussed the social and economic crisis of Richmond's inner-city neighborhoods in 1957, they had already framed the problem in terms of its political impact. Neither whites nor blacks could mistake the meaning of their analysis or the political implications of the social changes that were undermining the old order.[48]

What unleashed the political ramifications of social change in all three cities were the devastating effects of massive urban renewal. What began in all three cities as a sort of removal of marginal settlements of blacks in areas of the center city better suited to other uses became a wholesale black removal and the final building block in the separate city process begun more than one-half century earlier. From the late 1950s through the late 1960s, all three cities to varying degrees endowed urban renewal planners with the power to determine the character of the new segregated city. By the end of the process, however, the black community, which had been the main target of urban renewal, was poised to use the planning process to gain power in the city. The separate and renewed southern city was soon to become, in a political sense, the black metropolis. The legacy of urban renewal, to varying degrees in all three cities, accounted for the transformation of black protest into black power. In the case of Richmond, a protracted legal battle over a racially motivated annexation in 1970 resulted in court-mandated restructuring of government that produced the city first black majority city council and a black mayor in 1977. Although the politics of urban renewal was a mobilizing factor in the black community and the socio-political effects of massive displacement of blacks in mid-1960s through the early 1970s perpetuated the process of white flight from the city and, thus, strengthened the position of black voters, urban renewal was not the decisive issue in Richmond that it was in Atlanta in the emergence of black political power. In Memphis the maintenance of a governmental structure that failed to give the black community sufficient political representation blunted the political fallout in of one of the urban South's most "renewed" cities where black displacement was substantial. It was in Atlanta that the effects of urban renewal were immediate and profoundly political, where the seemingly unchallengeable political coalition fashioned by Hartsfield and bestowed on Ivan Allen collapsed in the face of emerging black political dominance.

Renewal in Atlanta: Prelude to Political Power

Atlanta's urban renewal and highway construction program during the 1950s and 1960s had a catastrophic effect on the social structure of the city. Between 1956, when the bulldozers got rolling, and 1966, according to the calculations of the city's own consultants, 67,000 persons were uprooted for the sake of a "new" Atlanta. In part because of dislocations associated with urban renewal, but also owing to fundamental limitations in the approach, neighborhood renewal "became a source of further disillusionment among the poor of Atlanta." Clarence Stone contends that the dominance of business interests, with their eyes riveted firmly on the needs of the downtown, explains why poorer neighborhoods either were exploited or neglected by the renewal process. The professed goals of eliminating slums and rehousing displacees in decent dwellings were only partially accomplished. "Some housing was built," notes Stone, "but not in the numbers or in the locations desired by low-income citizens." In fact, argues historian Ronald Bayor, in all stages of urban renewal in Atlanta "more housing was destroyed than was built or repaired." During the 1950s renewal "consisted of tearing down slums for commercial rebuilding; in the second stage of the 1960s slum clearance was used for the needs of the city—a stadium, civic center, expressway." The housing needs of those affected, which was by and large Atlanta's black citizenry, mattered relatively little in the rebuilding schemes.[49]

The organizational structure of the urban renewal process provided ample opportunity for business involvement while minimizing input from the neighborhoods. The Urban Renewal Policy Committee (URPC) was made up of the AHA commissioners (as AHA carried out urban renewal) and members of the aldermanic urban renewal committee. According to Stone, "business leaders were given easy and direct access to the early stages of renewal policy making, while other groups, in particular those with a neighborhood base, had only the opportunity to react to plans that were already fully developed." Even though the city created the Citizens Advisory

Committee for Urban Renewal (CACUR) in the late 1950s, neighborhood interests proved to be secondary even to this group. In fact, the urban renewal program that the citizens were supposed to create had been outlined for nearly a decade by the Atlanta Metropolitan Planning Commission.[50]

Atlanta secured legislative authority in 1947 to establish the Metropolitan Planning Commission, jointly funded by DeKalb and Fulton counties and the city. Creation of the planning commission, the first completely publicly-funded metropolitan planning group in the nation, was a necessary prelude to implementation of a major annexation—Atlanta's "last big annexation"—that aimed at expanding the electorate and at providing additional space for development. In 1949 a study commission created by the Georgia General Assembly examined the issues of local governance in the *Plan for Improvement* and sanctioned the addition of approximately 100,000 persons and 82 square miles of county land to Atlanta. The plan was approved in an advisory referendum in 1950, in part because of the strong backing supplied by the Atlanta Negro Voters League as well as other leading white business and civic organizations, and went into effect on January 1, 1952.[51]

Shortly after the annexation took effect, the Metropolitan Planning Commission released a prospectus for redevelopment of Atlanta entitled *Up Ahead* that addressed both the issues of desired public improvements in the central business district (including massive slum clearance to make way for business expansion) and the need for the "conservation of existing neighborhoods and improved housing for all groups." It explicitly referred to the need for "Negro expansion areas" in response to black "deconcentration." The report called for public actions to reduce residential densities, remove blighted areas, "improve the racial pattern of population distribution and make the best possible use of central land areas." In anticipation of full-scale redevelopment, the city used public housing construction to foster black migration to the south and west of the downtown. Two public housing projects, the 990–unit Carver Community in Southside completed in 1953 and the Perry Homes (1,000 units) that opened in the West Side in 1955, helped "to guide and concentrate the distribution" of blacks following the 1952 annexation. In conjunction with expressway construction (which preceded the beginning of urban renewal in 1959), "the major outlines of a resettlement policy were thus evident: low-income families in the central sector would be moved to selected outlying districts. Westside, Southside, and later East Atlanta would absorb displacees and immigrants. . . . Northside would remain white. Government actions, 'gentlemen's agreements,' and white business backing converged behind this policy. As the urban renewal program reached fruition, it became a major arena in which this still-emerging policy was tested," notes Stone. Until the mid-1960s it was the policy of Atlanta not to use urban renewal areas for low-income housing to facilitate black settlement.[52]

For this reason, throughout the 1950s and 1960s "renewal policy was widely opposed in the black community." The city's first trial run with urban renewal was a proposal in 1950 to redevelop the predominantly white Hemphill Avenue area near the Georgia Institute of Technology. Hemphill residents and businesses, as well as residents of another neighborhood slated to receive a public housing project to accommodate the renewal displacees, challenged the whole notion of urban renewal. Fearing a permanent coalition opposed to redevelopment of any sort, the proponents quietly shelved the project and looked for another place to begin. Black leaders were concerned that a similar move would be made toward their corner of the central business district—the Auburn Avenue black business district—and vowed to resist any clearance program. In fact, the Central Atlanta Improvement Association (CAIA) soon proposed the clearance of McDaniel Street, a black area near Auburn, for industrial use. As in Hemphill, the residents (this time predominantly black) and the property owners (who were largely white) challenged the project, although the Urban League lent crucial backing and helped to get the proposal through a divided Board of Aldermen. In 1953, however, the Georgia Supreme Court ruled the urban renewal legislation invalid, and it was not until 1955 that a constitutional amendment enabled Atlanta to become involved in the federal urban renewal program. The Central Atlanta Plan, prepared in 1955 by the CAIA but with assistance from the Metropolitan Planning Commission, delineated an ambitious slum-clearance program centered around the redevelopment of the Butler Street and Rawson-Washington areas. To secure African-American support for urban renewal, a third project involving rehabilitation and land acquisition in the Atlanta University area was included. This satisfied not only the Atlanta University leadership but also the Urban League. The problem of replacement housing for displaced blacks—a concern of the Atlanta Baptist Ministers' Union—was to be resolved through more public housing units as well as involvement in the FHA's 221 program for moderate-income housing produced by nonprofit organizations. The plan also called for clearance of two remote neighborhoods for possible redevelopment of black-occupied housing.[53]

The original proposal was scaled down when it became evident in 1957 that local bond revenues were not enough to cover city costs. The three downtown projects were trimmed slightly, and a clearance proposal for a black shopping center and industrial site, as well as a large rehabilitation project in the Atlanta University area, were deleted. The larger clearance project adjacent to Morris Brown College remained, as "failure to provide in our planning for the needs of Morris Brown College might jeopardize support of the Urban Renewal Program by much of the Negro civic and church leadership." Even though "black interests were also offered opportunities to attain their goals," the prime beneficiaries of the modified plan remained the white downtown business interests. Yet, it was white neighborhood opposition to the 221 program that threatened to derail urban renewal for a second time, because the city needed to demonstrate that it could handle the displacement problem. Initially, Mayor Hartsfield tried to avoid direct involvement in conflicts over where to locate 221 projects. In 1958, however, he came out openly for the subsidized housing program and appointed a citizens advisory committee to find ways to implement it. Only Hartsfield's support of rehousing through the 221 program kept blacks in the renewal coalition.[54]

Pressure to take seriously the agreement to rehouse blacks in new federally assisted units came from a grass roots organization called the Localities Committee. It appealed to federal officials to hold off on releasing renewal funds because the citizen participation and relocation components of the Atlanta plan did not meet federal standards. It objected to the boundaries selected for the projects and pointed to the excessive scale of center city displacement that would result from implementation of the plan and elevated concern over the relocation issue to a prominent place on the agenda of the urban renewal advocates. In November 1958 the Board of Aldermen approved construction of 1,000 public housing units even though it had no specific place to put them, which proved to be another stumbling block.[55]

The CIAI objected to downtown areas such as in Buttermilk Bottom, a slum area to the east of the central business district, for public housing, and aldermen and white members of the CACUR rejected remote locations. After a year of searching the AHA found two sites, one in the West Side (Bowen Homes—650 units) and the Egleston site just to the east of downtown. The Egleston side engendered the most controversy, not simply because it violated the CIAI position that public housing should be kept out of the core but also because the city's refusal to rezone the site for public housing once it had been selected could breed disenchantment and hostility in the black community. African-American militants might use the Egleston controversy to undermine cooperation between whites and blacks on urban renewal. "Among the backers of urban renewal," Stone notes, "there was some general concern that the program might be endangered by the displacement of moderate leaders in the Black community. Apprehension extended to the possibility that blacks might bring suit for public housing desegregation and that blacks might disregard existing racial agreements and expand into several white residential areas."[56]

Despite unanimous support from the urban renewal coalition for the Egleston rezoning, it lost by a single vote in the Board of Aldermen. The vice-mayor who cast the decisive vote paid for his lack of sensitivity to the black community when he was voted out of office in 1961. Despite widespread dissatisfaction with the defeat of the Egleston project, the moderates, led by A.T. Walden, retained their position of leadership in the black community and remained solid backers of the city's renewal program. The masses of black voters proved their loyalty to their leadership by giving "overwhelming electoral support to Ivan Allen, the 1962 mayoral candidate backed by the business community" and by black leaders.[57]

What made the Egleston issue so significant was that it compounded the already difficult problem of finding areas for new housing for blacks. At a 1959 hearing before the U.S. Commission on Civil Rights regarding housing in Atlanta, black leaders, many of whom were solidly behind the urban renewal program, castigated the city for creating an "artificial" land shortage for blacks. The president of the EREB testified that segregated housing in Atlanta was "hallowed by the long and continuing support it has had from government." Yet, what he failed to emphasize was that it was a tradition sanctioned by his own organization in an effort to manage racial change in Atlanta's neighborhoods.[58]

Hartsfield downplayed "official involvement in the racial transition of residential areas" and rejected the idea of using the CACUR or any other official body to oversee "research and analysis of housing patterns and housing needs . . . and coordination of public and private activities related to the acquisition and development of sites" for new housing. He preferred to work through unofficial groups such as the WSMDC while the Metropolitan Planning Commission quietly conducted the necessary background research. In early 1959 the commission prepared a detailed and confidential commentary on racial housing trends and land availability in thirty-six study areas that was presented to the "Housing Needs Panel" of the CACUR. The study indicated that there was a need for 21,700 additional housing units for black occupancy over the next five years but that at present there were commitments for only 7,500 housing units. This housing demand translated into a land area of 2,640 acres for new housing development and assumed that one-quarter of the demand would be met by "normal shifts of housing from white to the Negro market." Yet, the study also noted that a considerable number of the neighborhoods into which blacks desired to move were resolved to resist the transition process. In Grove Park, for example, white resistance to black in-migration remained strong in 1959, but black desire for homes was even greater. As a result, some blacks purchased homes in the neighborhood and rented to whites while waiting for the transition to occur.[59]

In contrast to Hartsfield's preference for official detachment, a key recommendation of this survey of housing problems was the need for direct involvement by the city in planning for future black housing areas. He stated that "planning will be needed with respect to making additional land available for non-white occupancy. The Mayor's Citizens Advisory Committee on Urban Renewal is expected to prepare recommendations on this matter."

Indeed, the essential thrust of his study was to project housing trends resulting from displacement of African-Americans caused by public projects. The hiring of a housing coordinator operating out of the Metropolitan Planning Commission in 1959 represented a further step toward institution-alizing racial housing matters in the official planning organization. As Jim Parham noted in a speech to the EREB in September 1959, his job as housing coordinator was to "document housing needs, neighborhood trends, market prices, transition areas, potential development areas, overcrowded areas . . . to alleviating tension and threat of violence in transition areas . . . locating land for the possible relocation of families displaced by urban renewal . . . [and] to assist in the formation of neighborhood improvement clubs in the already developed 221 housing areas so that critics of the program cannot point to these areas and make the claim that the slum dweller has merely transferred his habits to a new location." Even though Hartsfield preferred that control of black residential migration be exercised through private channels, by 1959 the process had become public and intimately connected to the ambitious urban renewal program that had not been fully conceived when he formed the WSMDC in 1952. Yet, as Stone correctly surmised, "throughout the Hartsfield era the city planned rehousing programs only as a way of meeting relocations needs, never as an effort to improve housing per se; even the building of relocation facilities was always limited by the availability of 'acceptable' sites."[60]

The muted protest from African-American leaders over the perpetuation of residential segregation and the unresponsiveness of city leaders to unmet housing needs owed to numerous factors, one of which was that black real estate brokers derived a lot of business from massive relocation of blacks, even under the restrictions imposed by groups such as the WSMDC. In addition, support for renewal enlisted white business backing for the con-troversial federal 221 housing program that provided black developers with a highly marketable commodity. Another incentive was that renewal bene-fited directly black institutions such as the Atlanta University complex. Knowing that the WSMDC and its technical advisor Bob Stuart provided a direct line to the mayor and to the renewal coalition, Atlanta University President Rufus E. Clement joined the renewal coalition as early as 1955. In addition to campus expansion, Clement saw federally financed redevelop-ment as the basis for widespread improvements of the entire black West Side. Clement sought the following black community improvements: (1) Business expansion, particularly of the Hunter Street business district; (2) traffic improvement; (3) new close-in private enterprise housing; (4) rehabilitation rather than clearance of existing housing; (5) industrial expansion in the area east of Northside Drive; and (6) development of civic and park centers. Clement's priorities represented more than just a wish list of disconnected public improvements; they were the skeleton of the physical components of the separate black city that had begun to coalesce out of the neighborhoods and institutions of West Atlanta. Even though blacks got relatively few of their items in the original renewal plan, Clement retained "wholehearted support" for the basic plan that kept "redevelopment of the Atlanta University Center Area as a part of . . . city-wide redevelopment," even when it became evident that the black community would bear the full brunt of renewal activities. Moreover, Clement obviously had a preconception of the segregationist implications of West Atlanta's redevelopment. As he concluded, "we recognize the fact that not all of this is by any means a slum area, although considerable portions may be so defined. The entire area, however in our opinion, is *the natural area into which we must expand,* and all of the area will greatly benefit by any rehabilitation program which is thoughtfully and carefully worked out."[61]

The 1960s brought changes not only in renewal policy but also in the black response to it. Under the mayoralty of Ivan Allen, Jr., beginning in 1962, there was more intensive activity, especially surrounding the construction of a civic center and a stadium, and as a result "widespread protests, and sharp confrontation" took place. The turbulence of the Allen regime strained the coalition between whites and blacks and provided a political environment within which increased citizen and neighborhood participation challenged the prevailing power structure. Some of the increased friction between whites and blacks (and blacks against blacks) was an inevitable product of participation by new groups sanctioned by federal policies under the Community Action Program (1964), the Model Cities Program (1966), and the Neighborhood Development Program (1968). Yet, local resistance to replacement housing efforts (either public housing or federal 221 housing) generated political pressures on the renewal coalition not only from displacees but also from the federal officials who so generously supplied Atlanta with urban renewal funds and who reminded Atlanta's coalition "that the approval of further renewal applications would be contingent upon a request for additional public housing."[62]

The replacement housing controversy focused on Buttermilk Bottom where the downtown business leaders wanted to put the new civic center. The Urban League favored clearance of the Bottom because of its dilapidated condition, but regarded it as an appropriate site for new black housing. The director of the Urban Renewal Department, Malcolm Jones, opposed full-scale clearance of the Bottom because likely protests from the black community might jeopardize the entire renewal program. The city received approval from the federal government in the fall of 1964 for use of the Early Land Acquisition Procedure, which allowed a site to be secured for redevelopment prior to official approval and execution of the urban renewal process. Allen got the business community, the Board of Aldermen, the media, and the AHA to line up behind the proposal, and the housing authority tried to anticipate community criticism by reserving 300 units in the newly constructed Bowen Homes for displacees. What Allen did not anticipate was the furor over demolition of C.W. Hill Elementary School to provide space for the auditorium as the first pillar of the civic center. The Atlanta Negro Voters League through its leader Jessee Hill charged that the city had failed to consult the community and requested federal officials to suspend funding for renewal. The refusal of the Board of Education to stop the AHA from taking the school resulted in city black leaders announcing in April 1965 that they would now "demand complete desegregation" of schools. (See Chapter 3.) Although the protest did not promote the school removal, the crisis ended with the city's agreement "to accelerate city-wide school desegregation."[63]

By fall 1965 the controversy spilled over into the recently designated urban renewal area of Bedford-Pine when the city announced that another 966 families must be relocated. Three black ministers whose churches served the neighborhood (all of whom had been displaced by urban renewal before coming to Bedford-Pine) and two white businessmen formed a grass roots protest group called U-Rescue, which stood for "Urban Renewal Emergency, Stop, Consider, Understand, Evaluate." The group held mass meetings in the neighborhoods, adopted resolutions opposing specific measures (but never urban renewal per se), and drew on the media to publicize their critique of urban renewal. U-Rescue secured a commitment from the Board of Aldermen and the AHA that the neighborhood would remain predominantly residential after redevelopment. The city agreed to have U-Rescue's leadership serve as the liaison with redevelopment officials and agreed to a strategy that "the project would consist largely of rehabilitation," with spot clearance on a "block-by-block basis."[64]

U-Rescue succeeded in forestalling the complete removal of residential uses in Bedford-Pine but failed to reduce the incidence of displacement. It secured a commitment for 350 units of public housing in the area and some assurances that there would be an attempt to build some moderate-income housing under the FHA 221(d)(3) program. Although it excelled in "pressing the claims of . . . the natural neighborhood," there was no resulting "redirection of urban renewal policy" for the city as a whole.[65]

The construction of Atlanta's new stadium on urban renewal land south of the central business district further illustrated Allen's unresponsiveness to the need for new black housing close to the center city. Actually, the original plan for the site was a white public housing project to serve as a buffer between the central business district and black neighborhoods in South Atlanta. Black leaders strenuously objected to this proposal because it would do nothing for the housing needs of their community. Allen preferred the stadium and secured from the city planning staff a feasibility study to support the stadium as the best use of the land. It was obvious, notes Bayor, that "black housing demands were not met at a time of extensive housing shortages for black families."[66]

The rehousing of displaced blacks in western and southern sections of the city reinforced the pattern of residential settlement that had been nurtured so meticulously through the public housing program and the efforts of the WSMDC. By the late 1960s 83 percent of Atlanta's public housing units were located in the West Side area, with the rest situated in the southeast for "white" occupancy. The Atlanta chapter of the National Association for the Advancement of Colored People (NAACP) protested to Washington and requested a cutoff of federal funds "until all discriminatory practices are eliminated and a balanced dispersion of public housing units is accomplished." Zoning that allowed high-density developments only in black areas reinforced the pattern. In a 1970 analysis of the city zoning plan, Samuel I. Spector contended that Atlanta used zoning "to preserve the status quo and to segregate the white and nonwhite populations." Even the federal government's refusal to approve new housing projects in these "racially-impacted areas" after 1967 did not alter the city's refusal to site assisted housing outside the separate city that had been created for black Atlantans. The Mayor's Housing Resource Committee, set up in 1966 to study housing needs and possible sites for development, tried to break the impasse in 1968 when it proposed rezoning a number of sites to achieve greater dispersal of new black housing. Even though the Atlanta Chamber of Commerce supported the recommendation, opposition from the Board of Aldermen, the AHA, and, ultimately, Mayor Allen, defeated the plan. Faced with the city's intransigence, federal officials eventually backed off their ruling and allowed more black housing in impacted areas. The only change apparent in this controversy was the new attitude at least some Atlanta black leaders had toward continued concentration of black housing in all-black areas.[67]

The city's recalcitrance when it came to making sites outside the separate city available for new black housing was complicated by a sudden resistance to black migration into transitional neighborhoods. During his first year in office Allen ordered that barricades be built across Peyton Road to prevent the infiltration of blacks into the all-white Peyton Forest neighborhood. The briefness of "Atlanta Wall's" existence did not lessen the outrage among blacks over this overt effort to curtail their residential mobility and to undermine the neighborhood-negotiation process pioneered by the defunct WSMDC. Allen contended that he decided to construct the barricade as a way to prove to whites that their neighborhood would be protected and also to free up for development an 800-acre tract on the black side that previously served as a racial buffer. The protest among blacks concerning the wall was led by an ad hoc group known as the All-Citizens Committee for Better City Planning who told Allen that "this move to wall in Negroes will not be tolerated at election time and purchasing time." According to Allen, the protest did not bring down the wall, although he admitted that it demonstrated the folly of his action. It was the Fulton County Superior Court that ordered removal of the barricade, an action that Allen undertook within minutes of the court decision.[68]

The Peyton Wall incident not only brought national attention to race relations in Atlanta but also undermined the traditional practices of controlling black residential mobility. A housing study by the Southern Regional Council (SRC), released after the incident, noted that the "city's planning and zoning policies were once bent toward the maintenance of racial boundaries and the confinement of the Negro population through the use of barriers and buffers." After the Peyton Road conflict was resolved, there was a substantial easing of such application of public policy. Yet, as evidenced by the city's continued opposition to public housing sites outside the separate city, as well as its reuse of urban renewal lands and the location of highways, Atlanta's planners and policymakers simply pulled back the lines of resistance in select neighborhoods and took their stand along a broader perimeter that separated whites from blacks. Despite Allen's contention that when he left office in the late 1960s, "there was complete desegregation of all public facilities in Atlanta," and that "in some areas black and white were living in the same neighborhoods, thanks to even-tempered white residents who saw that the real enemy was the unscrupulous 'blockbusting' realtor rather than the Negro neighbor," Atlanta was, in fact, a far more racially segregated city at the neighborhood and community levels than when he came into office eight years earlier.[69]

Between 1940 and 1960 the residential segregation index for the city rose from 87.4 to 93.6 on the eve of Allen's two terms as mayor. Between 1960 and 1970, the segregation index stayed in the nineties. A 1965 study by the Atlanta Bureau of Planning found that even though blacks represented 43.5 percent of the city's residents, they occupied only 22 percent of the city's land. The planners contended that "there would be more than enough land for construction of Negro housing—as well as all that is needed for whites—if it were not for the restrictions inherent in our community customs." Whereas urban renewal created vast tracts of land potentially available for new housing, blacks found little to praise in the rehousing efforts of the process by the end of the 1960s. White Atlantans extolled the elaborate transformation of the Buttermilk Bottom slum into an impressive collage of motels, office buildings, and high-rises, but black Atlantans pointed out how it had not changed anything for them and had been done at their expense. The *Atlanta Inquirer* noted that blacks "lived for years in Buttermilk Bottom . . . until the powers saw a great real estate value and then most of us were shifted" into new slum areas. The Atlanta Community Relations Commission noted in 1968 two problems compounded by the urban renewal program over the past decade, "the shortage of adequate low-income housing and segregated housing patterns in most communities of Atlanta."[70]

Further evidence that renewal failed to address key problems in Atlanta's impoverished pockets was the riot in September 1966 in the "Summerhill" ghetto adjacent to one bold symbol of urban renewal, the Atlanta stadium. Following the shooting of a African-American automobile theft suspect on September 6, Stokely Carmichael and Student Nonviolent Coordinating Committee members toured the area and denounced this case of police brutality. Over a four-day period, there was one death, twenty injuries, and 140 persons arrested. Black leaders created a "community council" to restore order and to counter the efforts of the militants to provoke further resistance. Despite the relative mildness of the violence, the riot of 1966 "revealed the depths of frustrations and deprivations still remaining in the lower income black neighborhoods of the city. After more than two decades of growing political influence, the black leadership of Atlanta and its white allies had failed to tackle adequately the assorted problems of the black majority—the poor—in the city." Urban renewal in Atlanta, as it had in Memphis and Richmond, contributed to the final shaping of the separate city. In the process it also served to debilitate the black community more thoroughly than any other public policy institution of the 1950s and 1960s. It proved to be as contentious as had been the school desegregation matters and mobilized blacks to turn the social and economic liabilities of the separate city into a potent political asset by the late 1960s.[71]

5

Race, Class, and the New Urban Politics

In August 1993 the Richmond *Times Dispatch* published a weeklong feature series entitled, "Divided We Stand." The idea for the series stemmed from a comment by former President Jimmy Carter that many American metropolitan areas—and he cited Atlanta, Washington and Chicago as examples—suffered from deep divisions that represented profound disparities between the living conditions of their residents. "The sharpest divides—black vs. white, rich vs. poor, city vs. suburb—are as vivid in Richmond as anywhere in the nation," observed *Times-Dispatch* reporter Michael Paul Williams.[1] Indeed, by the early 1990s in Atlanta, Memphis, and Richmond, the divisions along race and income lines were far more vividly etched than they had been a half century earlier when the federal government first sought to define a national urban policy agenda. We have attempted to describe the nature of the divisions as an interracial matter and also to show that within the black community there were sharp divides as well. The Civil Rights movement of the 1960s removed major barriers to black integration into the larger metropolitan community through such efforts as open housing, enforcement of voting rights, reinvestment in urban minority neighborhoods, various antipoverty programs, and nondiscrimination and affirmative action in employment, to name the most important areas. Yet, the separate black city that had emerged during the era of legally recognized segregation persists into the postsegregation era.

The evidence from Atlanta, Memphis, and Richmond overwhelmingly points to *increased segregation since the 1960s* and the persistence of the separate city. But the urban social dynamic at work was far more complicated than merely the enlargement of the black community. For one thing, there has been a significant degree of black dispersion into predominantly white neighborhoods throughout the metropolitan area. Yet, this dispersion (or integration) by blacks was limited largely to more affluent blacks. It was counterbalanced by increasing concentrations of lower-income blacks in core urban neighborhoods on a geographical scale that makes the notion of a separate black city more valid in the early 1990s than it was in the 1960s. Segregation of poor blacks from more affluent blacks residing in other areas of the metropolitan community generated a growing disadvanted subpopulation in the urban South.

Our study of black community development and empowerment in three leading southern cities from the 1940s through the 1960s has attempted to explain how urban America, in the words of the distinguished urban historian Richard C. Wade, "wandered into the dark streets and dangerous alleys of evergrowing ghettos, deepening pockets of hopelessness and despair, and dangerous prospects of impending disorder. Instead of incorporation," he continues, "we find separation; instead of mutual respect, we find mutual fear; instead of hope for a better future, we find expectations of increased contention." Wade's appraisal of the deep racial and class divisions of the American metropolis is sustained not only by our findings but also by a growing social science literature that documents the persisting problems of America's predominantly black urban underclass since the 1960s. Social theorist Paul Peterson suggests that the term *underclass* has become so widely used because it accurately connotes "the paradox of poverty in an otherwise affluent society that seems to have made strenuous efforts to eradicate this problem."[2]

We have described the failings of urban public policy in confronting race and poverty problems as well as supported the notion of a growing black urban underclass isolated racially from both the larger metropolitan area within a separate black city and a growing black middle class, many of whom moved out of core neighborhoods. William Julius Wilson's contention that the historic black community was undermined by federal policies that dispersed and stratified it within the broader metropolitan community is substantiated, at least in part, by our analysis of public policy and neighborhood change in all three cities both prior to and in the decades immediately following World War II. We concentrated essentially on the period when federal and local public policy first began to deal directly with the social and economic fabric of all three cities, ending our story at the point where such major federal initiatives as the War on Poverty and the full apparatus of civil rights enforcement were just gearing up. Wilson contends that in the wake of these policy initiatives, the historic black community dissipated, leaving behind a disadvantaged, resource-poor black underclass. Although our study is supportive of this viewpoint, the evidence we have gathered from three southern cities suggests several noteworthy modifications to the Wilson thesis.[3]

First, as late as the mid-1960s, there was little evidence in any of the three cities that the historic black community had begun to erode. If anything, the maturing of the black separate city in Atlanta, Memphis, and Richmond that occurred at the same time that a younger generation of civil rights activists pushed adamantly for black integration within the larger community, shows the sustained vitality of the historic black community. It is also important to note that through the 1960s there was still strong support within the black community for the idea that maintenance of the separate city had distinct economic and political advantages. Thus, as the black civil rights activists pressed forth with an agenda to dismantle the system of segregation and inequalities, the combined effects of white resistance to integration, public policies that furthered racial and class isolation, and the internal social dynamics of the black community itself, particularly in the political realm, perpetuated, indeed led to the physical expansion, of the black separate city. The exodus of the black middle class from the historic black community was as much a product of this physical expansion of the historic black community beyond its previously constricted boundaries as it was simply a case of abandonment of less advantaged neighbors by the middle class.

What we also demonstrated, however, is that the separate city played a critical historic role in developing black economic and political power and that blacks by the 1970s became a legitimate political force in all three cities. We also showed that public policy issues related to public housing, neighborhood preservation, urban renewal, and highway development generally contributed to the destabilization of the social fabric of all three cities and in so many essential ways failed to close the racial and social gaps. The policy revisions in the 1970s that corrected many of the past deficiencies by emphasizing neighborhood upgrading did not, however, appreciably benefit the most needy.

To examine more fully the Wilson argument, it would be necessary to go beyond the topics of our study, which is the urban black community prior to 1965, and examine closely black suburbanization since then. Space does not allow for a thorough analysis of black suburbanization, but it is possible, however, to look briefly at this phenomenon in one of our three case studies (Atlanta) and also to examine quickly the social and economic changes within the black separate city since the 1960s in our other two cases (Richmond and Memphis). Yet, to understand the increasing concentration of the urban needy, one must look beyond social factors to assess political and economic variables. The problems of black disadvantaged neighborhoods in the city are, in David Rusk's view, a problem of what he has termed urban "inelasticity" that has been particularly pervasive in the Rustbelt cities but is also an emerging problem in the Sunbelt. Rusk suggests that cities that failed to grow larger in order to capture a share of suburbanization evidenced inelasticity and were the cities that faced the most severe cases of decline and decay. All three of our cities were rated by Rusk as having some degree of elasticity, with Memphis rated the most elastic of the three (owing obviously to its vigorous annexation campaigns prior to the 1980s). Richmond was rated as "medium inelastic," and Atlanta showed the lowest elasticity. Inelastic cities, according to Rusk's theory, support suburbanization at the expense of urban vitality; they are cities "where racial prejudice has shaped growth patterns" and also are places that tend to be "more segregated than elastic areas."[4]

In "inelastic" Atlanta, rapid black suburbanization has been a notable feature of the changing metropolitan social structure. In the Atlanta metropolitan area, according to the 1990 census, the majority of blacks reside not in the city but in the adjacent suburbs. A study of black suburbanization and housing quality in Atlanta in the mid-1980s by Robert H. Thomas found that the city's African-Americans "left more densely populated areas for the relatively spacious suburbs," and that "blacks are not moving solely to neighborhoods of poor housing outside the central city boundaries." Only 18 percent of Atlanta's black suburban families had incomes below the poverty line in 1980. Even though most studies agree that blacks in suburbia possess housing that is considerably older and less valuable than that of whites, "the dispersal of increasingly larger numbers of blacks into white communities in selected metropolitan areas has opened a door that can only lead to future qualitative and quantitative gains," both in housing and in the quality of community life. As historian David R. Goldfield observed in the case of Atlanta, "the urban black middle class is becomeing detached from the rest of the black population," especially since "fair housing laws, greater affluence and the absense of exclusionary traditions in the new out-towns have accelerated middle-class black suburbanization."[5]

It has not been just affluent African-American who have left older inner-city neighborhoods in Atlanta, however. The city's belt of poverty, its zone of the disadvantaged, is predominantly black and extends throughout the south side of the city, reaching into adjacent DeKalb County. This one area accounts for nearly three-quarters of Atlanta's 214,517 poor identified in the 1980 census. Declining housing stock in this impoverished zone further compounds the problem of outmigration by the moderate-income and non-poor blacks. At the same time, as revealed in a 1988 investigative series by the *Atlanta Journal* and the *Atlanta Constitution* entitled "The Color of Money," it was revealed through an analysis of mortgage lending practices that discrimination was rampant largely in that belt of impoverished neighborhoods entending from Atlanta's south side into DeKalb and Fulton counties. The suburbanization of blacks in this portion of the Atlanta metropolis really constituted only the extension of the black separate city across the urban boundaries.[6]

Richmond

Richmond offers a compelling case of change within a black separate city that had come to dominate the city. "Three decades of ever-so-slow integration" was how the Richmond *Times-Dispatch* described it in 1993.[7] For one thing, there was only one small section of Richmond in west end that was

99+ percent white and substantially fewer areas (than in 1960) that were more than 80 percent occupied by whites. Clearly, blacks in Richmond in the 1990s were substantially more widely dispersed than they had been thirty years earlier. Part of this can be explained by the growth in the overall black population (by 21,000 persons) coupled with the loss of almost 40,000 white residents during this period. Yet, a major contributing factor was the thinning out of the historical center of black population due to various public improvement projects and housing abandoned in decayed core neighborhoods. These two factors made it necessary for blacks to seek alternative affordable housing in other parts of the city. In the meantime, the increase of black neighborhoods overwhelmingly composed of low-income families and individuals confirmed the precarious state of the black separate city by the 1980s. Even when African-Americans joined the march to suburbia in Richmond, most new black suburbanites found homes in those inner suburban neighborhoods that constituted an extension of the separate city across urban boundaries. The separate city, which had previously been an exclusively central city phenomenon, had been transformed by the 1980s and 1990s into a metropolitan condition.

By the 1980s the black community in Richmond was substantially more segregated at the neighborhood level than it had been in the 1960s. Nearly 40 percent of the city's census tracts were more than 75 percent black occupied in 1980. Over the preceding decade, seven tracts had gone from mixed-racial to a predominantly black population. In the city's east end, only one census tract (tract 211) was less than 50 percent black occupied, and that tract had increased its white occupancy owing largely to a precipitous decline in the black population base. In fact, the overall white population of tract 211 was halved between 1970 and 1980. Tract 211 encompassed one of the city's largest urban renewal sites, the Fulton Redevelopment Project, which largely accounted for the catastrophic drop in population during the 1970s. From a population of 3,062 in 1970, tract 211 plummeted to a population base of just 739 residents ten years later. Overall, owner occupancy dropped by nearly one-half, although there was a slight increase in the number of white owner-occupants. Renter-occupied units decreased from 498 to 38 over the same period. Yet, in adjacent tract 212, where all 440 owner-occupant units in 1970 were claimed by whites, by 1980 there were more black owner-occupants in the tract and also far fewer impoverished black families and individuals.

Census tract 211 underscored the dilemma of change sweeping through many of Richmond's core neighborhoods, where gentrification and urban renewal promoted increases in homeownership for both blacks and whites (albeit disproportionately favoring whites) and an improved income profile, but at the cost of massive (and seemingly irreversible) population losses. What the census figures also failed to indicate precisely in Richmond's core neighborhoods was how nearly two decades of intensive public investment in urban revitalization had not been sufficient to counteract the process of physical and social decay. According to a 1989 study of housing abandonment in Richmond, of the 1,995 vacant units in the city's core neighborhoods, 1,154 were deteriorated or dilapidated. The decline in population and the increasing incidence of segregation owed, in large measure, to a substantial reduction in the stock of habitable housing units after the 1960s and the failure of urban revitalization initiatives to replenish the lost units with new structures. In tract 211, as in so many other Richmond neighborhoods, the city's impoverished past and its precarious future merged.[8]

There were other disturbing indicators in the demographics of the 1980s. A solid belt of predominantly white neighborhoods dominated the city's west end both north and south of the James River, although a greater degree of residential integration characterized those neighborhoods south of the James River that had become part of Richmond as a result of the 1970 annexation. These southside neighborhoods were the scene during the early 1970s of a rather dramatic exodus of white residents when that area became part of the city. One effect of this white flight was the sudden availability of a rich supply of quality homes at bargain prices that were gobbled up by black professionals and whites interested in living close to the city but in a suburban-style setting. The concurrent implementation of the federal and state fair housing laws reinforced the market trend to integrate these neighborhoods and in the 1990s they remain one of the few racially integrated residential areas in the city.

Directly across the James River the west end neighborhoods of Tuckahoe and Windsor Farms remained almost purely white in occupancy. Census tracts 501, 502, and 503 had a combined black population in 1970 of 16 persons. By the 1980 census, the number had increased to just 35, which represented 0.5 percent of their total population. Yet, even in these exclusively white neighborhoods, as in the black neighborhoods in the east end, northside, and southside, there was an unmistakeable pattern of population decline through the 1970s and 1980s that pointed to the underlying frailty of the separate city, even when it involved an affluent population as in the west end neighborhoods. In the case of Richmond, as in Memphis, the separate city of the late twentieth century, compared to the variegated social city of the early twentieth century, lacked the means to attract and sustain population densities necessary to support vital urban institutions. This point is underscored if we look again at the less affluent, and largely black-occupied, east end neighborhoods in Richmond. Two east end census tracts, 205 and 208, experienced a doubling of their white population between 1970 and 1980, largely as a result of gentrification promoted by the Historic Richmond Foundation in the Church Hill neighborhood. Yet, in these two substantially revitalized tracts the overall population plunged from 7,810 residents to 4,545 and based on 1989 data there were at least 150 deteriorated or dilapidated vacant structures in these two tracts alone. The inability to attract a sufficient quantity of new white or black residents to this area owed in no small measure to its proximity to the city's major clustering of public housing complexes that provided the institutional foundation for residential segregation in the area in the first place. Only a small segment of whites chose to reside in Richmond's black separate city, and they live largely within a racial and economically homogeneous enclave.[9]

Memphis

The racial residential patterns that appeared in Memphis in the aftermath of the Martin Luther King assassination in 1968 differ little from Richmond's. Between 1970 and 1980 fourteen new census tracts were added to the forty-one tracts that already boasted a black population in excess of 75 percent. Overall, the percentage of tracts with a black population in excess of 75 percent was nearly the same in Memphis (42%) as in Richmond (39%). Exactly the same proportion of tracts (4%) registered a decline in black population during the 1970s. The failure of attempts to alter the historic pattern of concentrating low-income public housing in central Memphis and south Memphis neighborhoods added to the expansion of the black separate city. Immediately following the assassination of King and the ensuing violence that swept through Memphis, city leaders began for the first time to confront seriously the neighborhood and housing issues that had been left to fester over the previous ten years. Formation of the Memphis-Shelby County Citizens' Advisory Committee late in 1969 to bring blacks and whites together to discuss neighborhood concerns was a belated and tentative step toward a citizen-based biracial planning process. Concurrently, under the leadership of Memphis Housing Authority Commission Chairman Paul Borda, the city's dormant public housing program was resuscitated, and despite continual opposition from white neighborhoods, over 2,500 federally assisted low-rent housing units were constructed throughout the city between 1968 and 1971.[10]

The battle over the location of public housing in Memphis neighborhoods that erupted during the summer of 1968 focused on a proposal by the Memphis Housing Authority (MHA) to build a 300–unit turnkey housing project in Frayser, a predominantly white, blue-collar neighborhood in a newly annexed area. Borda pressed city leaders in the postriot months to seek federal housing assistance aggressively to address the city's black housing problem, which he regarded as a contributing factor in the violence. Yet, when the MHA announced plans to construct public housing in Frayser, nearby residents not only banded together to pressure city council to reject the necessary rezoning but also filed a court suit to prevent any future use of the property for low-income housing. According to Mayor Henry Loeb, who openly opposed the Frayser location, public housing should be built "in a place where it is wanted," and the Frayser residents were justified in their opposition. Council member Lewis Donaldson told a mass rally of 700 persons sponsored by the East Frayser Civic Club that the turnkey project was "nothing more than enforced blockbusting." He preferred building such projects in black neighborhoods rather than having the federal government "become an agency of social experimentation." Bowing to the intense neighborhood opposition, the Memphis City Council rejected the rezoning needed to build the project by a vote of seven-to-five but agreed to seek Department of Housing and Urban Development (HUD) approval to allow the units to be shifted to an alternative site. As proponents of the project noted, however, the council action not only delayed needed low-income housing, but also it established a precedent for neighborhood protest that jeopardized the future of low-income housing in the city.[11]

In late September 1970 Borda expressed his frustration to Loeb over the difficulty of securing city support for public housing. In particular, he noted that the Operation Breakthrough Program submitted to HUD in the aftermath of the 1968 riots to address the severe housing problems for blacks in Memphis had not received a "show of confidence and support of the 'City Fathers'." Since the Frayser controversy, he continued, "we have not been able to get enough sites approved for the authorized 2,000 units on our books." The major impediment was site selection, with only ten of the forty-three sites submitted by developers approved by all city agencies. "On this basis," Borda concluded, "how can we get sites for the next 2,000 units we have asked to be authorized?"[12]

In June 1969 the MHA went back to the city council with an alternative site for the 300–unit project slated for Frayser, and, again, neighborhood residents registered a vocal protest. This time, however, the 300 persons who showed up at the council meeting to protest were equally divided among white and black residents. This time the council voted, with only one dissenter, to approve the rezoning of a 40-acre parcel in a newly annexed area of south Memphis. Unlike the predominantly white Frayser, the transitional nature of the southwest Memphis neighborhood made it a prime candidate for low-rent housing, because Memphis intended to place the burden of public housing in the city's black separate city. Yet, it is significant to note that African-Americans now joined whites to challenge the process of segregating low-income assisted housing in black neighborhoods. Beside clamoring for an end to segregation, black representatives on city council after 1968 also lent support to neighborhood revitalization efforts to preserve established areas rather than further displace blacks.[13]

Much has been written about Atlanta as a showcase for neighborhood planning enthusiasm in the 1970s, but Memphis also responded to neighborhood needs with an ambitious plan of its own. Like so many cities, Memphis's neighborhood-planning process flowed directly from the prerequisites of the Community Development Block Grant (CDBG) program begun in 1974. Whereas the MHA had functioned in the past as the de facto neighborhood-planning agency, the city established a new Division of Housing and Community Development to oversee CDBG activities and selected a forty-member citizen-based Action Program Advisory Committee to develop a ranking system to determine which neighborhoods should receive funds. The vast majority of the neighborhoods deemed eligible for assistance were in Memphis's black areas, but there was a catch. The ranking system employed in Memphis, as in so many other cities, gave preference to moderate-income neighborhoods with a relatively high proportion of home owners and consistently ranked lower on the priority list poorer neighborhoods with greater needs. The idea was to preserve and upgrade the more viable black neighborhoods with less costly needs, given that there simply was not enough CDBG funds to make a difference in the most deteriorated areas. The strategy was widely referred to as "triage," and it was the spacious residential pockets accommodating disadvantaged blacks that were deemed the neighborhood "patients" too critically wounded to save. The policy in Memphis, as in Richmond, was to allow core neighborhood to die from resource deprivation and to allow the market to find a new future use.[14]

As a result, neighborhood planning in Memphis during the 1970s and 1980s did little to affect the fundamental income, housing, and poverty problems of the most depressed black neighborhoods. Only one bona fide lower-income Memphis black neighborhood, New Chicago, received community development aid, and only after an intense political skirmish. On the other hand, the Douglass neighborhood in north Memphis, where middleclass blacks had settled in the early 1900s (and that had been a showcase for city-sponsored rehabilitation since the 1950s), received a substantial commitment from the city's CDBG funds. Overall, however, the city's commitment to neighborhood planning led to a significant redistribution of resources to black neighborhoods.

All but one of the nine Memphis neighborhoods selected for initial funding were black-occupied. Moreover, between 1975 and 1982, the city committed more than $80 million to neighborhood-improvement efforts. Even with this vast infusion of public funds, Memphis planners were still unable to show conclusively that their efforts had made a difference either in improving the most deteriorated black neighborhoods that seemed to be spreading or in halting the flight of the middle class, both black and white, from the city's neighborhoods.

In Atlanta and Richmond, as well as Memphis, the neighborhood planning movement, launched in the era of protest and brought to fruition as black power increased, did make some notable contribution to the black community. Especially after 1974, black neighborhoods were the major recipients of community-improvement funds. Neighborhood preservation replaced neighborhood removal as the cornerstone of public policy in all three cities. Because the demographic revolution that characterized the 1940 through 1960 period had already run its course and Atlanta, Memphis, and Richmond were now more rigidly divided along race and class than they had been in 1940, the preservation strategy also had the effect of freezing the social and racial composition of the separate city. It is interesting to note that demographer Karl Taeuber found in an update of his racial residential segregation index (using 1980 census data) that all three cities showed decreasing degrees of segregation between 1970 and 1980. Richmond's segregation index was the lowest, dropping from 91 (out of 100) in 1970 to 79 in 1980. Both Atlanta and Memphis, which scored a 92 on the index in 1970, fell to 86 and 85 in 1980, respectively.[15] Obviously, neighborhood change continued to occur in the 1970s, but in no sense did it approach the magnitude of the preceding three decades. If there was an appreciable dip in the segregation index, as in the case of Richmond between 1970 and 1980, it represented the opening up of new neighborhoods to black occupancy that by the early 1990s had nearly all been absorbed by the expanding separate city.

The Attainment and Limitation of Black Political Independence

The development of racially defined separate cities in Atlanta, Memphis, and Richmond eventually led to the election of African-American mayors and majority black city councils. Black empowerment was a product of three important factors. One factor was demographic change. Given the heavy white outmigration to the suburbs, the black proportion of the total population in all three localities continued to rise until it exceeded the 50 percent mark. Census figures reveal that each city reached that mark in different decades with Atlanta becoming majority black in 1970 (51.4%), Richmond majority black in 1980 (51.3%), and Memphis majority black in 1990 (54.8%). As black populations grew, the political influence wielded by the African-American communities increased as well. Demographic change alone, however, does not fully account for the growth of black political independence. Memphis is a case in point. In spite of significant increases in the black population, Memphis lagged behind both Atlanta and Richmond in terms of substantive black representation in city hall. As recently as 1991, for example, when the Memphis black population exceeded 51 percent, only three of thirteen city council members and only three of nine school board members were black. Richmond, by contrast, lacked a black majority in the population until 1980 and, yet, had a majority black city council and a black mayor by 1977.[16]

A second factor contributing to black empowerment was legal intervention. The Civil Rights movement gave rise to legislation and court action that
removed the legal barriers to black voting. The 1965 Voting Rights Act, for
example, spurred voter registration throughout the South. It was also the
legal instrument used by a black plaintiff who challenged the 1970 annexation by the City of Richmond of 23 square miles from Chesterfield County.
The plaintiff charged that the annexation, which added 47,000 people (97%
of whom were white) to the city's population and which had not been cleared
by the federal government as called for under Section 5 of the Voting Rights
Act, was designed to dilute the black vote. Indeed, after the annexation, the
black proportion of the population dropped overnight from 52 percent to 42
percent. Litigation over the annexation, however, prompted a U.S. Supreme
Court order that led to the abolition of at-large city council elections and the
creation of nine single-member districts. The special election held under the
new voting system resulted in a 5/4 black majority council that, at its
inaugural meeting following the election, proceeded to elect the first black
mayor in Richmond's history.[17]

In 1991 the U.S. Justice Department lodged a suit against Memphis's
system of electing representatives to the city council and the school board.
The Department contended that the majority-vote elections for city council
and the school board and the representational system of the two bodies (6
at-large seats on the 13–member council and 2 at-large seats on the 9–member
school board) worked against the election of blacks. Also, as then U.S.
Attorney General Richard Thornburgh said, "The adoption of these electoral
devices in Memphis has been paralleled by a continuing and aggressive
program of annexing predominantly white areas into the city." As of July
1994, the suit was still pending before the courts, and the only change in the
electoral system that had occurred was the abolition of the majority-vote
requirement. Significantly, however, it was that change that led directly to
the election of Willie W. Herenton in 1991 as Memphis's first black mayor.
He won the mayoral election, beating white incumbent Richard Hackett with
49.45 percent of the total vote. His margin of victory was a razor-thin 172
votes out of a total of 247,919 votes cast. Had there been a run-off election,
as would have been necessary under the old system, Memphis might still be
one of only a few major American cities with a black majority and without a
black mayor. The point is that the election of Memphis's and Richmond's
first black mayors resulted in part from significant changes in the law and
court mandates.[18]

The third factor leading to black empowerment was political mobilization. The discontent within the black community that earlier found expression in protest demonstrations and acts of civil disobedience was turned to
voter education and registration. In addition, the Civil Rights movement
produced a new generation of black leaders who were less interested in

brokering elections among white candidates and more concerned about the election of blacks to public office. Atlanta's Andrew Young and Richmond's Henry Marsh, III, former mayors of their respective cities, were both members of the Civil Rights generation—Young as one of Dr. Martin Luther King, Jr.'s, key lieutenants and Marsh as a protégé of Oliver Hill, a noted attorney who played a leading role in the 1954 *Brown* decision. "Without question," Roger Biles wrote in a recent study of black mayors, "the increased activism of the 1950s and 1960s spilled over into politics as previously disengaged blacks, emboldened by courtroom and legislative triumphs, began to believe that 'black power' could be translated into meaningful reform."[19] Atlanta, in particular, illustrates this phenomenon in that the sit-in movement ushered in a period of greater black political independence. After the student-led protests, the coalition involving the white corporate elite and the conservative black elite broke apart. Black political independence meant that whatever alliances between the black voter and the white business community emerged in the future would be more ad hoc in nature, unlike the more stable coalition that typified the Hartsfield/Allen regimes, and structured in such a way that blacks no longer would assume a subservient role.

Richmond, too, provides solid evidence of the importance of political mobilization for achieving political independence. The Crusade for Voters, born during the Massive Resistance era, was a very effective instrument in generating votes in the African-American community. From its inception in 1956 until the mid-1960s, although not sufficiently strong to elect its own slate of candidates to city council, the Crusade was a decisive factor in determining which white candidates were elected. Given its sway in the black community and its ability to deliver a solid bloc of votes, the Crusade was on occasion able to extract concessions from the conservative white power structure in the form of appointments of blacks to city boards and agencies and the adoption of public policy favorable to the black community. By the late 1960s, however, the Crusade was able to elect some of its own candidates to city council on the strength of the black vote alone.[20]

Atlanta
Demographic change, legal intervention, and political mobilization all led to black political independence in the separate city, although the story of independence varies depending on whether one is discussing Atlanta, Memphis, or Richmond. For Atlanta blacks, political independence reached its zenith with the election of Maynard Jackson in 1973. From the late 1940s until 1969, the black vote was crucial to the election of business-oriented white mayors. With its control of city hall assured, the corporate elite was quick to extol the racial amity that existed in Atlanta and to capitalize on William Hartsfield's decades-old slogan that Atlanta was "a city too busy to hate." Such was easy, however, when policymaking authority remained in the hand

of whites. The tenuous nature of the biracial partnership became evident in 1969, however, when the candidate supported by the business establishment and by outgoing Mayor Ivan Allen was defeated by Allen's vice-mayor for eight years, Sam Massell. Massell was Jewish and that alone put him outside the Protestant-oriented power structure. Moreover, Massell's labor support and liberal inclinations made him a maverick of sorts. During the campaign, he attacked the political influence of business and his run-off election victory was made possible by a sizeable African-American vote. As Alton Hornsby noted when assessing the 1969 election, "The invincible coalition of upper income white voters and the solid black vote had been disrupted." That same election also led to the election of Maynard Jackson as vice-mayor. Jackson was to the black establishment as Massell was to the white establishment—an outsider. Unlike Massell, however, who lost the support of the white power structure and received only 18 percent of the white vote, Jackson wound up getting support from several well-placed black leaders and garnered 99 percent of the black vote.[21]

By 1973, in addition to representing over 50 percent of the total population, blacks also accounted for 49.9 percent of Atlanta's voting-age population and 49 percent of all registered voters. Corporate Atlanta saw the handwriting on the wall. Sam Massell, who four years earlier had appealed to the black voter, now turned his back on the very constituency that had been so important to his 1969 victory. Indeed, his reversal was evident shortly after he took office. In an effort to establish rapport with the corporate community, he supported several business-sponsored initiatives, including the development of a rapid transit system (MARTA). In 1971 and 1972 Massell spoke with alarm about the exodus of whites to the suburbs and lobbied for state legislation that would have added 50,000 people, most of whom were white, to the city's population. The timing was such that the new citizens would be able to vote in the 1973 election. The legislation died in committee, but the fact that Massell instigated the legislation seriously damaged his standing in the black community. Also, during the 1970 garbage strike, Massell engendered black opposition because he refused to negotiate with the strikers, most of whom were black.[22]

The 1973 run-off election was a head-on collision between Massell and Jackson. Jackson had come come close to winning the general election in a multicandidate field (he pulled 47 percent of the total vote), but in the run-off, he received overwhelming support from the African-American community (95 percent of the black vote) and 17 percent of the total white vote. Jackson's lopsided black vote was due to the fact that demographic trends and political change already pointed to the strong possibility that an African-American could be elected mayor, but also because Jackson himself was a very strong, articulate candidate. Perhaps the single most important factor, however, was the sharp reaction among blacks to Massell's racist appeals to whites during the final days of the campaign. The appeals backfired in that not only did they solidify the black community, prompting 67 percent of black registered voters to show up at the polls (in contrast to a 55% white voter turnout), but also they contributed to Jackson's support within the moderate white community. In fact, the black voter turnout was so significant that Jackson could have won the election without a single white vote! Such is the power of black political independence.[23]

The once-close relationship between the business elite and city hall broke apart during Jackson's first four-year term. As Jackson gave ear to neighborhood groups and grass roots interests, it became evident to corporate Atlanta that it would not be accorded the same privileged access it enjoyed under previous regimes. Jackson instituted a neighborhood-based planning process with the city divided into twenty-four neighborhood planning units. Neighborhood groups became much more involved in public affairs. They also formed a powerful lobby against the construction of more expressways. Jackson-sponsored initiatives such as affirmative action, residency requirements for all appointed municipal officials, and minority set-aside programs (the latter designed to allocate a certain percentage of city-sponsored capital projects to African-American businesses) deepened the divide between the new political administration and the old corporate elite. Adding to the business community's resistance to the mayor was Jackson's threat to deposit municipal money in Birmingham banks if Atlanta banks refused to name women and minorities to their boards. Jackson also displaced a white police chief considered racially insensitive by blacks and, in so doing, created an ugly standoff between the fired chief and the acting chief whom Jackson appointed. The result of these and other flash points led to a series of articles in the *Atlanta Constitution* that lamented the breakdown of the business-government alliance.[24]

Jackson won reelection in 1977. Black political independence led to his victory, but the victor assumed a much less independent posture over the next four years. Given the mutual dependence of government and business (with government needing a strong tax base and the access to capital and business needing political contacts and ready access to policymaking authority), and given also the accommodation that the black middle was seeking with the white corporate elite, Jackson's second term saw the beginning of a restored relationship between city hall and the city's economic notables. Jackson proved in his second term to be much more responsive to business interests, pushing economic development projects, for example, and meeting much more regularly with business leaders. In a interesting turn of events, unlike the 1970 garbage strike during which Vice-Mayor Jackson marched with the strikers, when a garbage strike in 1977 led to a breakdown in negotiations, Mayor Jackson decreed that strikers who did not return to work would be fired.[25]

It was not until the election of Andrew Young, however, that the alliance between business and government was restored to a state much like that of the Hartsfield era when the black middle class and the white upper class locked arms. Young was determined to avoid the problems that plagued Jackson during his first term of office by maintaining close communication with the city's business leaders and by devoting much of his efforts to downtown development. Unlike Jackson, Young proved less sensitive to neighborhood interests, supporting, for example, expressway connectors in downtown that cut through neighborhoods. One of the largest downtown projects that Young championed was the redevelopment of Underground Atlanta, a 1970s tourist attraction noted for its location under highway and street networks. The assortment of entertainment and retail shops had declined over the years largely because of crime problems. Young envisioned a new complex that was safe and that would generate new hotel development, attract 150 businesses, generate 3,000 new jobs, and pump additional revenue into the municipal coffers. He succeeded in getting a multimillion dollar commitment from several prominent business leaders and persuaded city council to contract with the Rouse Company to design the new complex. Young was a superb salesman. Young showcased Atlanta during the 1988 National Democratic Convention and as a former member of Congress and as U.S. ambassador to the United Nations during the Carter presidency, he had acquired an impressive list of contacts and spent a considerable amount of time traveling across the country and to other parts of the world selling Atlanta as a place to do business. Recounting in his farewell address the accomplishments of his two terms in office, he pointed with pride that his administration "sent a message to the world that we know how to do business." His numerous trips out of the city, although applauded by corporate leaders, were criticized by those who wanted the mayor to focus on the home front and attend to the crime, housing, and drug problems that were ballooning in the inner city. Those problems, however, only got worse as Young's "public purpose capitalism" (the term he used to describe his efforts to involve private business in public interest projects) took center stage. Black political independence during the Young era did not mean independence from the white business community. Quite the contrary. The ties between government and business, once ruptured and then restored in Maynard Jackson's two terms, became stronger under Andrew Young and resembled the almost inseparable relationship between the political and commercial elites that had characterized Atlanta's postwar years. The difference in the era of black independence was that city hall was now heavily influenced by a black mayor and a black majority city council.[26]

Under the city's charter, Young could not serve more than two terms, and when the 1989 election was held, Maynard Jackson was back on the scene, after having served as a successful bond lawyer and developing strong working relationships with Atlanta's business community. With blacks clearly in control of the electoral process, the election turned on which black candidate would be elected. Given his campaign's emphasis on the need for downtown development, the protection of neighborhood interests, and social equity, Jackson had a broad-based appeal to upper-income whites and middle-class blacks and, thus, won the election with a handsome 79 percent majority, winning all 187 precincts. Jackson's administration proved friendly to Atlanta's bankers and developers, although he also spoke of the need for additional low-income housing, including single-room occupancy units for the homeless. In spite of criticism from community activists that, in regard to housing and other social issues, Jackson was long on talk and short on action, the mayor proved adept at maintaining strong support from many quarters of the city and clearly would have been reelected had he decided to run for reelection. He stunned the city, however, when he announced in June 1993 that his health problems prevented his seeking a fourth term. The business community immediately turned to Andrew Young, but he, too, also declined to run. When the 1993 election was held, City Councilman Bill Campbell was elected mayor, marking the first time in Atlanta history that a black who lacked significant ties to the civil rights community assumed the city's highest elected position.[27]

Richmond

Black political independence came to Richmond in 1977. Unlike Atlanta, Richmond never experienced strong biracial partnerships either prior to 1977 or afterward. The relationships between the Crusade for Voters and the Richmond power structure was dissimilar to that between the Atlanta Negro Voters League and the Atlanta power structure. Given Richmond's conservative, race-conscious white aristocracy and corporate elite, which held the reins of power during the 1950s and the 1960s, blacks were forced to develop earlier than Atlanta blacks a much more independent posture. The creation of the Crusade itself was an effort to develop political self-reliance. Under the leadership of the Crusade, blacks abandoned single-shot voting and voted for a full slate of candidates. With the growth of the black population and the vast increases in black voter registration that the Crusade masterminded, the Crusade engaged in balance-of-power politics. The Crusade, through its endorsement of white candidates, sought to incur debts from whites elected with black support.[28]

By 1966 Richmond's black population stood at 48 percent. Moreover, thanks to the effective work of the Crusade, black voter registration increased in the two years between 1964 to 1966 by 65 percent, pushing the number of black registered voters from just over a fourth of the total to over a third. As a consequence, the Crusade for Voters acquired enough clout that it dropped the practice of supporting "safe" whites and began endorsing several "long-shot" candidates who stood a good chance of winning on the basis of the black vote alone. One of those "long-shot" candidates was Henry L. Marsh, first elected to the city council in 1966 and, reelected in 1968 and in 1970. The 1972 election was enjoined by federal court action as were the next two elections while the courts wrestled with suits generated over the contested annexation of 1970. As noted, when a special election was called in 1977, Henry Marsh became the first black mayor of Richmond. His election by a majority vote of city council stemmed from the fact that five blacks were elected in 1977 to the nine-member city council. The new majority, meanwhile, stemmed primarily from three factors: (1) Shifts in the city's population; (2) increased black voter registration and voter turnout (by 1977 blacks represented 45 percent of all registered voters); and (2) a court-mandated election system that was instituted as a remedy for the racially impermissible boundary expansion.[29]

Marsh and his allies on council signaled shortly after they assumed power that a new day had dawned and that business as usual was no longer acceptable. The first major confrontation between Marsh and the business community was over the incumbent white city manager, William Leidinger, a public administrator who had been appointed prior to the 1977 election and who enjoyed strong support in the board rooms of corporate Richmond. Finding Leidinger to be unresponsive to the sentiments of the new council, Marsh and the other black members of council asked him to resign. Leidinger refused and proceeded to take his case to the city's top business leaders. Perhaps the most humiliating experience in Marsh's tenure was a summons for him and the other black council members to appear before Richmond's economic notables and explain why it was necessary to fire the manager. The corporate elite was in no mood for conciliation. Marsh was told that unless the council dropped their plans to fire the city manager, business leaders would oppose a major new downtown development project and that some business owners would move their operations out of the city. Marsh and his allies remained firm, however, and the city manager was replaced in 1978. As one observer noted, "Economic power had run into political power and it had lost."[30] Marsh's experiences with the white business community during his first term was similar to those of Maynard Jackson's. They both disrupted the understandings that had long existed between public and private sphere of influence, and, as a consequence, they both met strong resistance from the commercial elite.

In spite of the confrontation with the business community over the firing of the city manager, Marsh was a realist and understood the need for the city to maintain a healthy economy. Business leaders, meanwhile, understood the reality that a healthy business climate could not develop with racial animus and that business itself would suffer should racial conflict get out of hand. During the Marsh years, groundwork was laid for a major new public-private partnership known as "Richmond Renaissance." Joining white economic power and black political power, Richmond Renaissance was an organization whose initial efforts were to strengthen the city's retail core. James Rouse was enlisted to develop a downtown festival marketplace to re-attract to Richmond's department stores city and suburban shoppers, who years earlier had begun spending their money in the regional shopping malls outside the city. Although Marsh was no longer mayor when the market-place opened in 1985, his work with the business community secured the foundation. Marsh, like Jackson, was much more oriented to neighborhoods than his white predecessors. The percentage of capital budget allocations directed to neighborhood projects, for example, increased from 48 percent of the total to 75 percent. Community Development Block Grant funding tended to focus on smaller, neighborhood-oriented projects with one highly visible project allocated to each council district. Also like Jackson, Marsh diversified the composition of government agencies. Between 1976 and 1981, Marsh and the city council increased the number of blacks serving on boards and commissions by 43 percent and the number of women by 40 percent.[31]

Marsh was displaced as mayor in 1982 by Roy West, a black school principal and a political maverick with no links to Richmond's civil rights community. Marsh remained on the council because he had won election from his district. The 1982 council remained majority black with five blacks and four whites. In a strange twist of history, William Leidinger, the city manager fired in 1978, ran for council and was elected in 1980 and again in 1982.[32] Marsh remained very unpopular with Leidinger and the other white members of council. Having defeated a Marsh supporter and knowing that it took only five votes to become mayor, West became the center of attention. Marsh and his three remaining allies courted West as did the four white members of council. At the first meeting of the new council in July 1982 when the mayor for the next two years was selected, West voted for himself and received the votes of the four white members, thus becoming the new mayor of Richmond.

West's election represented a new period in Richmond politics. Given the single-member district system of election and the continued growth of the black population, black majorities on council would be a fixture for the foreseeable future. No longer was it a question of whether an African-Ameri-can would be elected, but which African-American. The separate black city of Richmond has always been diverse, but during the 1960s and the 1970s it was necessary to close ranks in order to extract concessions from white politicians whose elections required black support. The disputes within the black community were contained and fought out privately. During the 1980s and early 90s, however, the disputes were much more visible, and the Crusade was no longer able to contain the conflict. Blacks ran against other blacks, and the alliances on council were less predictable, although racial divisions were still very apparent because the majority of black council members leaned left politically and the majority of white council members leaned right.[33]

Notwithstanding the fact that West voted frequently with the white members of the council, he did institute a minority set-aside program similar to the one Maynard Jackson established in Atlanta. It was later challenged and declared unconstitutional by the U.S. Supreme Court. West strengthened the alliance between white business leaders and black politicians that had gotten off to a shaky start during Marsh's administration. West gave voice to the more conservative forces in the black community, and through partnership with the white business establishment helped to usher in an era of centrist politics in Richmond. West's biggest problem, however, were West himself. On one occasion, he verbally abused parents who had opposed actions he had taken at the school where he was principal. Even his former supporters found themselves the object of West's often irrational attacks. Illustrative of the bizarre events that occurred during West's tenure was the time he shot himself in the hand with a pistol and claimed, at least initially, that the injury had been sustained in a fall. He later changed his story to square with the facts. By 1988, West's support as mayor had eroded to the point that, rather than face defeat by a vote of council (of which he was still a member), he decided not to run for another term as mayor. When the votes were cast, West, once again, sided with the white members of council, and a white mayor was elected, although Mayor Geline Williams's tenure was only two years.[34]

In 1990 Walter Kenney, a longtime supporter of Henry Marsh and the Crusade, was elected mayor and reelected in 1992. Reflective of the shifting alliances in Richmond politics and the aimless course of the Crusade for Voters, the Crusade in 1992 dropped Kenney as one of its endorsees but included Roy West and Geline Williams.[35] Kenney's mayoralty was not distinguished by policy initiatives, as was the case with Henry Marsh's, nor was it distinguished by the dominance of the incumbent's personality, as was the case with Roy West. Black political leaders in Richmond today operate without the clear agenda that once characterized the Crusade when it was mobilizing Richmond's separate city for political independence. Absent significant increases in the city's white population and efforts by whites to reestablish control of council, and absent also the emergence of a policy agenda among black leaders, the Richmond black community will continue to speak with many voices with the discord becoming more apparent as the class divisions among African-Americans grow wider and wider.

Memphis

Blacks in Memphis did not experience political independence until 1991. Until that year Memphis was one of a very few major American cities with a black majority without a black mayor and majority black city council. Moreover, for a period of forty years, dating from 1951, only two blacks had won contested citywide elections. By 1991 only 3 of the 13 members of council and only 3 of the 9 members of the school board were black. Like Richmond, Memphis also lacked strong biracial coalitions, except for a brief moment between 1955 and 1959 when reformist mayor Edmund Orgill sought to establish a relationship with blacks that differed from that of Boss Crump whose black support was generated out of fear, intimidation, and patronage. Orgill, while disavowing the tactics of the Crump machine and setting Memphis on a more progressive course, proved a disappointment to the black community. As the 1959 election revealed, when Orgill and his allies in the business and professional community refused to support black candidates, blacks found that they could not rely on white reformers to help to secure their political independence. As a consequence, from 1959 forward, Memphis blacks charted a separate course, forming only temporary alliances with white candidates who would exchange favor for favor, black support for substantive concessions. The reform movement itself was short-lived as reformers were displaced by white reactionaries. For the long period stretching from the 1960s through the 1980s, Memphis blacks, like their Richmond counterparts, had to contend with very conservative forces in the white community. Given its racial climate, one made worse by the 1968 assassination of Dr. Martin Luther King, Jr., Memphis was never identified as a New South city, and its corporate elite could never engage in the kind of clever sloganeering that made Atlanta famous. Memphis was not "a city too busy to hate."

The inability of Memphis blacks to become incorporated in city government was a combination of factors. One of the major factors was the electoral system. The fact that only two blacks had won citywide elections from 1951 to 1991 stemmed largely from the requirement, recently overturned by federal court action, that the successful candidate had to acquire more than 50 percent of the vote. In addition, six of the thirteen council positions are at-large seats. (Earlier in this chapter, it was noted that, as of July 1994, a suit was still pending before the federal courts regarding the combination of an at-large and a ward system of electing city council members and members of the school board).[36] Another factor that has made the attainment of black political independence difficult is lack of unity within the black community. The first black mayor was elected only after efforts to select a consensus candidate. Before the election, several blacks were planning to run, including then NAACP Executive Director Benjamin Hooks and D'Army Bailey, the attorney instrumental in converting the motel where Dr. King was killed into the National Civil Rights Museum. Ironically, the consensus-building effort itself led to dissension. Harold Ford, a member of the U.S. House of Representatives long involved in Memphis politics, called a meeting of the city's black leaders that was closed to whites and the press. That meeting led to dissent among community activists, as well as whites living in the city's Poplar Corridor (a comparatively liberal white middle-class section of Memphis that in the past had proved willing to vote for black candidates). Black activists, decrying the elitism of a Ford and others associated with the summit, convened a meeting of their own called the "Peoples Convention."

Still another factor impeding black empowerment has been the lack of voter participation, most noticeable among the growing numbers of poor blacks who are moving to Memphis from Mississippi and eastern Alabama. The city, in 1991, had one of the highest concentrations of poor blacks in the United States. A voter-registration drive in preparation for the election failed to meet the goal of registering 40,000 blacks. Only 5,700 blacks registrants were added to the rolls.[37]

The consensus candidate who emerged from meetings in the black community was Willie W. Herenton, Memphis's first black superintendent of schools who later became a major contender for the superintendent of schools in Atlanta. He won the election by only 172 votes. Along with Herenton came new black majorities on the city council and the school board. Given the disunity that existed in the black community prior to his election, however, it was not surprising that his first 100 days in office were difficult. Black council members challenged many of his moves, particularly Herenton's decision to select a white utilities executive to succeed him in case of an emergency. Another sore spot was Herenton's failure to return phone calls from black leaders on council, prompting Dr. James Ford, the city council chairman to remark, "he [Herenton] doesn't even communicate with me. If this doesn't get better, he won't last very long."[38] Acting on the advice of Maynard Jackson and Andrew Young, Herenton placed heavy emphasis on downtown development and, thus, early in his administration sought and secured support from major white business leaders.

It is much too early to assess the impact of black political independence in Memphis. One matter is certain, however. Black leaders in all three cities, Memphis, Richmond, and Atlanta, face pressures that no white mayor had to confront. What any black leader must acknowledge today are the vast limitations of political independence. In many respects, black political independence has proved to be a cruel hoax. Just as African-Americans acquired power to control their own destiny, the cities over which they preside are collapsing. Throughout the urban South, black poverty has increased. Blacks who are employed are concentrated in the lowest paying jobs. Atlanta's large predominantly black residential zone in downtown is the second poorest neighborhood in the United States. Richmond's poorest neighborhoods, almost totally African-American, rival in despair those of Atlanta's. In a 1986 study of 43 middle-size cities in the United States (ranging from 150,000 to

450,000 people), Richmond, it was revealed, was both the richest and the poorest. Richmond's West End neighborhood south of Cary Street was the single most affluent neighborhood of any neighborhood in the forty-three cities. Meanwhile, with the exception of Atlanta's poor neighborhoods, Richmond's were the poorest in the survey. According to the mayors of Memphis and Shelby County, of cities with populations exceeding 500,000, Memphis has the largest proportion of blacks living in poverty and on welfare than any other city in the nation.[39]

Along with the highly concentrated sections of abject poverty in the inner cities of Atlanta, Memphis, and Richmond come rising rates of violent crime (often drug-related), homelessness, health problems, low levels of educational achievement, and deteriorating infrastructure. All three cities are losing population as middle-class blacks and whites increasingly move to the suburbs. As important, if not more important as far as the public economy is concerned, is the loss of business to the suburbs. In 1960 Atlanta, for example, contained 90 percent of the jobs in the metropolitan area. By 1980 the city's share had dropped to 42 percent. Just as the demands for services increase, the ability to deliver the services decline. No longer can the cities look to the federal government for assistance, not since the vast cutbacks in federal aid during the 1980s. With the nation's mounting debt and with the election of President Clinton based on a successful suburban strategy designed to woo disaffected Democrats who had been voting for Republican presidential candidates back to the party, mayors cannot expect Washington to target central cities for massive infusions of federal money. State government will not be inclined to assist cities, either, not as the suburbs gain larger numbers of seats in the legislature. In short, cities will have to rely increasingly on their own resources and to seek partnerships with business and suburban governments. As historian David Goldfield observed, "Implicit in the equation between black political power and white economic power is the notion that politics in the 1990s is often a question of resources. If politics is a question of resources, then black politicians have few of those resources, and their black constituents even fewer." Black leaders, understandably, have been wary of discussions of regional reform calling for consolidation of government. All three cities have used such efforts to dilute the black vote. But it is also not in the interest of black mayors to preside over the death of their communities. They may need as never before to work cooperatively with their suburban political leaders in seeking regional approaches to poverty, crime, education, and health care. Public-private partnerships have meant, so far, a policy agenda heavily tilted toward downtown development with virtually no attention to the growing social problems in inner-city neighborhoods. How can black leaders address those problems and still keep the alliance with the business community? Perhaps Michael Lomax, the former chair of the Fulton County Commission and 1993 Atlanta mayoral candidate, said it best when he remarked, "We'll see these problems [of the black underclass] addressed when the business community understands the total cost." Black independence, after all of the struggle and hardship, had itself become a struggle in a period of scarce resources. As a consequence, the separate city now finds its political independence offset by the necessity to maintain a dependence on white corporate power.[40]

The economic divisions of all three cities, indeed, of cities throughout the South and the rest of the nation, are still largely definable by race. As long as the black community continues to function as a society separate from and unequal to the larger society, it will never achieve the kind of independence that will enable it to control its own destiny. Moreover, the movement of middle-class blacks out of the older districts to the suburbs may well expand the boundaries of the separate city, but it also drains the historic black neighborhoods of the urban core of important resources and networks. Those African-Americans unable to leave now constitute the poorest of the poor, and the institutions that once nourished the neighborhoods and sustained the economic, religious, and cultural life of the residents are collapsing. Their collapse brings about the dissolution of the material and psychological support so important for upward mobility. In the wake of the exodus are inner-city areas whose citizens live in fear and without hope and whose problems defy solution by the most committed leaders of city government. Meanwhile, the operation of the private market, still controlled by white institutions and interests, enriches the suburbs and starves the central city at the very moment that national and state governments grow more distant from the concerns of African-American leaders of the central city. Ironically, the separate city made black political independence possible, but a separate city devoid of economic power poses hard questions about the very meaning of independence.

Notes

1. The Rise of the Separate City

1. William J. Wilson, *The Truly Disadvantaged*; Charles Murray, *Losing Ground*.

2. Wilson, *Disadvantaged*, pp. 137–38.

3. Horace R. Cayton and St. Clair Drake, *Black Metropolis: A Study of Negro Life in a Northern City*; Arnold Hirsch, *Making the Second Ghetto: Race and Housing in Chicago, 1940–1960*.

4. Hirsch, *Second Ghetto*. See also, John F. Bauman, *Public Housing, Race and Renewal: Urban Planning in Philadelphia, 1920–1974*, chap. 5; Raymond A. Mohl, "Race and Space in the Modern City: Interstate-95 and the Black Community in Miami," pp. 3–4; and Elijah Anderson, *Streetwise: Race, Class and Change in an Urban Community*, p. 57.

5. Gilbert Osofsky, *Harlem: The Making of a Ghetto, Negro New York, 1890–1930*, p. 128; Allen Spear, *Black Chicago: The Making of a Negro Ghetto, 1890–1920*; Kenneth A. Kusmer, *A Ghetto Takes Shape: Black Cleveland, 1870–1930*; Joe W. Trotter, Jr., ed., *Black Milwaukee: The Making of an Industrial Proletariat*; Henry Louis Taylor, Jr., "City Building, Public Policy, and the Rise of the Industrial City, and Black Ghetto-Slum Formation in Cincinnati, 1850–1940," in Henry Louis Taylor, Jr., ed., *Race and the City: Work, Community, and Protest in Cincinnati, 1820–1970*, pp. 156–57; Emmett J. Scott, *Negro Migration during the War*; James Weldon Johnson, *Black Manhattan*, pp. 146–47; William M. Tuttle, Jr., *Race Riot: Chicago in the Red Summer of 1919*, p. 163.

6. Gunnar Myrdal, *An American Dilemma: The Negro Problem and Modern Democracy*, p. 188; Blaine A. Brownell, "The Urban South Comes of Age, 1900–1940," in Blaine A. Brownell and David R. Goldfield, eds., *The City in Southern History: The Growth of Urbanization in the South*, p. 138.

7. Brownell, "Urban South Comes of Age," p. 138.

8. David Ward, *Poverty, Ethnicity and the American City, 1840–1925: Changing Conceptions of the Slum and the Ghetto*, pp. 146, 217.

9. August Meier and Elliott Rudwick, *From Plantation to Ghetto*. See also Robert C. Weaver, *The Negro Ghetto*, and Kusmer, *A Ghetto Takes Shape*.

10. Kenneth B. Clark, *Dark Ghetto: Dilemmas of Social Power*, pp. 22, 24. Sociologist Lee Rainwater, in *Behind Ghetto Walls: Black Family Life in a Federal Slum* (1970), implies that a single large public housing project in St. Louis, Pruitt-Igoe, constituted a ghetto in the 1960s.

11. Cayton and Drake, *Black Metropolis*, pp. 113, 204–06.

12. Allen H. Spear, "Preface," in Johnson, *Black Manhattan*, pp. vi–vii; Johnson, *Black Manhattan*, pp. 148–59.

13. Johnson, *Black Manhattan*, p. xv.

14. Christopher Silver, "The Racial Origins of Zoning: Southern Cities from 1910 to 1940," pp. 189–205.

15. Robin D.G. Kelly, "The Black Poor and the Politics of Opposition in a New South City, 1929–1970," in Michael B. Katz, ed., *The "Underclass" Debate: Views from History*, pp. 293–333. For another southern urban case of black community development that involved differing race experiences based on class factors, see Earl Lewis, *In Their Own Interests: Blacks in Twentieth-Century Norfolk* (Berkeley: Univ. of California Press, 1990).

2. Community Change and Community Leadership

1. Benjamin E. Mays, *Born to Rebel: An Autobiography*, pp. 67, 276.

2. George B. Tindall, *The Emergence of the New South, 1913–1945*, p. 719.

3. Raymond Gavins, *The Perils and Prospects of Southern Black Leadership: Gordon Blaine Hancock, 1884–1970* .

4. Ibid., pp. 186–89, 146. The development of the SRC included a series of meetings following the initial Durham gathering, all of which involved Hancock's leadership (see pp. 128–55). See also Edward F. Burrows, "The Commission on Interracial Cooperation, 1919–1944: A Case History of the Interracial Movement in the South."

5. Gavins, *Perils*, pp. 33–35, 44–50, 148–59, 180–90. See also Richmond Council of Social Agencies, *The Negro in Richmond, Virginia*.

6. David M. Tucker, *Lieutenant Lee of Beale Street*, pp. 43–67, 78, 127–33.

7. Baltimore *Afro-American*, June 8, 1929, cited in Tucker, *Lieutenant Lee*, p. 66.

8. Pittsburg *Courier*, April 3, 1943, cited in Tucker, *Lieutenant Lee*, p. 133–34.

9. Richard C. Wade, *Slavery in the Cities: The South, 1820–1860*; Ira Berlin, *Slaves without Masters: The Free Negro in the Antebellum South*; Robert E. Perdue, *The Negro in Savannah, 1865–1900*; Howard N. Rabinowitz, *Race Relations in the Urban South, 1865–1890*, pp. 329–30. See also John W. Blassingame, "Before the Ghetto: The Making of the Black Community in Savannah, 1865–1880," pp. 463–88.

10. Rabinowitz, *Race Relations*, pp. 332, 333, 339; C. Vann Woodward, *The Strange Career of Jim Crow*.

11. Richard J. Hopkins, "Status, Mobility, and the Dimensions of Change in a Southern City: Atlanta, 1870–1910," p. 227; Ray Stannard Baker, *Following the Color Line*, provides a detailed discussion of the 1906 race riot. See also Michael J. O'Connor, "The Measurement and Significance of Racial Residential Barriers in Atlanta, 1890–1970," p. 28.

12. Dwight Fennel, "A Demographic Study of Black Business, 1905–1908, with Respect to the Race Riot of 1906"; O'Connor, "Racial Residentail Barriers," p. 33; "Historical Trends in Negro Population Areas," memorandum, n.d., Atlanta City Planning Commission Papers, Atlanta Historical Society.

13. Gilbert T. Stephenson, "The Segregation of the White and Negro Races in Cities," pp. 2–9; Roger L. Rice, "Residential Segregation by Law, 1910–1917," pp. 179–99; *Carey et al. v. City of Atlanta et al.*, 143 Ga. 192, 84 S.E. 456 (1915); *Harden v. City of Atlanta*, 147 Ga. 248, 93 S.E. 401 (1917).

14. Silver, "Racial Origins of Zoning."

15. Bruno Lasker, "The Atlanta Zoning Plan," p. 17; Robert Whitten, "Letter to Editor," *Survey* 48 (June 15, 1922): 418–19; *Smith v. City of Atlanta*, 161 Ga. 769, 132 S.E. 66 (192).

16. Warren H. Manning, "Atlanta—Tomorrow a City of a Million"; E. Bernard West, "Black Atlanta—Struggle for Development, 1915–1925," pp. 25–48; Dana F. White, "The Black Sides of Atlanta: A Geography of Expansion and Containment, 1970–1870," pp. 199–225.

17. Robert A. Thompson, Hylan Lewis, and David McEntire, "Atlanta and Birmingham: A Comparative Study in Negro Housing," in Nathan Glazer and David McEntire, eds., *Housing and Minority Groups* (Berkeley: Univ. of California Press, 1960), pp. 19, 28–30; Howard L. Preston, *Automobile Age Atlanta: The Making of a Southern Metropolis, 1930–1935*, pp. 103–10; O'Connor, "Racial Residential Barriers," pp. 100–04; Michael L. Porter, "Black Atlanta: An Interdisciplinary Study of Blacks on the East Side of Atlanta, 1890–1930," pp. 26, 37. Meadow Brook (1917) was the first black subdivision developed on Atlanta's West Side.

18. The role of the West Side Mutual Development Committee (WSMD), created by Mayor William Hartsfield in 1952, in the neighborhood-planning process in Atlanta will be discussed more fully in Chapter 4. The files of the WSMDC are contained in the Atlanta City Planning Commission Papers, Atlanta Historical Society.

19. Memorandum, M.D. Carrell to Colonel Horatio B. Hackett, May 19, 1934, Atlanta Project Files H-1100, Record Group 196, Records of the Public Housing Administration, National Archives; Peter E. Arnold, "Public Housing in Atlanta."

20. Richmond City Planning Commission, "Population by Race, Richmond, Virginia, 1870–1964," Staff Report, RCPC, n.d., Richmond Department of Planning and Community Development Library, Richmond; White, "Black Site of Atlanta."

21. "An Ordinance to Secure for White and Colored Residents Respectively the Separation of Residences for Each Race," April 19, 1911, Ordinances and Resolutions of the City of Richmond, September 1910–August 1911, Ordinances and Resolutions of the City of Richmond, September 1910–August 1912 (Richmond: Saunders, 1913), pp. 166–67; Barbara J. Flint, "Zoning and Residential Segregation: A Social and Physical History, 1910–1940," p. 302; Brockenbrough Lamb, "Legal Aspects of Zoning Laws," *Virginia Municipal Review* 1 (March 1924): 75–83; *City of Richmond et al. v. Deans*, 37 F. (2nd) 712–713 (January 14, 1930); *Virginia Municipal Review* 7 (February 1930): 27; George C. Wright, "The NAACP and Residential Segregation in Louisville, Kentucky, 1914–1917," pp. 39–54.

22. Charles Knight, *Negro Housing in Certain Virginia Cities*, pp. 38–39; Rabinowitz, *Race Relations*, pp. 98, 105–06, 112–13, 231; Zane L. Miller, "Urban Blacks in the South, 1865–1920: The Richmond, Savannah, New Orleans, Louisville, and Birmingham Experience," pp. 201–02.

23. Although there is no concise history of Jackson Ward, Miller, in "Urban Blacks in the South," offers a useful sketch through 1920 (in Schnore, *New Urban History*). See also Carroll R. Minor, "The Institutional Life of Negroes in Richmond." Richmond Department of Planning and Community Development, *Conservation Plan for the Central Wards Conservation Area*, contains a historical sketch of the area.

24. *Housing Betterment* 2 (July 1913): 18–19; *Housing Betterment* 6 (December 1917):

60–61; *Housing Betterment* 8 (June 1919): 110; *Housing Betterment* 8 (September 1919): 109–10.

25. Knight, *Negro Housing*, pp. 103, 106; RCSA, *Negro in Richmond*, pp. 65–75.

26. Correspondence connected with the low-income housing projects in Richmond during the 1930s can be found in Box H-168, Records of the Public Housing Administration, and Group H-4101 and H-4103, Records of the Federal Emergency Administration of Public Works (FEAPW), National Archives, Washington, D.C. See in particular George W. Howell and James H. Rhorer to Director of Housing Division, April 16, 1935, Group H-4101, Records of FEAPW.

27. Richard D. Stimson to A.R. Clas, July 2, 1935; William H. Schwarzschild to A.R. Clas, July 10, 1935; Real Estate Appraisal Company of Richmond to A.R. Clas, August 27, 1935; A.R. Clas to Colonel H.B. Hackett, August 26, 1935; A.R. Clas to William H. Schwarzchild, September 30, 1935; William H. Schwarzchild to A.R. Clas, September 23, 1935; W.L. Ransome, L.A. Reid, and J.M.C. Ramsey to A.R. Clas, October 1, 1935, Group H-4101 and H-4103, Records of FEAPW.

28. Cited in Pat Jones, "Human Misery in Slum Area Presents Problem to Richmond."

29. Thomas J. Woofter, *Negro Problems in Cities*, pp. 79, 137, 139–40; Leigh D. Fraser, "A Demographic Analysis of Memphis and Shelby County, Tennessee, 1820–1972," p. 25, Table 5. Fraser demonstrates that there was actually a net natural decrease in the black population of Shelby County (which includes Memphis) of 162 persons during the 1930–1940 decade.

30. Harland Bartholomew, *A Comprehensive City Plan, Memphis, Tennessee* (Memphis: City Plan Commission, 1924), pp. 117–27; First Annual Report, City Plan Commission, 1921, p. 2, cited in Blaine A. Brownell, "The Commerical-Civic Elite and City Planning in Atlanta, Memphis and New Orleans in the 1920s," p. 358; Robert A. Sigafoos, *Cotton Row to Beale Street: A Business History of Memphis*, pp. 152–54.

31. Oral History Interview with Blair T. Hunt by Ronald Walter (typed transcript), Memphis-Shelby County Public Library, Memphis.

32. WPA Housing Survey, p. 17; cited in Sigafoos, *Cotton Row*, pp. 179–83; Memphis Housing Authority, *Ten Years in Housing: Memphis Housing Authority, 1947–48 Annual Report*, p. 18; David Tucker, *Memphis after Crump: Bossism, Blacks and Civic Reformers, 1948–1968*, especially chap. 1.

33. Memphis's first two public housing projects, Dixie Homes and Lauderdale Court, were built under the PWA program and completed in 1938, at a total cost of $6.6 million.

34. U.S. Census of Population, 1940, Statistics for Census Tracts, Atlanta, Memphis, and Richmond.

35. Ibid.

36. Gloriastene Thompson, "The Expansion of the Negro Community in Atlanta, Georgia, from 1940 to 1958," p. 9; Charles S. Johnson, *Patterns of Negro Segregation*; White, "Black Sides of Atlanta," p. 222.

37. See White, "Black Sides of Atlanta."

38. MHA, *Ten Years in Housing*.

39. See Tucker, *Memphis since Crump*, pp. 69, 91, 172.

40. See Christopher Silver, *Twentieth Century Richmond: Planning Politics and Race*, pp. 223–30, 329–30.

41. Homer Hoyt, *The Structure of Residential Neighborhoods to American Cities*, pp. 42–53, 168.

42. Tim Wheeler, "Church Hill: Gaslight Affluence, Poverty Share Streets," Richmond *Times-Dispatch*, August 7, 1977.

43. For a detailed (and sympathetic) assessment of the Crump machine in Memphis, see William D. Miller, *Memphis during the Progressive Era*, and *Mr. Crump of Memphis*. Far more critical is Tucker, *Memphis since Crump*, pp. 17, 22–39.

44. Annette E. Church and Roberta Church, *The Robert R. Churches of Memphis*, pp. 184–85; Lester C. Lamon, *Black Tennesseans, 1990–1930*, pp. 297–99.

45. Lamon, *Black Tennesseans*, p. 98.

46. According to Bunche, "Paine fulfilled part of his agreement by appointing three, rather than the requested six, blacks to the detective force. However, one died; the other two were suspended after a run-in with white hoodlums." Ralph J. Bunche, *The Political Status of the Negro in the Age of Franklin D. Roosevelt*, p. 495; Walter P. Adkins, "Beale Street Goes to the Polls," p. 38; Mingo Scott, Jr., ed., *The Negro in Tennessee Politics and Governmental Affairs, 1865–1965* p. 117.

47. Adkins, "Beale Street Goes to the Polls," pp. 40–44; Robert A. Lanier, *Memphis in the Twenties: The Second Term of Mayor Rowlett Paine, 1924–1928*, pp. 130–32.

48. Bunche, *Political Status of the Negro*, p. 499; Tucker, *Memphis since Crump*, pp. 18–19; Church and Church, *The Robert R. Churches*, pp. 184–85; Hunt interview, pp. 14–15, 18.

49. Tucker, *Memphis since Crump*, p. 20.

50. Kate Born, "Memphis Negro Workingmen and the NAACP," pp. 102–03.

51. Adkins, "Beale Street Goes to the Polls,"p. 107; Herbert P. Jones, "Dr. Joseph Edison Walker: The Era of Good Feelings, Memphis 1948–1958," pp. 8–11; Hunt interview, p. 19.

52. T.J. Johnson, *From the Driftwood of Bayou Pierre*, p. 72; Jones, "Dr. Joseph Edison Walker," pp. 11, 73; *Memphis World*, June 13, 1950.

53. Tucker, *Memphis since Crump*, pp. 21, 56–57, 64, 76; Jones, "Dr. Joseph Edison Walker," pp. 11–13.

54. Gloria Brown Melton, "Blacks in Memphis, Tennessee, 1920–1955: A Historical Study," p. 315; David Tucker, *Black Pastors and Leaders: Memphis, 1819–1972*, pp. 102–18; Jones, "Dr. Joseph Edison Walker," pp. 14–15; Randolph Meade Walker, "The Role of the Black Clergy in Memphis during the Crump Era," pp. 38–39.

55. Bunche, *Political Status of the Negro*, pp. 488, 490–91; Clarence A. Bacote, "The Negro in Atlanta Politics," pp. 342–43.

56. See August Meier and David Lewis, "History of the Negro Upper Class in Atlanta, Georgia, 1890–1958," pp. 128–39.

57. Robert J. Alexander, "Negro Business in Atlanta," pp. 454-55.

58. Porter, "Black Atlanta," Table 4, p. 157, and Table 18, pp. 291–93; Alexander, "Negro Business in Atlanta, pp. 460–61; Atlanta University, *Business Enterprise Owned and Operated by Negroes in Atlanta, Georgia, 1944* (Atlanta: Atlanta Univ., 1944), pp. 11–37, 52–56.

59. Porter, "Black Atlanta," p. 343.

60. Alexander, "Negro Business in Atlanta," pp. 451–64.

61. Anne L. Branch, "Atlanta and the American Settlement House Movement," pp. 36–51; Peter E. Arnold, "Public Housing in Atlanta: A National First," p. 11.

62. Memorandum from William B. Hartsfield to W.H. Aiken et al., December 8, 1952, in City of Atlanta, Bureau of Planning Records, Box 3, Atlanta Historical Society; Atlanta *Constitution*, April 30, 1960; Alexander, "Negro Business in Atlanta," p. 460.

63. Bunche, *Political Status of the Negro*, p. 488; Bacote, "Negro in Atlanta Politics," pp. 343-45.

64. Bunche, *Political Status of the Negro*, p. 490; Bacote, "Negro in Atlanta Politics," pp. 345–49.

65. Bacote, "Negro in Atlanta Politics," pp. 349–50.

66. A.J. Dickinson, "Myth and Manipulation: The Story of the Crusade for Voters in Richmond, Virginia: A Case Study of Black Power in a Southern Urban Area,", p. 12.

67. Richmond *Afro-American and Richmond Planet*, January 29, 1983, pp. C9, C2, C8, C9–C10.

68. Bunche, *Political Status of the Negro*, pp. 131, 438; Andrew Buni, *The Negro in Virginia Politics, 1902–1965*, pp. 121–22.

69. Buni, *Negro in Virginia Politics*, p. 123.

70. Ibid., pp. 153–55; Richmond *Afro-American*, January 29, 1983, p. F2.

71. Buni, *Negro in Virginia Politics*, p. 157; Richmond *Afro-American*, January 29, 1983, p. F2; Richmond Citizens' Association, *Workers' Guide, 1947 Charter Campaign*; Richmond *Times-Dispatch*, October 27, 1947; Dwight Carter Holton, "Power to the People: The Struggle for Black Political Power in Richmond, Virginia," p. 31.

72. Holton, "Power to the People," pp. 43–46; Ladislas Segoe and Associates, *Recommended Plan of a System of Expressways for the Richmond Area, March 24, 1950*; Silver, *Twentieth Century Richmond*, pp. 183–97.

73. Holton, "Power to the People," p. 47.

74. Ibid., pp. 48–52; Richmond *Afro-American*, May 31, 1952.

75. Holton, "Power to the People," pp. 48–52.

3. School Desegregation and the Rise of Black Political Independence

1. See Morton Sosna, *In Search of the Silent South: Southern Liberals and the Race Issue*, pp. 121–39; Tucker, *Lieutenant Lee*, p. 138; Edward J. Meeman, *The Editorial We: A Posthumous Autobiography*, p. xx.

2. Virginius Dabney, *Across the Years*, p. 393.

3. Ibid., p. 392.

4. Ibid., p. 393.

5. Sosna, *In Search*, pp. 121–39. Sosna's chapter on Dabney also appears in Maurice Duke and Daniel P. Jordan, eds., *A Richmond Reader, 1733–1983*, pp. 381–97.

6. The editorial is included in the appendix of Dabney's *Across the Years*, pp. 391–96; the quote is from p. 394.

7. Ibid., pp. 394–96.

8. Ibid., pp. 164–65. Also see Sosna, *In Search*, p. 135–36.

9. Actually, the Southern Regional Council (SRC) was constructed on the foundations of an earlier organization, the Commission on Interracial Cooperation, that was formed after World War I to reduce the racial tensions and violence that had gripped the South after the war. Like the SRC, the Commission was headquartered in Atlanta and was biracial. For a discussion of the Commission, see Ann Wells Ellis,

"A Crusade against 'Wretched Attitudes': The Commission on Interracial Cooperation's Activities in Atlanta," pp. 21–44; Dabney, *Across the Years*, p. 164. Also see Harold H. Martin, *Ralph McGill, Reporter*, pp. 130–31, 187.

10. Hugh Davis Graham, *Crisis in Print: Desegregation and the Press in Tennessee*, pp. 40–41.

11. Calvin McLeod Logue, *Ralph McGill at Work*, pp. 73–77. For a good discussion of white southern liberals, see Sosna, *In Search*.

12. Virginius Dabney, telephone interview, May 23, 1985; Richond *Times-Dispatch*, May 18, 1954.

13. Richard Wilson, "Six Backed by RCA Win in Light Vote," Richmond *Times-Dispatch*, June 9, 1954, pp. 1, 5.

14. James Latimer, "No Specific Plans Voted at Meeting Here," Richmond *Times-Dispatch*, June 11, 1954, p. 1.

15. Doug McAdam, *Political Process and the Development of Black Insurgency, 1930–1970*, offers solid empirical evidence that widespread segregationist activity followed rather than triggered black protest (see pp. 142–43). See also Buni, *Negro in Virginia Politics*, p. 177; Numan V. Bartley, *The Rise of Massive Resistance: Race and Politics in the South during the 1950s*, pp. 143, 341.

16. Bartley, *Rise of Massive Resistance*, p. 82. See also Aldon D. Morris, *The Origins of the Civil Rights Movement: Black Communities Organizing for Change*, pp. 48, 81–82.

17. James Jackson Kilpatrick, *The Southern Case for School Segregation*, p. 8; Bartley, *Rise of Massive Resistance*, pp. 126–29.

18. Bartley, *Rise of Massive Resistance*, pp. 131–32. See also J. Harvie Wilkinson, III, *Harry Byrd and the Changing Face of Virginia Politics, 1945–1966* p. 129.

19. Bartley, *Rise of Massive Resistance*, p. 131.

20. Wilkinson, *Harry Byrd*, p. 128.

21. Massive Resistance legislation plus the antecedents of the legislation are discussed thoroughly in several works, including Robbins L. Gates, *The Making of Massive Resistance: Virginia's Politics of Public School Desegregation, 1954–1956*; James W. Ely, Jr., *The Crisis of Conservative Virginia: The Byrd Organization and the Politics of Massive Resistance*; and Benjamin Muse, *Virginia's Massive Resistance*.

22. Muse, *Virginia's Massive Resistance*, p. 47; Buni, *Negro in Virginia Politics*, pp. 185–86.

23. Buni, *Negro in Virginia Politics*, p. 187; Muse, *Virginia's Massive Resistance*, p. 48; "Number of Registered Voters," October 5, 1957, and October 4, 1958, Office of the Registrar, Richmond, Virginia.

24. Gates, *Making of Massive Resistance*, p. 154; Wilkinson, *Harry Byrd*, pp. 125–27; Population figures for 1956 were interpolated by using 1950 and 1960 census tract data from the U.S. Bureau of the Census. Voter-registration figures for 1956 were acquired from the Office of the Registrar, Richmond, Virginia.

25. Buni, *Negro in Virginia Politics*, p. 154; See also Dickinson, "Myths and Manipulations," pp. 24–25; 12–14.

26. See Rutledge M. Dennis, "Du Bois and the Role of the Educated Elite," pp. 388–402; John V. Moeser and Rutledge M. Dennis, *The Politics of Annexation: Oligarchic Power in a Southern City*, p. 34.

27. Dwight Carter Holton, " 'Power to the People'," pp. 65–67.

28. Ibid., pp. 69–73.

29. Oscar Renal Williams, III, "The Civil Rights Movement in Richmond and Petersburg, Virginia, During 1960," M.A. thesis, Virginia State University, 1990, pp. 40–49.

30. Holton, " 'Power to the People'," p. 73; John V. Moeser and Rutledge M. Dennis, "The Role of an Urban Elite in a Municipal Annexation Dispute," *Urban Affairs Papers* 2 (4) (Fall 1980): 7.

31. Moeser and Dennis, "Role of Urban Elite," pp. 8–10, 12; Allan Statton Hammock, "The Leadership Factor in Black Politics: The Case of Richmond, Virginia," Ph.D. diss., University of Virginia, 1977, p. 50.

32. Bartley, *Rise of Massive Resistance*, p. 275; Gates, *Making of Massive Resistance*, pp. 210–13; Lori L. Herrell, "Segregation, Desegregation, Resegregation: Legal Efforts for Integration of Richmond Public Schools," p. 3.

33. Richmond *News Leader*, August 1960, quoted in James A. Sartain and Rutledge M. Dennis, "Richmond, Virginia: Massive Resistance without Violence," in Charles V. Willie and Susan Greenblatt, eds., *Community Politics and Educational Change: Ten School Systems under Court Order* (New York: Longman, 1981), pp. 221–22.

34. Ely, *Crisis of Conservative Virginia*, pp. 134–35. See also Mildred Davis Bruce, "The Richmond School Board and the Desegregation of Richmond Public Schools, 1954–1971," p. 96.

35. Ed Grimsley, "Building of Two Schools Authorized by Council," Richmond *Times-Dispatch*, May 7, 1960, p. 4; Edward A. Mearns, Jr., "Virginia," in U.S. Commision on Civil Rights, *Civil Rights U.S.A.: Public Schools, Southern States, 1962* (New York: Greenwood, 1968), pp. 190–91; Moeser and Dennis, *The Politics of Annexation*, pp. 35–41; Ely, *Crisis of Conservative Virginia*, pp. 181–82.

36. Gary C. Leedes and James M. O'Fallon, "School Desegregation in Richmond: A Case History," p. 3; Sartain and Dennis, "Richmond, Virginia," p. 219; James L. Doherty, *Race and Education in Richmond*, p. 57.

37. Robert A. Pratt, *The Color of Their Skin: Education and Race in Richmond, Virginia, 1954–1989*, p. 27. See also Mark Johnson, "Strife That Was Avoided Made Sit-In News Here."

38. Bruce, "Richmond School Board and Desegregation," pp. 87–89, 91.

39. *Warden et al. v. School Board of the City of Richmond et al.*, civ. no. 2819, E.D. Va., July 5, 1961, 6 *Race Relations Law Reporter* 1025 (1961).

40. Leedes and O'Fallon, *School Desegregation in Richmond*, pp. 1–2.

41. Ibid., p. 5–6.

42. See Herrell, "Segregation, Desegregation, Resegregation;" p. 7; Leedes and O'Fallon, "School Desegregation in Richmond," pp. 6–9; Sartain and Dennis, "Richmond, Virginia," pp. 222–23.

43. Herrell, "Segregation, Desegregation, Resegregation," pp. 8–10; Leedes and O'Fallon, "School Desegregation in Richmond," pp. 9–14; Sartain and Dennis, "Richmond, Virginia," pp. 223–24.

44. Bartley, *Rise of Massive Resistance*, pp. 143–44, 288.

45. Tennessee Code, Section 49–1742, quoted by Willie W. Herenton, "A Historical Study of School Desegregation in the Memphis City Schools, 1954–1970," pp. 54–56.

46. Robert Lee Walker, "Equality or Inequality: A Comparative Study of Segregated Public Education in Memphis, Tennessee, 1862 to 1954," pp. 5–6; Herenton,

"Historical Study of School Desegregation," pp. 59–62; Tucker, *Memphis since Crump*, pp. 118–19.

47. Harry Holloway, *The Politics of the Southern Negro: From Exclusion to Big City Organization*; Tucker, *Memphis since Crump*, p. 119.

48. Herenton, "Historical Study of School Desegregation," p. 54; Tucker, *Memphis since Crump*, pp. 51–52.

49. William E. Wright, *Memphis Politics: A Study in Racial Bloc Voting*, p. 6; Tucker, *Memphis since Crump*, p. 77. No official voter-registration figures prior to 1958 are available for Memphis. The 1955 registration figures are taken from Tucker's *Memphis since Crump*.

50. Melton, "Blacks in Memphis," pp. 315–16; Scott, *Negro in Tennessee Politics*, 118–20; Wright, *Memphis Politics*, p. 6; Jones, "Dr. Joseph Edison Walker," p. 12.

51. Melton, "Blacks in Memphis," p. 317; Walker, cited in Scott, *Negro in Tennessee*, p. 118; Tucker, *Memphis since Crump*, pp. 64–65.

52. Melton, "Blacks in Memphis," pp. 318–19.

53. Ibid., pp. 330–31; David M. Tucker, *Black Pastors and Leaders: Memphis, 1819–1972*, pp. 107–10.

54. Wright, *Memphis Politics*, p. 6; Tucker, *Black Pastors*, p. 110–11; Tucker, *Memphis since Crump*, p. 77; Melton, "Blacks in Memphis," p. 331.

55. Cited in Wright, *Memphis Politics*, p. 6; U.S. Commission on Civil Rights, *Hearings before the U.S. Civil Rights Commission*, held in Memphis Tennessee, January 25–26, 1962, p. 130.

56. Tucker, *Memphis since Crump*, p. xi.

57. Stephen M. Findlay, "The Role of Bi-Racial Organizations in the Integration of Public Facilities in Memphis, Tennessee, 1954–1964," pp. 7–8; Ann Trotter, "The Memphis Business Community and Integration," in Elizabeth Jacoway and David R. Colburn, eds., *Southern Businessmen and Desegregation* (Baton Rouge: Louisiana State Univ. Press, 1982), pp. 282–300; Tucker, *Memphis since Crump*, pp. 85–86; Holloway, *Politics of Southern Negro*, p. 281.

58. Melton, "Blacks in Memphis, "p. 334; Tucker, *Memphis since Crump*, pp. 82–83, 85–86; Findlay, "Role of Bi-Racial Organizations," pp. 11, 13.

59. Tucker, *Memphis since Crump*, p. 85; "Mayor Orgill's Statement Regarding Segregation," Edmund Orgill Papers; Orgill to Gordon Hollingsworth, March 15, 1956, Orgill Papers.

60. Tucker, *Memphis since Crump*, pp. 84–85.

61. Selma S. Lewis, "Social Religion and the Memphis Sanitation Strike," pp. 66–70; Trotter, "Memphis Business Community," p. 286; Findlay, "Role of Bi-Racial Organizations," pp. 10–12, 14–15.

62. For a good discussion of the forces that contributed to the creation of the MCCR, see Findlay, "Role of Bi-Racial Organizations," pp. 12–20. See also Benjamin Muse, *Memphis*, pp. 17–22; Lewis, "Social Religion," p. 72; Tucker, *Memphis since Crump*, pp. 119–21.

63. Trotter, "Memphis Business Community," pp. 286–87; Muse, *Memphis*, pp. 21–22; Lewis, "Social Religion," pp. 73–74; Tucker, *Memphis since Crump*, pp. 29, 126; Findlay, "Role of Bi-Racial Organizations," p. 29.

64. Jones, "Dr. Joseph Edison Walker," pp. 16–18; Tucker, *Memphis since Crump*, p. 97.

65. Holloway, *Politics of the Southern Negro*, p. 281; Tucker, *Memphis since Crump*, p. 101; Wright, *Memphis Politics*, pp. 7, 9.

66. Wright, *Memphis Politics*, p. 9.

67. Memphis, Tennessee, Office of the Registrar, City Registration Figures for 1959; Scott, *Negro in Tennessee Politics*, p. 144.

68. Wright, *Memphis Politics*, p. 15.

69. Tucker, *Memphis since Crump*, pp. 96, 102–105; Wright, *Memphis Politics*, pp. 17–18.

70. Wright, *Memphis Politics*, p. 20.

71. Ibid., pp. 24–25; Tucker, *Black Pastors and Leaders*, p. 112.

72. Wright, *Memphis Politics*, p. 12.

73. Ibid., pp. 28–31. See also Lamon, *Blacks in Tennessee*, p. 104.

74. Wright, *Memphis Politics*, pp. 30–35. See also Holloway, *Politics of the Southern Negro*, pp. 282–86.

75. Herenton, "Historical Study of School Desegregation," p. 64; Russell Sugarmon, Jr., "Breaking the Color Line in Memphis, Tennessee," in Alan F. Westin, ed., *Freedom Now!*, p. 165. Also, for a good discussion of the Memphis sit-ins, see U.S. Commission on Civil Rights, *Hearings before the U.S. Commission on Civil Rights*, pp. 94–112.

76. Herenton, "Historical Study of School Desegregation," pp. 64–66.

77. Muse, quoted in Holloway, *Politics of the Southern Negro*, p. 287; U.S. Commission on Civil Rights, *Hearings before the U.S. Commission on Civil Rights*, pp. 107–08.

78. U.S. Commission on Civil Rights, *Hearings before the U.S. Commission on Civil Rights*, p. 145; Tucker, *Memphis since Crump*, pp. 121–22; G.W. Foster, Jr., "Memphis," in U.S. Commission on Civil Rights, *Civil Rights U.S.A.: Public Schools, Southern States, 1962*, (New York: Greenwood, 1968), p. 145; Stimbert, cited in Tucker, *Memphis since Crump*, p. 122.

79. Foster, "Memphis," pp. 144–45.

80. Ibid., pp. 147–48; U.S. Commission on Civil Rights, *Hearings before the U.S. Commission on Civil Rights*, p. 14.

81. Foster, "Memphis," p. 145.

82. Ibid., p. 148; cited in the *Washington Post*, October 4, 1961, p. A5.

83. Foster, "Memphis," p. 148; "A Race Relations Chronicle," *Memphis* 8 (October 1983): 54.

84. Herenton, "Historical Study of School Desegregation," pp. 67–68.

85. Ibid., pp. 70–75.

86. Ibid., pp. 76–82.

87. Ibid., pp. 83–92.

88. See, for example, Numan Bartley's *The Rise of Massive Resistance*, pp. 128–29, pp. 75, 131, 137, 236.

89. Quoted in ibid., pp. 218–19; pp. 54, 75, 182–83, 223–24.

90. Virginia H. Hein, "The Image of 'A City Too Busy to Hate': Atlanta in the 1960s," p. 207.

91. Bartley, *Rise of Massive Resistance*, p. 332; Alton Hornsby, Jr., "A City That Was Too Busy to Hate," in Jacoway and Colburn, *Southern Businessmen and Desegregation*, p. 124.

92. Hein, "Image," pp. 205–06.

93. Harold H. Martin, *William Berry Hartsfield: Mayor of Atlanta*, pp. 134–36.

94. Hein, "Image," p. 205; Bartley, *Rise of Massive Resistance*, p. 333.

95. Ivan Allen, Jr., with Paul Hemphill, *Mayor: Notes on the Sixties*, p. 32.

96. Allen, *Mayor*, pp. 32–33; Clarence N. Stone, *Regime Politics: Governing Atlanta, 1946–1988*, p. 47; Bartley, *Rise of Massive Resistance*, p. 334.

97. McGill, cited in Logue, *Ralph McGill*, p. 230; Stone, *Regime Politics*, p. 47; Bartley, *Rise of Massive Resistance*, p. 335; Hornsby, "City Too Busy to Hate," p. 126.

98. Hornsby, "City Too Busy to Hate," p. 127.

99. Martin, *Ralph McGill*, p. 179; Hornsby, "City Too Busy to Hate," pp. 128, 131–32.

100. Hornsby, "City Too Busy to Hate," p. 133.

101. Bacote, "Negro in Atlanta Politics," p. 344.

102. Ibid.

103. Ibid. See also Mary Louise Frick, "Influences on Negro Political Participation in Atlanta, Georgia," p. 17.

104. In some respects, Georgia's county unit system was similar in operation to the national Electoral College for presidential elections. Under the system each county was given unit votes equal to twice the number of members the county had in the Georgia House of Representatives. In an election the winner of a plurality of popular votes would receive the county's entire unit vote. Given the malapportioned state legislature in which rural populations had a disproportionate share of the seats, the county unit system clearly hurt politicians whose support resided largely in urban areas. In some cases, a rural vote was worth thirty times the vote coming from a city. See Frick, "Influences," pp. 17–18.

105. Bacote, "Negro in Atlanta Politics," pp. 345–46; Robert A. Holmes, "The University and Politics in Atlanta: A Case Study of the Atlanta University Center," pp. 52–53; Martin, *William Hartsfield*, p. 50; Frick, "Influences," p. 50.

106. Martin, *William Hartsfield*, pp. 50–51; Stone, *Regime Politics*, pp. 29–30.

107. Holmes, "The University and Politics," p. 53; Frick, "Influences," pp. 51–63; William Hartsfield, cited in Martin, *William Hartsfield*, pp. 46, 87–89; Hein, "Image," p. 209.

108. William Charles Hamann, "A Study of Voting Participation, 1945–1955, in an All Negro Precinct in Atlanta, Georgia," p. 63; Bacote, "Negro in Atlanta Politics," p. 349.

109. Stone, *Regime Politics*, pp. 30–31; cited in Martin, *William Hartsfield*, pp. 41–42.

110. Martin, *William Hartsfield*, p. 68.

111. Holmes, "The University and Politics," p. 7; Mays, *Born to Rebel*, p. 289.

112. Ibid. Mays, *Born to Rebel*, p. 290.

113. Holmes, "The University and Politics," p. 7.

114. Jack L. Walker, "The Functions of Disunity: Negro Leadership in a Southern City," pp. 228–29. See also Jack L. Walker, "Protest and Negotiation: A Case Study of Negro Leadership in Atlanta, Georgia," p. 116–17; Mays, *Born to Rebel*, pp. 290–92; John V. Petrof, "The Effect of Student Boycotts upon Purchasing Habits of Negro Families in Atlanta, Georgia," pp. 266–70.

115. Mays, *Born to Rebel*, p. 293; Stephen Burman, "The Illusion of Progress: Race and Politics in Atlanta, Georgia," p. 445.

116. Allen, *Mayor*, p. 36.

117. William B. Hartsfield, Oral History Interview, January 6, 1966, Special Collections, Robert W.Woodruff Library, Emory University, Atlanta, pp. 5–6.

118. Ibid., pp. 7–18.

119. Ibid., pp. 8, 12–13. See also Allen, *Mayor*, pp. 36–37; Walker, "Functions of Disunity," p. 229.

120. Allen, *Mayor*, pp. 37–38; Fred Powledge, *Black Power, White Resistance: Notes on the New Civil War*, p. 105.

121. Mays, *Born to Rebel*, p. 293; Hornsby, "City Too Busy to Hate," p. 135; Allen, *Mayor*, p. 39.

122. Allen, *Mayor*, pp. 39–42.

123. Walker, "Functions of Disunity" and "Protest and Negotiation."

124. Hein, "Image," pp. 206–07; Stone, *Regime Politics*, p. 103; McGill, cited in Logue, *Ralph McGill*, p. 225.

125. Hornsby, "Negro in Atlanta Politics," pp. 9–11.

126. Ibid., pp. 11–12.

127. Barbara L. Jackson, "Desegregation: Atlanta Style," p. 47.

128. Stone, *Regime Politics*, p. 103, 60–67.

129. Jackson, "Desegregation," pp. 47–48.

130. Ibid., p. 47; Stone, *Regime Politics*, pp. 104–06.

4. Neighborhood Restructuring

1. Charles W. Williams, Jr., "Two Black Communities in Memphis"; Mary W. Scott, *Old Richmond Neighborhoods*; White, "Black Sides of Atlanta," pp. 199–225; Homer Hoyt, *The Structure and Growth of Residential Neighborhoods in American Cities*.

2. See Mark I. Gelfand, *A Nation of Cities: The Federal Government and Urban America, 1933–1965*.

3. Norman J. Johnston, "Harland Bartholomew: His Comprehensive Plans and the Science of City Planning"; Harland Bartholomew, "Neighborhood Rehabilitation and the Taxpayer," p. 57; Reginald Isaacs, "The Neighborhood Unit as an Instrument for Segregation," pp. 215–19; Harland Bartholomew, *A Report upon the Comprehensive City Plan*, and *A Master Plan for the Physical Development of the City, Richmond, Virginia*.

4. William B. Hartsfield to W.H. Aiken et al., December 8, 1952, West Side Mutual Development Committee Papers (WSMDC); Robert B. Fairbanks, "The Good Government Machine: The Citizens Charter Association and Dallas Politics, 1930–1960," pp. 133–34.

5. W.H. Aiken et al. to Frank Carter, March 27, 1953, WSMDC papers. Ronald H. Bayor contends that the work of the WSMDC demonstrated the ability of Atlanta blacks to influence (but not dominate) postwar urban policy in the city. "At no time were blacks totally at the mercy of white planners and city officials. The initial movement into the westside before 1945 and the usually successful attempts afterward to expand their residential area indicate that black leaders were not powerless." See "Spatial and Racial Planning in Atlanta," p. 2.

6. *Atlanta Constitution*, December 1, 1934; Charles F. Palmer, *Adventures of a Slum Fighter*; Arnold, "Public Housing," pp. 9–18.

7. Howard Weaver Pollard, "The Effect of Techwood Homes on Urban Development in the United States," pp. 25, 27, 30, 34–35; M.D. Carrel to Colonel Horatio B. Hackett, May 19, 1934, Memorandum on Atlanta Housing Project, File H-1100, Record Group 196, Records of the Public Housing Administration (PHA). Pollard, "Effect of Techwood Homes," pp. 36–37.

8. Pollard, "Effect of Techwood Homes," p. 38; Arnold, "Public Housing," pp. 28–29.

9. Pollard, "Effect of Techwood Homes," p. 19; Atlanta *Journal*, September 30, 1934; Frederic J. Paxom to Frances Perkins, March 6, 1934; Application of the Home Improvement League, Atlanta, January 29, 1934; Renewal of Application, Home Improvement League, Atlanta, August 31, 1935, F-H432, PHA.

10. Memorandum and Report on Techwood and University Housing Projects, Atlanta, Georgia, January 9, 1934, File-H-1100, PHA.

11. Arnold, "Public Housing," pp. 44–56.

12. Memphis Housing Authority, *Ten Years in Housing*, p. 18; Sigafoos, *Cotton Row*, pp. 179–80, 182; Tucker, *Memphis since Crump*, chap. 1.

13. Roger Biles, *Memphis in the Great Depression*, pp. 94–96.

14. *Memphis World*, February 28, 1947; October 22, 1948; May 10, August 12, 1955; Melton, "Blacks in Memphis," pp.308–09.

15. *Memphis World*, June 10, 24, November 18, 28, 1952.

16. Memphis *Commercial Appeal*, February 20; August 18, 1956; Memphis *Press-Scimitar*, January 9, 1956; February 25, 1958.

17. Silver, *Twentieth Century Richmond*, pp. 146–48, 150–54, 166–67, 196, 264, 270, 297.

18. Jones, "Human Misery;" Richmond *Times-Dispatch*, September 4, 5; October 2, 1940; Richmond *New Leader,* February 26, August 21, 1941, April 24, 1942; April 28, 1943; Silver, *Twentieth Century Richmond,* p. 150–54; Negro Housing and Miscellaneous Correspondence, Records of the War Industries Board, National Archives, Washington, D.C.

19. For a detailed discussion of the highway controversy in Richmond, see Silver, *Twentieth Century Richmond*, pp. 183–97; The slashing editorials of James J. Kilpatrick in the Richmond *News Leader* during the 1950s rallied the opponents of the public housing and slum-clearance initiatives of the Richmond Redevelopment and Housing Authority. Although successful in preventing Richmond involvement in urban renewal until the late 1950s, and even then through a relatively small effort, the construction of public housing proceeded briskly, largely to accommodate blacks displaced by a variety of public improvements projects, especially highways construction.

20. Atlanta *Journal and Constitution*, July 28, 1968, quoted in Arnold, "Public Housing," pp. 65–66; Atlanta Metropolitan Planning Commission, *Up Ahead* (Atlanta: The Commisssion, 1952), p. 58. The American Public Health Association published *Planning the Neighborhood* (1948), which underscored the risk of planned integration and recommended adherence to the principle that neighborhood planning should safeguard existing social relations and not introduce change. See Samuel Adams, "Blueprint for Segregtion: A Survey of Atlanta Housing," p. 77.

21. O'Connor, "Racial Residential Barriers in Atlanta," p. 104; "Governor Gets in Mozeley Park Row," *Atlanta Journal*, February 15, 1949; "Mayor Tries to End Row over Negro Home Limits," Atlanta *Constitution*, February 15, 1949; Dan Carter, "Compromise Effected in Mozeley Park Row"; Thompson, Lewis, and McEntire, "Atlanta and Birmingham," pp. 26–30.

22. Thompson, Lewis, and McEntire, "Atlanta and Birmingham," p. 30; White, "Black Side of Atlanta," p. 220.

23. Robert C. Stuart to W.O. Duvall, March 19, 1954; Memorandum on Recent Development Concerning Center Hill-Grove Park; Stuart to Marvin Overstreet, President, West Side Corporation, March 12, 1956, WSMDC Papers.

24. Stuart to Overstreet, pp. 2–3; Stuart to Duvall, March 19, 1954; William B. Hartsfield to Charles Donaldson, Chief of Construction, City of Atlanta, March 20, 1954, WSMDC Papers.

25. Atlanta Urban League, *A Report of the Housing Activities of the Atlanta Urban League, November 28, 1951,* WSMDC Papers.

26. Thompson, Lewis, and McEntire, "Atlanta and Birmingham," pp. 22–25.

27. Stuart to Hartsfield, January 10, 1957; "Policy Statement by West Mutual Development Committee, Draft for Staff Discussion, July 23, 1958, WSMDC Papers.

28. Ibid.

29. "Immediate Needed Community Improvements," memorandum to WSMDC by the EREB, March 8, 1955; Hartsfield to Stuart, March 5, 1955; "Agreement between Southwest Citizens Association et al.," February 18, 1954, WSMDC Papers; Ronald Bayor, "Roads to Racial Segregation: Atlanta in the Twentieth Century."

30. Letter to Collier Heights Residents from WSMDC and Advisory Panel, March 5, 1954; Letter to Collier Heights Residents from Advisory Panel, February 11, 1954; Collier Heights Civic Club, "Committee Report" (including map), January 15, 1954; S.B. Avery, Present of Southwest Citizens Association to Members of the Atlanta Real Estate Board, January 28, 1954.

31. Memorandum, Stuart to C.R. Allen, November 26, 1956; Letter from WSMDC to Friend in the Delmar Lane Area, November 8, 1956; "To Real Estate Brokers and Home Mortgage Brokers," WSMDC, January 14, 1955; Memorandum, Stuart to Adamsville Civic Representatives, January 14, 1955; Stuart to Hartfield, July 29, 1958, WSMDC Papers.

32. Draft, "Proposal for West Atlanta Planning Council," December 23, 1953, discussed September 20, 1954, WSMDC Papers.

33. George Goodwin to Stuart, January 25, 1954; Memorandum, Wyont B. Bean and Stuart to Mayor and Board of Aldermen, City of Atlanta, August 20, 1958; S.B. Avery to Hartsfield, March 24, 1955, with the following P.S. to Stuart: "I trust the committee (WSMDC) will be expanded as we have so often discussed"; Stuart, "Outline Draft of Atlanta Plan for Race Relations," July 16, 1955; Robert Thompson, "Some Factors Affecting Race Relations in Atlanta, Georgia," typed ms., December 13, 1956, WSMDC Papers.

34. Memorandum, "Report on Grove Park Transition Area," August 26, 1960, WSMDC Papers.

35. Stuart to E.A. Gilliam, Alderman, City of Atlanta, February 6, 1957, WSMDC Papers.

36. Memorandum, Stuart to Bob Allen, April 2, 1957, re: Preliminary Thoughts on Neighborhood Improvement Program; Memorandum, Bob Allen to Stuart, April 5, 1957, re: More Preliminary Thoughts on a Neighborhood Improvement Program, WSMDC Papers.

37. Burt Sparer, Regional Planner, Metropolitian Planning Commission to Hartsfield, January 28, 1958.

38. *Annexation: A Must for a Growing Memphis,* p. 4; Memphis *Commercial Appeal,*

August 25, 1957; see Edmund Orgill Papers, especially Orgill to Edward R. Richmond, June 6, 1957, Mississippi Valley Collection, Memphis State University.

39. Memphis *Commercial Appeal*, February

40. Charles A. Caldwell, "War Declared on Slums, Meeting Plans Attack"; Robert Gray, "Way to End Slums Pictured in Report to City's Officials"; James Gunter, "$3,362,538 in Federal Money Allocated to Memphis for Job of Clearing, Using Slum Areas"; Memphis *Commercial Appeal*, July 7, 8, 10, 1957.

41. "Clubs Will Protest Negro Housing Plan," Memphis *Commercial Appeal*, February 25, 1958; Orgill to W.D. Galbreath, Jr., and Fred Davis, n.d., in Memphis-Shelby County Planning Commission, 1959 Folder, Mayor's Files, Memphis-Shelby County Public Library Archives; Orgill to Commissioner Claude A. Armour, July 9, 1957, Orgill Papers; Memphis *Press-Scimitar*, February 25, 1958; Tucker, *Memphis since Crump*, pp. 65–78, 95, 98–99.

42. *Master Plan for Richmond, 1946*, pp. 13–14, 21, 57, 128, 130–33, 151; Harland Bartholomew, "The Neighborhood—Key to Urban Redemption," pp. 243–47.

43. Richmond Department of Public Works, *Statistical Data Relative to Housing*.

44. Richmond *Times-Dispatch*, February 16; March 29; October 16, 1950; April 1, September 28, 1952; Richmond *News Leader*, November 21, 1951; April 1, July 12, 22, September 23, October 3, 9, 10, 27, November 7, 10, 11, 17, 1952.

45. Richmond *Afro-American*, June 24, 1954.

46. Richmond *News Leader*, June 30, July 1, 12, 19, August 4, 6, 7, 9, 1955.

47. Silver, *Twentieth Century Richmond*, pp. 227–29.

48. Richmond *Times-Dispatch*, January 14, 15, 19, 1957, March 16, 17, 1959.

49. Eric Hill Associates, *City of Atlanta, Georgia Report on Relocation of Individuals, Families and Businesses: Atlanta Community Improvement Program*; Clarence Stone, *Economic Growth and Neighborhood Discontent: Systems Bias in the Urban Renewal Program of Atlanta*, p. 4; Bayor, "Expressways," p. 3.

50. Stone, *Economic Growth*, pp. 35–36.

51. Ibid., p. 48; *Up Ahead*, p. 57; Bradley R. Rice, "Atlanta: If Dixie Were Atlanta," pp. 35–36. See also Bradley R. Rice, "The Battle of Buckhead: The Plan of Improvement and Atlanta's Last Big Annexation," pp. 5–22; Douglas Cater, "Atlanta: Smart Politics and Good Race Relations," p. 21.

52. Stone, *Economic Growth*, pp. 52–53; Bayor, "Expressways," p. 4.

53. Stone, *Economic Growth*, pp. 58–64; Atlanta *Daily World*, March 23, 1950.

54. Stone, *Economic Growth*, pp. 64–67.

55. Ibid., pp. 67–69.

56. Ibid., p. 70.

57. See Chapter 3 for a discussion of the Allen mayoralty in Atlanta.

58. U.S. Commission on Civil Rights, *Hearing, Atlanta*, p. 542, 547.

59. Stone, *Economic Growth*, pp. 72–73; memorandum, "Rough Draft Comments of Study Areas," Housing Needs (Negro), Metropolitan Planning Commission, Confidential Draft, as Adopted, February 3, 1959; discussion outline, Confidential Special Meeting on Housing Needs, Citizens Advisory Committee on Urban Renewal, February 4, 1959, WSMDC Papers.

60. Stone, *Economic Growth*, p. 80; Joseph Gross, "A Survey of Housing Needs in the City of Atlanta," prepared for the Urban Renewal Department of the City of Atlanta, 1958; "First Speech to Empire Real Estate Board," September 1959, typed

notes, James Parham, Housing Coordinator, Atlanta Metropolitan Planning Commission, WSMDC Papers.

61. Rufus E. Clements, President, Atlanta University to Stuart, August 18, 1955, WSMDC Papers.

62. Stone, *Economic Growth*, p. 95.

63. Ibid., pp. 99–106.

64. Ibid., pp. 107–09.

65. Ibid., p. 113.

66. Bayor, "Expressways," p. 8.

67. Ibid., pp. 9–13; Samuel Ira Spector, "Municipal and County Zoning in a Changing Urban Environment," pp. 5–6.

68. Allen, *Mayor*, pp. 71–72; Bayor, "Roads to Segregation," p. 15.

69. Allen, *Mayor*, p. 90; Southern Regional Council, "Proposed Immediate Steps on the Immediate Problem: Housing Discrimination and Low-Cost Housing Shortages," n.d., Southern Regional Council Papers, Woodruff Library, Atlanta University, cited in Bayor, "Roads to Segregation."

70. See Karl E. Taeuber, "Residential Segregation in the Atlanta Metropolitan Area," pp. 155–56; Bayor, "Expressways," p. 20; Hein, "Image," pp. 218–19.

71. Hornsby, "Negro in Atlanta Politics," pp. 20–21.

5. Race, Class, and the New Urban Politics

1. Michael Paul Williams, "Sharp or Subtle, Lines of Race, Wealth, Culture Persist," p. 1.

2. Richard C. Wade, "The Enduring Ghetto: Urbanization and the Color Line in American History," p. 6; Paul Peterson, "The Urban Underclass and the Poverty Paradox," p. 4.

3. Wilson, *Disadvantaged*, pp. 137–38.

4. David Rusk, *Cities without Suburbs*.

5. Robert H. Thomas, "Black Suburbanization and Housing Quality in Atlanta," p. 26; Christopher Silver, "Housing Policy and Suburbanization: An Analysis of the Changing Quality and Quantity of Black Housing in Suburbia since 1950," in Jamshid A. Momeni, ed., *Race, Ethnicity, and Minority Housing in the United States*, p. 69–88; David R. Goldfield, "Black Political Power and Public Policy in the Urban South," p. 172.

6. Carla J. Robinson, "Racial Disparity in the Atlanta Housing Market," pp. 85–109.

7. "Divided We Stand," Part II, Race and Resentment, Richmond *Times-Dispatch*, August 23, 1993.

8. Christopher Silver et al., "Survey of Vacant Residential Units in Richmond Core Neighborhoods."

9. U.S. Census, 1970 and 1980, Richmond Census Tracts.

10. See Henry Loeb Papers, correspondence with Paul Borda, Chairman of Memphis Housing Authority, in Memphis-Shelby County Public Library Archives, Memphis; and Public Record and Oral History Collection, Memphis Sanitation Strike and M.L. King, Jr., Assassination, Mississippi Valley Collection, Memphis State University, Memphis.

11. Borda to Loeb, September 21, 1970; Loeb to Mrs. Paul Kramer et al., August 22, 1968, Loeb Papers; Memphis *Press-Scimitar* (August 14, September 25, 1968).

12. Borda to Loeb, September 21, 1970; Jesse Turner to Loeb, n.d. (probably late 1968), Loeb Papers.

13. Loeb to Wyeth Chandler and Billy Hyman, September 21, 1970, Loeb Papers.

14. Division of Housing and Community Development, *APAC Recommendations, 1978–1981* (Memphis, March 1978).

15. Cited in Robert Bullard, "Blacks and the American Dream of Housing," p. 55. See also Karl Taeuber, "Racial Residential Segregation."

16. U.S. Department of Commerce, Bureau of Census, Census Tract Statistics for 1970, 1980, and 1990. In addition, Richmond, like Atlanta, would have become majority black in 1970 had it not been for the 1970 annexation of 47,000 whites from neighboring Chesterfield County. For a detailed account of the racial politics surrounding the annexation, see Moeser and Dennis, *The Politics of Annexation;* "Memphis Election System Challenged," *Atlanta Journal-Constitution,* 16 February 1991, p. A3.

17. Moeser and Dennis, *The Politics of Annexation.*

18. "Memphis Election System Challenged," p. A3; "Herenton Is Elected Mayor of Memphis by 172 Votes," *Wall Street Journal,* 7 October 1991, p. A16.

19. Roger Biles, "Black Mayors: A Historical Assessment," p. 114.

20. Dwight Carter Holton, " 'Power to the People'."

21. Hornsby, "Negro in Atlanta Politics," p. 25. See also Burman, "Illusion of Progress," pp. 445–46. On the black vote in the election, see Alton Hornsby, "Negro in Atlanta Politics," p. 26; Mack H. Jones, "Black Political Empowerment in Atlanta: Myth and Reality," p. 99; Stone, *Regime Politics,* pp. 78–79.

22. U.S. Department of Commerce, Bureau of Census, Census Tract Statistics for 1970 and 1980. Voting-age population was interpolated for the year 1973 by using 1970 and 1980 Census Tract Statistics as benchmark figures; voting-registration figures were acquired from the Office of the Georgia Secretary of State, Elections Division. Voter-registration figures for the City of Atlanta consist of the totals for those portions of Fulton and DeKalb counties falling inside the city's boundaries. To approximate the number of DeKalb County registered voters living in Atlanta, the authors examined the percentage of DeKalb registrants living in Atlanta from 1972 to 1984. Finding that for twelve out of the thirteen years between 1972 and 1984, 6 percent of all DeKalb registered voters lived in the city (in 1981 the figure was 5%), the authors applied the same percentage for each year from 1958 through 1971. On Masselli's loss of support, see Jones, "Black Political Empowerment," pp. 99–104; Duncan R. Jamieson, "Maynard Jackson's 1973 Election as Mayor of Atlanta," p. 16.

23. Jones, "Black Political Empowerment," pp. 107–08.

24. Stone, *Regime Politics,* pp. 85–91.

25. Jones, "Black Political Empowerment," p. 115; Stone, *Regime Politics,* pp. 92–94.

26. Carol Pierannunzi and John D. Hutcheson, Jr., "Electoral Change and Regime Maintenance: Maynard Jackson's Second Time Around," p. 152; Alton Hornsby, Jr., "Andrew Jackson Young: Mayor of Atlanta, 1982–1990," pp. 159, 159–82.

27. Kristine F. Anderson, "Atlanta's Jackson Back in Familiar Mayor Role," p. A6; Pierannunzi and Hutcheson, "Electoral Change and Regime Maintenance," p. 153; Anderson, "Atlanta's Jackson Back in Familiar Mayor Role"; Ronald Smother, "Councilman's Victory in Atlanta Mayoral Runoff Signals New Era," p. A16.

28. John V. Moeser, "City Politics since '48: Three Distinct Periods," p. F3.

29. Moeser and Dennis, *Politics of Annexation*, pp. 60–70. City of Richmond, Office of the Registrar.

30. Moeser and Dennis, *Politics of Annexation*, p. 181.

31. Peter J. Roggemann, "Does a Ward System Better Serve Low Income and Minority Neighborhoods? The Case of Richmond, Virginia," pp. 31, 44; Moeser, "City Politics since '48."

32. Tom Campbell, "Mrs. Dell Unseated; Leidinger Returned," p. A1.

33. Moeser, "City Politics since '48."

34. Biles, "Black Mayors," p. 121; Robert Holsworth, "Council Elections: Where Are the Issues?" *Style*, 10 May 1988, p. 59; Lisa Antonelli Bacon, "Roy West Evens the Score," *Style*, 6 October 1992, p. 17; Michael Paul Williams, "Williams Elected Mayor; McDaniel Is Vice Mayor," p. A1.

35. Rick Sauder, "City Council Facing Second Big Shake-Up," p. A1.

36. "Memphis Election System Challenged," p. A3.

37. Cynthia Mitchel, "Mayoral Race Splits Memphis Blacks," p. A3; Ronald Smothers, "Memphis Campaign is Racially Divisive," p. A14; Martha Brannigan, "Memphis, Poised to Elect a Black Mayor, Finds Blacks Can't Agree on a Candidate," p. A8.

38. Darryl Fears, "Honeymoon Is Over for Memphis Mayor," p. A3.

39. Goldfield, "Black Political Power," pp. 169–70; Eric Sundquist, "Violence Rules in Group Rest of U.S. Left Behind," *Richmond Times-Dispatch*, 15 June 1986, p. A1; Susan Chira, "Push for Better Schools in Memphis Takes on Importance for Nation."

40. William Schneider, "The Dawn of the Suburban Era in American Politics," pp. 33–44; Goldfield, "Black Political Power," pp. 171, 174; Lomax quoted in ibid., p. 179.

Bibliography

Primary Sources

Manuscripts

City of Atlanta, Bureau of Planning Records. Papers. Atlanta Historical Society.

City of Atlanta, Planning Commission. Papers. Atlanta Historical Society.

Hartsfield, William B. Oral interview, January 6, 1966. Special Collections, Robert W. Woodruff Library, Emory University, Atlanta.

"Mayor Orgill's Statement Regarding Segregation." Edmund Orgill Papers. Mississippi Valley Collection, Brister Library, Memphis State University.

Mayor's Files. Memphis-Shelby County Public Library Archives.

Negro Housing and Miscellaneous Correspondence. Records of the War Industries Board, National Archives, Washington, D.C.

Office of the Registrar. City Voter Registration Figures. Memphis, Tennessee.

Oral interview with Blair T. Hunt by Ronald Walter (typed transcript). Memphis-Shelby County Public Library, Memphis.

Public Record and Oral History Collection. Memphis Multimedia Archival Project: 1968 Sanitation Workers' Strike. Mississippi Valley Collection, Memphis State University, Memphis.

Records of the Federal Emergency Administration of Public Works, National Archives, Washington, D.C.

Records of the Public Housing Administration. National Archives, Washington, D.C.

Richmond City Planning Commission. Papers. Department Planning and Community Development Library, Richmond.

Voter Registration Figures. Office of the Registrar, Richmond, Virginia.

West Side Mutual Development Committee. Papers. Atlanta Bureau of Planning Files, Atlanta Historical Society.

Documents

Annexation: A Must for a Growing Memphis. (Memphis, September 1967).

Atlanta Urban League. *A Report of the Housing Activities of the Atlanta Urban League, November 28, 1951.* Revised June 18, 1951.

Bartholomew, Harland. *A Comprehensive City Plan, Memphis, Tennessee.* Memphis: City Plan Commission, 1924.

———. *A Master Plan for the Physical Development of the City, Richmond, Virginia.* Richmond: City Planning Commission, 1946.

———. *A Report on the Comprehensive City Plan, Memphis, Tennessee.* Memphis: City Planning Commission, 1940.

Carey et al. v. City of Atlanta et al. 143 Ga. 192, 84 S.E. 456 (1915).

City of Richmond et al. v. Deans. 37 F. (2nd) 712–713 (January 14, 1930).

Eric Hill Associates. City of Atlanta, Georgia Report on Relocation of Individuals, Families and Businesses: Atlanta Community Improvement Program. September 1966.

Harden v. City of Atlanta. 147 Ga. 248, 93 S.E. 401 (1917).

Kerner Commission. Report of the National Advisory Commission on Civil Disorders. New York: Dutton, 1968.

Ladislas Segoe and Associates. Recommended Plan of a System of Expressways for the Richmond Area, March 24, 1950. Richmond: City Planning Commission, 1950.

Memphis Housing Authority. Ten Years in Housing: Memphis Housing Authority, 1947–48 Annual Report. Memphis: Memphis Housing Authority, 1948.

Richmond Citizen's Association. Workers' Guide, 1947 Charter Campaign. Richmond: Richmond Citizens' Association, 1947.

Richmond Council of Social Agencies. The Negro in Richmond, Virginia. Richmond: Richmond Council of Social Agencies, 1929.

Richmond Department of Planning and Community Development. Conservation Plan for the Central Wards Conservation Area. Richmond: Planning and Community Development, 1976.

Richmond Department of Public Works. Statistical Data Relative to Housing. Richmond: Department of Public Works, 1939.

Ordinances and Resolutions of the City of Richmond, September 1910–August 1912. Richmond: Saunders, 1913.

Smith v. City of Atlanta. 161 Ga. 769, 132 S.E. 66 (1926).

U.S. Census of Population. 1940, 1950, 1960, and 1970. Statistics for Census Tracts, Atlanta, Memphis, and Richmond. Washington, D.C.

U.S. Commission on Civil Rights. Hearings before the U.S. Civil Rights Commission. Held in Memphis, Tennessee, January 25–26, 1962.

Newspapers

Atlanta Daily World, 1950.

Atlanta Journal and Constitution, 1934, 1949, 1960–69, 1991–92.

Baltimore Afro-American,1929–30.

Christian Science Monitor, 1991.

Memphis Commercial Appeal, 1953–58.

Memphis Press-Scimitar. 1953–56, 1968.

Memphis World. 1947–52.

New York Times. 1991–93.

Pittsburg Courier. 1943.

Richmond Afro-American and Richmond Planet. 1952–54, 1960, 1983–90.

Richmond News Leader. 1941–55, 1960.

Richmond Times-Dispatch. 1939–59, 1977, 1982–92.

Wall Street Journal. 1991.

Washington Post. 1961.

Secondary Sources

Abbott, Carl. The New Urban American: Politics in Sunbelt Cities. Chapel Hill: Univ. of North Carolina Press, 1981.

Adams, Samuel. "Blueprint for Segregation: A Survey of Atlanta Housing." New South 22 (Spring 1967).

Adkins, Walter P. "Beale Street Goes to the Polls." M.A. thesis, Ohio State Univ., 1935.

Alexander, Robert J. "Negro Business in Atlanta." *Southern Economics Journal* 17 (1951): 454–55.

Allen, Ivan Jr., with Paul Hemphill. *Mayor: Notes on the Sixties.* New York: Simon and Schuster, 1971.

Anderson, Elijah. *Streetwise: Race, Class and Change in an Urban Community.* Chicago: Univ. of Chicago Press 1990.

Anderson, Kristine F. "Atlanta's Jackson Back in Familiar Mayor Role." *Christian Science Monitor,* Sept. 12, 1991.

Arnold, Peter Edward. "Public Housing in Atlanta." *Atlanta Historical Bulletin* 13 (Sept. 1968): 9–18.

———. "Public Housing in Atlanta." M.A. thesis, Georgia State Univ., 1970.

Atlanta University. *Business Enterprise Owned and Operated by Negroes in Atlanta, Georgia, 1944.* Atlanta: Atlanta Univ., 1944.

Bacote, Clarence A. "The Negro in Atlanta Politics." *Phylon* (1955): 342–43.

Baker, Ray Stannard. *Following the Color Line.* New York: Doubleday, Page, 1908.

Bartholomew, Harland. "The Neighborhood—Key to Urban Redemption." *American Planning and Civic Annual.* Washington: American Planning and Civic Assoc., 1941, 243–47.

———. "Neighborhood Rehabilitation and the Taxpayer." *American City* 53 (Feb. 1938): 57.

Bartley, Numan V. *The Rise of Massive Resistance: Race and Politics in the South During the 1950s.* Baton Rouge: Louisiana State Univ. Press, 1969.

Bauman, John F. *Public Housing, Race and Renewal: Urban Planning in Philadelphia, 1920–1974.* Philadelphia: Temple Univ. Press, 1987.

Bayor, Ronald H. "Expressways, Urban Renewal and the Relocation of the Black Community in Atlanta." Unpublished paper, Organization of American Historians Conference, 1988.

———. "Roads to Racial Segregation: Atlanta in the Twentieth Century." *Journal of Urban History* 15 (Nov. 1988): 3–21.

———. "Spatial and Racial Planning in Atlanta." Unpublished paper, American Planning Association Conference, Atlanta, April 1989.

Berlin, Ira. *Slaves without Masters: The Free Negro in the Antebellum South.* New York: Pantheon, 1974.

Biles, Roger. "Black Mayors: A Historical Assessment." *Journal of Negro History* 77 (Summer 1992): 109–25.

———. *Memphis in the Great Depression.* Knoxville: Univ. of Tennessee Press, 1986.

Blassingame, John. "Before the Ghetto: The Making of the Black Community in Savannah, 1865–1880." *Journal of Social History* 6 (Summer 1973): 463–88.

Born, Kate. "Memphis Negro Workingmen and the NAACP." *West Tennessee Historical Society Papers* 28 (1974).

Branch, Anne L. "Atlanta and the American Settlement House Movement." *Atlanta Historical Bulletin* 12 (June 1967): 36–51.

Brannigan, Martha. "Memphis Poised to Elect a Black Mayor, Finds Blacks Can't Agree on a Candidate." *Wall Street Journal,* May 31, 1991.

Brownell, Blaine A. "The Commercial-Civic Elite and City Planning in Atlanta, Memphis and New Orleans in the 1920s." *Journal of Southern History* 41 (Aug. 1975): 339–68.

Brownell, Blaine A., and David R. Goldfield, eds. *The City in Southern History: The Growth of Urbanization in the South.* Port Washington, N.Y.: Kennikat Press, 1977.

Bruce, Mildred Davis. "The Richmond School Board and the Desegregation of Richmond Public Schools. 1954–1971." Ed.D diss., College of William and Mary, 1988.

Bullard, Robert D. "Blacks and the American Dream of Housing." In Jamshid A. Momeni, ed., *Race, Ethnicity and Minority Housing in the United States*, 53–68. Westport, Conn.: Greenwood, 1986.

Bunche, Ralph J. *The Political Status of the Negro in the Age of Franklin D. Roosevelt,*. Ed. and an introduction by Dewey H. Grantham. Chicago: Univ. of Chicago Press, 1973.

Buni, Andrew. *The Negro in Virginia Politics, 1902–1965*. Charlottesville: Univ. Press of Virginia, 1967.

Burman, Stephen. "The Illusion of Progress: Race and Politics in Atlanta, Georgia." *Ethnic and Racial Studies* (Oct. 1979).

Burrows, Edward F. "The Commission on Interracial Cooperation, 1919–1944: A Case History of the Interracial Movement in the South." Ph.D. diss., Univ. of Wisconsin, 1954.

Caldwell, Charles A. "War Declared on Slums, Meeting Plans Attack." Memphis *Press-Scimitar*, July 15, 1953.

Campbell, Tom. "Mrs. Dell Unseated; Leidinger Returned." *Richmond Times-Dispatch*, May 5, 1982.

Carter, Dan. "Compromise Effected in Mozeley Park Row." *Atlanta Journal*, Feb. 16, 1949.

Cater, Douglas. "Atlanta: Smart Politics and Good Race Relations." *Reporter*, July 1957.

Cayton, Horace R., and St. Clair Drake. *Black Metropolis: A Study of Negro Life in a Northern City*. New York: Harmont, Bromean, 1945.

Chira, Susan. "Push for Better Schools in Memphis Takes on Importance for Nation." *York Times*, Jan. 15, 1992, B-1.

Church, Annette E., and Roberta Church. *The Robert R. Churches of Memphis*. Ann Arbor, Michigan: Edward Brothers, 1974.

Clark, Kenneth B. *Dark Ghetto: Dilemmas of Social Power*. New York: Harper and Row, 1965.

Cowardin, Edward M., and Charles McGuigan. "Virginius Dabney." *Style Weekly*, Jan. 22, 1985.

Dabney, Virginius. *Across the Years*. Garden City, N.Y.: Doubleday, 1978.

Dennis, Rutledge M. "Du Bois and the Role of the Educated Elite." *Journal of Negro Education* 46 (Fall 1977): 388–402.

Dickinson, A.J. "Myth and Manipulation: The Story of the Crusade for Voters in Richmond, Virginia: A Case Study of Black Power in a Southern Urban Area." Honor's thesis, Yale Univ. 1967.

Doherty, James L. *Race and Education in Richmond*. Privately printed, 1972.

Duke, Maurice, and Daniel P. Jordan, eds. *A Richmond Reader, 1733–1983*. (Chapel Hill: Univ. of North Caroline Press, 1983.

Dunn, William, and Kevin Johnson. "Integration Not as Easy as Moving." *USA Today*, March 12, 1991.

Eisinger, Peter. *The Politics of Displacement: Racial and Ethnic Transition in Three American Cities*. New York: Academic Press, 1980.

Ellis, Ann Wells. "A Crusade against 'Wretched Attitudes': The Commission on Interracial Cooperation's Activities in Atlanta." *Atlanta Historical Journal* 23 (Spring 1979): 21–44.

Ely, James W., Jr. *The Crisis of Conservative Virginia: The Byrd Organization and the Politics of Massive Resistance*. Knoxville: Univ. of Tennessee Press, 1976.

Fairbanks, Robert. "The Good Government Machine: The Citizens Charter Association and Dallas Politics, 1930–1960." In Fairbanks Underwood and Kathleen

Underwood, eds., *Essays on Sunbelt Cities and Recent Urban America*. College Station: Texas A & M Univ. Press, 1990.

Fears, Darryl. "Honeymoon Is Over for Memphis Mayor." *Atlanta Journal and Constitution*, April 9, 1992.

Fennel, Dwight. "A Demographic Study of Black Business, 1905–1908, with Respect to the Race Riot of 1906." M.A. thesis, Atlanta Univ. 1977.

Findlay, Stephen M. "The Role of Bi-Racial Organizations in the Integration of Public Facilities in Memphis, Tennessee, 1954–1964." Unpublished research paper, History 7960, Memphis State Univ., 1975.

Flint, Barbara J. "Zoning and Residential Segregation: A Social and Physical History, 1910–1940." Ph.D. diss., Univ. of Chicago, 1977.

Foster, G.W., Jr. "Memphis." In U.S. Commission on Civil Rights, *Civil Rights U.S.A.: Public Schools, Southern States, 1962*. New York: Greenwood Press, 1968.

Fraser, Leigh D. "A Demographic Analysis of Memphis and Shelby County, Tennessee, 1820–1972." M.A. thesis, Memphis State Univ., 1974.

Frick, Mary Louise. "Influences on Negro Political Participation in Atlanta, Georgia." M.A. thesis, Georgia State College, 1967.

Gates, Robbins L. *The Making of Massive Resistance: Virginia's Politics of Public School Desegregation 1954–1956*. Chapel Hill: Univ. of North Carolina Press, 1962.

Gavins, Raymond. *The Perils and Prospects of Southern Black Leadership: Gordon Blaine Hancock, 1884–1970*. Durham: Duke Univ. Press, 1977.

Gelfand, Mark I. *A Nation of Cities; The Federal Government and Urban America, 1933–1965*. New York: Oxford Univ. Press, 1965.

Goldfield, David R. "Black Political Power and Public Policy in the Urban South." In Arnold R. Hirsch and Raymond A. Mohl, eds., *Urban Policy in Twentieth-Century America*, 169–170. New Brunswick, N.J.: Rutgers Univ. Press, 1993.

Goldsmith, William W., and Edward J. Blakely. *Separate Societies: Poverty and Inequality in U.S. Cities*. Philadelphia: Temple Univ. Press, 1992.

Graham, Hugh Davis. *Crisis in Print: Desegregation and the Press in Tennessee*. Nashville: Vanderbilt Univ. Press, 1967.

Gray, Robert. "Way to End Slums Pictured in Report to City's Officials." Memphis *Commercial Appeal*, Dec. 11, 1953.

Grimsley, Ed. "Building of Two Schools Authorized by Council." *Richmond Times-Dispatch*, May 7, 1960.

Gunter, James, "$3,362,538 in Federal Money Allocated to Memphis for Job of Clearing, Using Slum Areas. Memphis *Commercial Appeal*, Feb. 15, 1955.

Hamann, William Charles. "A Study of Voting Participation, 1945–1955, in an All Negro Precinct in Atlanta, Georgia." M.A. thesis, Emory Univ., 1955.

Hein, Virginia H. "The Image of 'A City Too Busy to Hate': Atlanta in the 1960s." *Phylon* (Fall 1972).

Herenton, Willie W. "A Historical Study of School Desegregation in the Memphis City Schools, 1954–1970." Ph.D. diss., Southern Illinois Univ., 1971.

Herrell, Lori L. "Segregation, Desegregation, Resegregation: Legal Efforts for Integration of Richmond Public Schools." Unpublished paper for History 490, Virginia Commonwealth University, 1985.

Hirsch, Arnold. *Making the Second Ghetto: Race and Housing in Chicago, 1940–1960*. Cambridge: Cambridge Univ. Press, 1983.

Holloway, Harry. *The Politics of the Southern Negro: From Exclusion to Big City Organization*. New York: Random House, 1969.

Holmes, Robert A. "The University and Politics in Atlanta: A Case Study of the Atlanta University Center." *Atlanta Historical Journal* 25 (Spring 1981).

Holton, Dwight Carter. " 'Power to the People': The Struggle for Black Political Power in Richmond, Virginia." Honor's thesis, Brown Univ., 1987.

Hopkins, Richard J. "Status, Mobility, and the Dimensions of Change in a Southern City: Atlanta, 1870–1910." In Kenneth T. Jackson and Stanley K. Schultz, eds., *Cities in American History*. New York: Knopf, 1972.

Hornsby, Alton, Jr. "Andrew Jackson Young: Mayor of Atlanta, 1982–1990." *Journal of Negro History* 77 (Summer 1992): 159–82.

———— "The Negro in Atlanta Politics, 1961–1973." *Atlanta Historical Bulletin* 21 (Spring 1977).

Hoyt, Homer. *The Structure and Growth of Residential Neighborhoods in American Cities*. Washington, D.C.: Government Printing Office, 1939.

Isaacs, Reginald. "The Neighborhood Unit as an Instrument for Segregation." *Journal of Housing* 5 (Aug. 1948): 215–19.

Jackson, Barbara L. "Desegregation: Atlanta Style." *Theory into Practice* 17 (Feb. 1978).

Jamieson, Duncan R. "Maynard Jackson's 1973 Election as Mayor of Atlanta," *Midwest Quarterly* 18 (1976): 16.

Johnson, Charles S. *Patterns of Negro Segregation*. New York: Harper and Brothers, 1943.

Johnson, James Weldon. *Black Manhattan*. With a Preface by Allen H. Spear. New York: Atheneum, 1968.

Johnson, Mark. "Strife That Was Avoided Made Sit-In News Here." *Richmond Times-Dispatch*, Feb. 18, 1990.

Johnson, T.J. *From the Driftwood of Bayou Pierre*. Louisville: Dunne Press, 1949.

Johnston, Norman. "Harland Bartholomew: His Comprehensive Plans and the Science of City Planning." Ph.D. diss., Univ. of Pennsylvania, 1964.

Jones, Herbert P. "Dr. Joseph Edison Walker: The Era of Good Feelings, Memphis, 1948–1958." Unpublished paper, Memphis State Univ. Library, 1983.

Jones, Mack H. "Black Political Empowerment in Atlanta: Myth and Reality." *Annals of the American Academy of Political Science* 439 (Sept. 1978).

Jones, Pat. "Human Misery in Slum Area Presents Problem to Richmond." *Richmond Times-Dispatch*, Jan. 15, 1939.

Kantrowitz, Barbara, and Pat Wingert. "A New Era of Segregation." *Newsweek*, 27 Dec. 1993, 44.

Kaplan, Marshall, et al. *The Model Cities Program: The Planning Process in Atlanta, Seattle, and Dayton*. New York: Praeger, 1970.

Katz, Michael B., ed. *The "Underclass" Debate: Views from History*. Princeton: Princeton Univ. Press, 1993.

Key, Valdimer Orlando, Jr. *Southern Politics in State and Nation*. New York: Alfred A. Knopf, 1950.

Kilpatrick, James Jackson. *The Southern Case for School Segregation*. New York: Crowell-Collier, 1962.

Knight, Charles. *Negro Housing in Certain Virginia Cities*. Richmond: William Byrd, 1927.

Kusmer, Kenneth A. *A Ghetto Takes Shape: Black Cleveland, 1870–1930*. Urbana: Univ. of Illinois Press, 1975.

Lamb, Brockenbrough. "Legal Aspects of Zoning Laws." *Virginia Municipal Review* 1 (March 1924): 75–83.

Lamon, Lester C. *Black Tennesseans, 1900–1930*. Knoxville: Univ. Tennessee Press, 1977.

Lanier, Robert A. *Memphis in the Twenties: The Second Term of Mayor Rowlett Paine, 1924–1928*. Memphis: Zenda Press, 1979.

Lasker, Bruno. "The Atlanta Zoning Plan." *Survey* 48 (April 22, 1922): 17.

Latimer, James. "No Specific Plans Voted at Meeting Here." *Richmond Times-Dispatch*, June 11, 1954.

Leedes, Gary C., and James M. O'Fallon. "School Desegregation in Richmond: A Case History." *University of Richmond Law Review* 10 (Fall 1975): 1-61.

Lewis, Selma S. "Social Religion and the Memphis Sanitation Strike." Ph.D. diss., Memphis State Univ., 1976.

Logue, Calvin McLeod. *Ralph McGill at Work*. Vol. 1 of *Ralph McGill: Editor and Publisher*. Durham, N.C.: Moore Publishing Co. 1969.

Long, Margaret. "Neighborhood Transition: The Moods and the Myths." *New South* 21 (Spring 1966): 36–45.

Manning, Warren H. "Atlanta—Tomorrow a City of a Million." *Atlanta Constitution Magazine*, March 3, 10, 1922.

Martin, Harold H. *Ralph McGill, Reporter*. Boston: Little, Brown, 1973.

———. *William Berry Hartsfield: Mayor of Atlanta*. Athens: Univ. of Georgia Press, 1978.

Mays, Benjamin E. *Born to Rebel: An Autobiography*. New York: Charles Scribner's Sons, 1971.

McAdam, Doug. *Political Process and the Development of Black Insurgency, 1930–1970*. Chicago: Univ. of Chicago Press, 1982.

Mearns, Edward A., Jr. "Virginia." In U.S. Commission on Civil Rights, *Civil Rights U.S.A.: Public Schools, Southern States, 1962*. New York: Greenwood Press, 1968.

Meeman, Edward J. *The Editorial We*. A posthumous autobiography compiled, edited, and with an introduction and afterward by Edwin Howard. Memphis: Edward J. Meeman Foundation, 1976.

Meier, August, and David Lewis. "History of the Negro Upper Class in Atlanta, Georgia, 1890–1958." *Journal of Negro Education* 28 (Spring 1959): 128–39.

Meier, August, and Elliott Rudwick. *From Plantation to Ghetto*, 3d ed. New York: Hill and Wang, 1976.

Melton, Gloria Brown. "Blacks in Memphis, Tennessee, 1920–1955: A Historical Study." Ph.D. diss., Washington State Univ., 1982.

Miller, William D. *Memphis During the Progressive Era*. Memphis: Memphis State Univ. Press, 1957.

———. *Mr. Crump of Memphis*. Baton Rouge: Louisiana State Univ. Press, 1964.

Miller, Zane L. *Suburb: Neighborhood and Community in Forest Park, Ohio, 1935–1976*. Knoxville: Univ. of Tennessee Press, 1981.

———. "Urban Blacks in the South, 1865–1920: The Richmond, Savannah, New Orleans, Louisville, and Birmingham Experience." In Leo Schnore, ed., *The New Urban History: Quantitative Explorations by American Historians*. Princeton: Princeton Univ. Press, 1975.

Minor, Carroll R. "The Institutional Life of Negroes in Richmond." M.A. thesis, Univ. of Richmond, 1933.

Mitchel, Cynthia. "Mayoral Race Splits Memphis Blacks." *Atlanta Journal and Constitution*, April 17, 1991.

Moeser, John V. "City Politics since '48: Three Distinct Periods." *Richmond-Times Dispatch*, April 6, 1986.

Moeser, John V., and Rutledge M. Dennis. *The Politics of Annexation: Oligarchic Power in a Southern City*. Cambridge, Mass.: Schenkman, 1982.

Mohl, Raymond A. "Race and Space in the Modern City: Interstate-95 and the Black Community in Miami." Unpublished paper presented at the American Planning Association Conference, Atlanta, Georgia, April 1989.

Morris, Aldon D. *The Origins of the Civil Rights Movement: Black Communities Organizing for Change*. New York: Free Press, 1984.

Murray, Charles. *Losing Ground*. New York: Basic Books, 1984.

Muse, Benjamin. *Memphis*. Atlanta: Southern Regional Council, 1964.

———. *Virginia's Massive Resistance*. Bloomington: Indiana Univ. Press, 1961.

Myrdal, Gunnar. *An American Dilemma: The Negro Problem and Modern Democracy*. New York: Harper and Brothers, 1944.

O'Connor, Michael J. "The Measurement and Significance of Racial Residential Barriers in Atlanta, 1890–1970." Ph.D. diss., Univ. of Georgia, 1977.

Osofsky, Gilbert. *Harlem: The Making of a Ghetto: Negro New York, 1890–1930*. New York: Harper and Row, 1966.

Palmer, Charles F. *Adventures of a Slum Fighter*. Atlanta: Tupper and Lowe, 1955.

Pearson, Paul M. "Federal Housing Projects for Negroes." *The Southern Workers* 65 (Nov. 1936): 371–79.

Perdue, Robert E. *The Negro in Savannah, 1865–1900*. New York: Exposition Press, 1973.

Peterson, Paul. "The Urban Underclass and the Poverty Paradox." In Christopher Jencks and Paul Peterson, eds., *The Urban Underclass*. Washington, D.C.: Brookings Institute, 1991.

Petrof, John V. "The Effect of Student Boycotts upon Purchasing Habits of Negro Families in Atlanta, Georgia." *Phylon* 24 (Fall 1963): 266–70.

Pierannunzi, Carol, and John D. Hutcheson, Jr. "Electoral Change and Regime Maintenance: Maynard Jackson's Second Time Around." *PS* (June 1990): 151–53.

Pollard, Howard Weaver. "The Effect of Techwood Homes on Urban Development in the United States." M.A. thesis, Georgia Institute of Technology, 1968.

Porter, Michael L. "Black Atlanta: An Interdisciplinary Study of Blacks on the East Side of Atlanta, 1890–1930." Ph.D. diss., Emory Univ., 1974.

Powledge, Fred. *Black Power, White Resistance: Notes on the New Civil War*. Cleveland: World Publishing, 1967.

Pratt, Robert A. *The Color of Their Skin: Education and Race in Richmond, Virginia, 1954–1989*. Charlottesville: Univ. Press of Virginia, 1992.

Preston, Howard L. *Automobile Age Atlanta: The Making of a Southern Metropolis, 1930–1935*. Athens: Univ. of Georgia Press, 1979.

Rabinowitz, Howard N. *Race Relations in the Urban South, 1865–1890*. New York: Oxford Univ. Press, 1978.

Rainwater, Lee. *Behind the Ghetto Wall: Black Family Life in a Federal Slum*. Chicago: Aldine, 1970.

Rice, Bradley R. "Atlanta: If Dixie Were Atlanta." In Rice and Richard M. Bernard, eds., *Sunbelt Cities: Politics and Growth since World War II*. Austin: Univ. of Texas Press, 1983.

———. "The Battle of Buckhead: The Plan of Improvement and Atlanta's Last Big Annexation." *Atlanta Historical Journal* 25 (Winter 1981): 5–22.

Rice, Roger, L. "Residential Segregation by Law, 1910–1917." *Journal of Southern History* 64 (May 1968): 179–99.

Ridgeway, James. "Atlanta Fights Poverty: Report from Another Battle Front." *New Republic* 152 (May 29, 1965): 12–14.

Robinson, Carla J. "Racial Disparity in the Atlanta Housing Market." *Reviews in Black Political Economy* 19 (Winter/Spring 1991): 85–109.

Roggemann, Peter J. "Does a Ward System Better Serve Low Income and Minority Neighborhoods? The Case of Richmond, Virginia." Unpublished paper presented to the Virginia Social Science Assoc., April 7, 1979.

Rusk, David. *Cities Without Suburbs*. Washington, D.C.: Woodrow Wilson Center Press, 1993.

Sartain, James A., and Rutledge M. Dennis. "Richmond, Virginia: Massive Resistance without Violence." In Charles V. Willie and Susan Greenblatt, eds., *Community*

Politics and Educational Change: Ten School Systems under Court Order. New York: Longman, 1981.

Saunder, Rick. "City Council Facing Second Big Shake-Up." *Richmond Times-Dispatch,* May 4, 1992.

Schneider, William. "The Dawn of the Suburban Era in American Politics." *Atlantic* 270 (July 1992): 33–44.

Scott, Emmett J. *Negro Migration during the War.* New York: Oxford Univ. Press, 1920.

Scott, Mary W. *Old Richmond Neighborhoods.* Richmond: William Byrd Press, 1950.

Scott, Mingo, Jr. *The Negro in Tennessee Politics and Governmental Affairs, 1865–1965.* Nashville: Rich Printing, 1964.

Sigafoos, Robert A. *Cotton Row to Beale Street: A Business History of Memphis.* Memphis: Memphis State Univ. Press, 1979.

Silver, Christopher. "The Changing Face of Neighborhoods in Memphis and Richmond, 1940–1985." In Randall M. Miller and George E. Pozzetta, eds., *'Shades of the Sunbelt': Essays on Ethnicity, Race, and the Urban South.* Boca Raton, Fla.: Florida Atlantic Univ. Press, 1989.

———. "Housing Policy and Suburbanization: An Analysis of the Changing Quality and Quantity of Black Housing in Suburbia since 1950." In Jamshid A. Momeni, ed., *Race, Ethnicity, and Minority Housing in the United States.* New York: Greenwood Press, 1986.

———. "The Racial Origins of Zoning: Southern Cities from 1910–1940." *Planning Perspectives* 6 (1991): 189–205.

———. *Twentieth Century Richmond: Planning, Politics and Race.* Knoxville: Univ. of Tennessee Press, 1984.

Silver, Christopher, et al. "Survey of Vacant Residential Units in Richmond Core Neighborhoods." Richmond: Virginia Commonwealth Univ., 1989.

Smother, Ronald. "Councilman's Victory in Atlanta Mayoral Runoff Signals New Era." *New York Times,* Nov. 11, 1993, A: 16.

———. "Memphis Campaign Is Racially Divisive." *New York Times,* Oct. 2, 1991.

Sosna, Morton. *In Search of the Silent South: Southern Liberals and the Race Issue.* New York: Columbia Univ. Press, 1977.

Spear, Allen. *Black Chicago: The Making of a Negro Ghetto, 1890–1920.* Chicago: Univ. of Chicago Press, 1967.

Spector, Samuel Ira. "Municipal and County Zoning in a Changing Urban Environment." Research Paper 53. Atlanta: Bureau of Business and Economic Research, Georgia State University, June 1970.

Stephenson, Gilbert T. "The Segregation of the White and Negro Races in Cities." *South Atlantic Quarterly* 13 (Jan. 1914): 1–18.

Stone, Clarence N. *Economic Growth and Neighborhood Discontent: Systems Bias in the Urban Renewal Program of Atlanta.* Chapel Hill: Univ. of North Carolina Press, 1976.

———. *Regime Politics: Governing Atlanta, 1946–1988.* Lawrence: Univ. Press of Kansas, 1989.

Sugarmon, Russell, Jr. "Breaking the Color Line in Memphis, Tennessee." In Alan F. Westin, ed., *Freedom Now!* New York: Basic Books, 1964.

Taeuber, Karl. "Racial Residential Segregation, 1980." Citizens Commission on Civil Rights, *A Decent Home.* Washington, D.C.: Center for National Policy Review, 1983.

———. "Racial Segregation: The Persisting Dilemma." *Annals of the American Academy of Political and Social Sciences* 422 (Nov. 1975): 87–96.

——— "Residential Segregation in the Atlanta Metropolitan Area." In Andrew M.

Hamer, ed., *Urban Atlanta: Redefining the Role of the City*. Atlanta: Georgia State Univ. Business Press, 1980.

Taylor, Henry Louis, Jr. *Race and the City: Work, Community, and Protest in Cincinnati, 1820–1970*. Urbana: Univ. of Illinois Press, 1993.

Thomas, Robert H. "Black Suburbanization and Housing Quality in Atlanta." *Journal of Urban Affairs* 6 (1984): 26.

Thompson, Gloriastene. "The Expansion of the Negro Community in Atlanta, Georgia, from 1940–1958." M.A. thesis, Atlanta Univ., 1959.

Thompson, Robert A., Hylan Lewis, and David McEntire. "Atlanta and Birmingham: A Comparative Study in Negro Housing." In Nathan Glazer and David McEntire, eds. *Housing and Minority Groups*. Berkeley: Univ. of California Press, 1960.

Tindall, George B. *The Emergence of the New South, 1913–1945*. Baton Rouge: Louisiana State Univ. Press, 1967.

Trotter, Ann. "The Memphis Business Community and Integration." In Elizabeth Jacoway and David R. Colburn, eds., *Southern Businessmen and Desegregation*. Baton Rouge: Louisiana State Univ. Press, 1982.

Trotter, Joe W., Jr., ed. *Black Milwaukee: The Making of an Industrial Proletariat*. Urbana: Univ. of Illinois Press, 1985.

Tucker, David M. *Black Pastors and Leaders: Memphis, 1819–1972*. Memphis: Memphis State Univ. Press, 1975.

———. *Lieutenant Lee of Beale Street*. Nashville: Vanderbilt Univ. Press, 1971.

———. *Memphis since Crump: Bossism, Blacks and Civic Reformers, 1948–1968*. Knoxville: Univ. of Tennessee Press, 1980.

Tuttle, William M., Jr. *Race Riot: Chicago in the Red Summer of 1919*. New York: Atheneum, 1974.

Wade, Richard C. "The Enduring Ghetto: Urbanization and the Color Line in American History." *Journal of Urban History* 17 (Nov. 1990): 4–13.

———. *Slavery in the Cities: The South, 1820–1860*. New York: Oxford Univ. Press, 1964.

Walker, Jack L. "The Functions of Disunity: Negro Leadership in a Southern City." *Journal of Negro Education* 32 (Summer 1963): 227–36.

———. "Protest and Negotiation: A Case Study of Negro Leadership in Atlanta, Georgia." In Harry A. Bailey, ed., *Negro Politics in America*. Columbus, Ohio: Charles E. Merrill, 1967.

Walker, Randolph Meade. "The Role of the Black Clergy in Memphis during the Crump Era." *West Tennessee Historical Society Papers* 33 (1979): 29–47.

Walker, Robert Lee. "Equality or Inequality: A Comparative Study of Segregated Public Education in Memphis, Tennessee, 1862 to 1954." Ed.D. diss., Western Colorado Univ., 1974.

Ward, David. *Poverty, Ethnicity and the American City, 1840–1925: Changing Conceptions of the Slum and the Ghetto*. Cambridge: Cambridge Univ. Press, 1989.

Weaver, Robert C. *The Negro Ghetto*. New York: Harcourt and Brace, 1948.

West, E. Bernard. "Black Atlanta—Struggle for Development, 1915–1925." M.A. thesis, Atlanta Univ., 1976.

Wheeler, Tim. "Church Hill: Gaslight Affluence, Poverty Share Streets." *Richmond Times-Dispatch*, Aug. 7, 1977.

White, Dana F. "The Black Sides of Atlanta: A Geography of Expansion and Containment, 1970–1870." *Atlanta Historical Journal* 26 (Summer-Fall 1982): 199–225.

Wilkinson, J. Harvie III. *Harry Byrd and the Changing Face of Virginia Politics, 1945–1966*. Charlottesville: Univ. Press of Virginia, 1968.

Williams, Charles W. Jr. "Two Black Communities in Memphis." Ph.d. diss., Univ. of Illinois-Urbana, 1981.

Williams, Michael Paul. "Sharp or Subtle, Lines of Race, Wealth, Culture Persist." *Richmond Times-Dispatch*, Aug. 22, 1993.

———. "Williams Elected Mayor; McDaniel Is Vice Mayor." *Richmond Times-Dispatch*, July 2, 1988.

Wilson, Richard. "Six Backed by RCA Win in Light Vote." *Richmond Times-Dispatch*, June 9, 1954.

Wilson, William J. *The Truly Disadvantaged.* Chicago: Univ. of Chicago Press, 1987.

Woodward, C. Vann. *The Strange Career of Jim Crow.* New York: Oxford Univ. Press, 1955

Woofter, Thomas J. *Negro Problems in Cities.* Garden City, New York: Doubleday, Doran, 1928.

Wright, George C. "The NAACP and Residential Segregation in Louisville, Kentucky, 1914–1917." *Register of the Kentucky Historical Society* 78 (Winter 1980): 39–54.

Wright, William E. *Memphis Politics: A Study in Racial Bloc Voting.* Eagleton Institute, Cases in Practical Politics, no. 27. New York: McGraw-Hill, 1962.

Index